PITTSBURGH
THE STORY OF A CITY

PITTSBURGH

THE STORY OF A CITY
1750-1865

By Leland D. Baldwin

ILLUSTRATIONS
BY WARD HUNTER

UNIVERSITY OF PITTSBURGH PRESS

SBN 8229-5216-5

Library of Congress Catalog Card Number 73-104172

Copyright © 1937 by the University of Pittsburgh Press
First printing 1937
Second printing 1938
Third printing 1947
Paperback reissue 1970

Manufactured in the United States of America

*This book is one of a series
relating Western Pennsylvania history
written under the direction
of the Western Pennsylvania Historical Survey
sponsored jointly by the
Buhl Foundation, the Historical Society
of Western Pennsylvania, and the
University of Pittsburgh*

Contents

Maps

(following Index)

Preface

THIS book is not for historians. If the formal history of Pittsburgh has not been sufficiently set forth, let no one seek to find a remedy here. This volume, rather, endeavors to draw for the general reader an impressionistic picture of the city's development; mass effects have been sought rather than minutiae, however significant, and feeling, drama, and atmosphere rather than textbook completeness. If in this search certain obscure facts have been romantically expanded for dramatic effect (such as Washington's dinner party in Semple's tavern) yet nothing essential or statistical has been altered. To save labor for those who would seek the sources on the section devoted to the beginning of the Revolution let it be understood that the account is conjectural beyond a few basic facts. And here I must also apologize to the shade of Lewis Evans. I have so distorted his *Analysis* that he could scarcely hope to recognize it, and in addition I have inserted many a brick from writers contemporary with Evans and have bound them together with modern mortar.

Locations of important places and events have been placed as accurately as existing data allowed, and choice has been made as carefully as possible when authorities disagreed. Anyone who definitely locates slips will confer a favor by communicating them to the author. The policy has been adopted of considering the streets that run part way from river to river as north and south streets, even though they do run cater-cornered to the cardinal points of the compass. Visited upon innocent future generations, this unwarranted directional ambiguity is certainly one of the crows that every Pittsburgher should pick with Town-planners Campbell and Woods when he meets them in the future life.

It is not my purpose to list the many books, newspapers, and manuscripts consulted in the preparation of this work, though by rights they deserve more than the graceful bow that is now accorded them. For research aid I thank Frank B. Sessa and John W. Harpster, both fellows of the Western Pennsylvania Historical Survey, and for editorial assistance Mary Jo Hauser, Elisabeth M. Sellers, and C. V. Starrett.

PITTSBURGH
THE STORY OF A CITY

Prologue

Lewis Evans, His Map

ABOUT the year 1750 the scarce-dispelled clouds of war between Great Britain and France began once more to lower, and it became apparent to the thin line of merchants and farmers along the Atlantic seaboard that the two nations would soon engage in a struggle for control of the Ohio Valley. As a consequence, Governor James Hamilton of Pennsylvania engaged Philadelphia's best-known cartographer, Lewis Evans—"a gentleman of great American Knowledge,"acclaimed Ben Franklin—to go on a secret mission to spy out the land across the mountain wall at the headwaters of the westward flowing rivers.

There is some doubt as to whether he undertook the journey, but at any rate he eventually published a *General Map of the Middle British Colonies of America* and accompanied it with an *Analysis* descriptive of the region included in the map. There is no better contemporary account of the West of that day than the *Analysis*; it was a narrative to titillate those nascent imperialists of the colonies, the land speculators and merchants, and the map, in its many pirated editions, became the cloudy pillar of the next generation on its westward march. Hence, without further parley, let Lewis Evans take the stand:

From this Rief of Rocks [*the fall line*], over which all the rivers fall, to that chain of broken hills, called the South Mountain (and in Virginia the Blue Ridge), there is a distance of 50, 60, or 70 miles of very uneven ground, rising sensibly as you advance further inland. The declivity of the whole gives great rapidity to the streams and impoverishes the soil by washing away the richer mould. The reason of which is this, when the country was cover'd with Woods, and the Swamps with brush, the rain that fell was detained by these interruptions, and so had time to insinuate into the Earth, and contribute to the springs and runs. But now the country is clear'd, the rain as fast as it falls, is hurried into the rivers, and washes away the earth and soil of our Naked Fields to an extent now little realized but which in time may turn a most fruitful land into a desert.

These inequalities render half the country not easily capable of culture, so that the inhabitants look with longing eyes upon the lands of the Six Nations to the Westward. It might seem that the labour of building new homes and clearing new Lands would make them reluctant to migrate, but it is not so. The people are of the lowest rank and least informed, of Mankind who have flowed in from *Germany*, *Ireland* and *the gaols of Great Britain*, or they are the children of such, born on the land or brought in very young, and are settlers by birth and profession. Their houses (save for some of the Gentry) are but Logs and as miserable and draughty as any in Ireland. The people are born and bred in the Woods and used to a life in such; they have been trained up to and serv'd (if I may so express myself) an apprenticeship to clearing lands and planting and ploughing amongst such; What to others would be hardship, is to them the natural Course of their Life.

Between the South Mountain and the *hither* chain of the Endless Mountains (often for Distinction called the North Mountain) there is a Valley of pretty even, good land, some 8, 10 or 20 miles wide, and is the most considerable quantity of valuable land that the English are possest of; and runs through New-Jersey, Pensilvania, Mariland and Virginia. The Scotch-Irish and Dutch have been cultivating it for twenty years past and have followed its course as far South as Carolina. The

2

Endless Mountains are not scattered and in lofty peaks over-topping one another, but stretch in long uniform ridges, scarce half a mile perpendicular in any place above the intermediate vallies. Their name is expressive of their extent, though no doubt, not in a literal sense. The further chain is called the Allegeni Ridge of Mountains. Except the further Ridges there is but little good land in the mountains; to be sure not one tenth part is capable of Culture, and what small matter there is, consists of extream rich Soil, the Lawns, on the river edges, being so much rich mud subsided there. Sundry Dutch and Scotch-Irish families have squatted in these vallies which are claimed as hunting preserves by the savages of the Six Nations. It was upon the complaint of these last that Governor Hamilton sent Secretary Peters and Interpreter Weiser with the magistrates of Cumberland County to invade their little Sanctuaries and burn their Log-houses to the ground and bind the Colonets to appear in court. They met with no resistence but on the Juniata where two of the inhabitants escaped from the hands of the sheriff and having got at some distance called, "You may take our lands and houses, and do what you please with them; we deliver them to you with all our hearts, but we will not be sent to jail!" Such is the spirit of these people that no measure that the governor can take is long of effect. It is said that they are already back on their Plantations, to the great chagrine of the Indians. These savages are alarmed at the swarm of strangers, and there is danger of a breach between them—the Irish are very rough to them. It may be proper to add that the cabbins which were burnt were of no considerable Value; being such as the country people erect in a day or two, and cost only the price of an entertainment.

To the North and Westward of the Endless Mountains is a country of vast extent, and in a manner as high as the mountains themselves through which great plateau the Ohio, called by the French La Belle Rivière, and its tributaries have cut their way; How far these plains extend is not known, for those most extensive plains of Ohio are part of them; which continue to widen as they extend farther Westward, even far beyond the Mississippi. And it must be said here that all America, East of

3

Mississippi, low lands, hills and mountains, is everywhere covered with Woods, except some interval spots of no great extent,
cleared by the European Colonets. Here are no Churches, Tow-
ers, Houses or peaked mountains to be seen from afar. To look
from the hills into the lower Lands, is but, as it were, into an
Ocean of Woods, swelled and deprest here and there by little
inequalities, not to be distinguished, one part from another, any
more than the waves of the real Ocean.

These are the three chief Roads (or I had better say Traders
Paths) from the Inhabitants to the Ohio: The first, wch lieth in
Pensilvania, is from Harrises Ferry on Susquehanna to Frankstown (whence it is call'd the Frankstown Path) on a Northern
Branch of the Juniata, thence across the Allegeni Mountains to
the Kishkimentas River (or Romanettoes Creek) and so to the
Ohio. The next also lies altogether within Pensilvania: it takes
a route by Shippensburg and the South branch of the Juniata
to the house of John Wray [*the site of Bedford*] (whence it is call'd
the Wraystown Path) and then crosses the Allegeni Mountain
to the Ohio. It is but little used by traders. The other, which we
may call the Virginia Path crosses the mountains from Ft. Cumberland on the Potowmack by way of Wills Creek and the Great
Meadows to the Forks of the Ohio. None of these roads are as
yet passable by wagons but the declivities are such that they
could with some labour be made suitable.

II

OF THE head of the River Ohio (which portion in the Indian
tongue is called Allegeni) I have little knowledge, but understand
that it is sufficiently deep for Canoes and Batteaux, which do
not draw above 15 inches water. These canoes, which in the tongue
of the country are named Perogues, are fashioned or hollowed
out from great logs; Batteaux, which is the French for Boats,
are formed of planks and flat-bottomed. The navigation from
Chartier's Old Town [*now Tarentum*], all the way down to the
Mississippi (which is at nine or ten hundred miles distance), has
been hitherto performed in very large wooden Canoes, which are
made of great length, as better fitted to steer against a rapid

stream; they are navigated down by two men, and upwards by four at least. Notwithstanding that the current is for the most part pretty moderate there are places where the boatmen must wade and hawl over the Rifts, and at le Tart's Falls they are obliged to hawl the Canoes with Ropes in coming up, for near a furlong along the south east side. The Great Fall [*now Louisville*] is about half a mile rapid water, which however is passable, by wading and dragging the Canoe against the stream, when lowest; and with still greater ease, when the water is raised a little. Ohio, as the Winter snows are thawed, by the warmth or rains in the Spring, rises in vast floods, which continue of some height for at least a month or two. The stream is then excellently fitted for large vessels of 100 or 200 Tons which may go to the Sea with safety, so that in process of time, large Ships may be built upon Ohio, and sent off to Sea with the heavy produce of the country, and sold with the cargoes.

Ohio has many Branches, which furnish good navigation to the adjacent parts, but the most considerable of these is the Monaungahela much distinguished by its Royley Water which joins the Ohio (or Allegeni) near the confines of this Province. The land between the Forks of the Ohio is low swampy ground, much infested with venomous Serpents and Muskeetose, and subject to be overflowed every spring; but the land surrounding is very high (I had almost said mountainous) so that a noble prospect may be had from any point. The River Youghiogani joins the Monaungahela at some distance above the Forks and as it descends from the direction of the Potowmack is likely in time to become a link in the sole passage from Ohio to the Ocean. From the branches of Ohio there are many portages to Lake Erie, notably through Canawagy Creek and a lake called Jadághque [*Chautauqua*], and from French Creek; while from Beaver Creek which flows into Ohio where it fetches a Compass and turns to the South one may portage to the Cayahoga and so into the lake. These rivers, however, are but seldom navigated by our people; because the great number of Pack-horses necessary to carry their goods to Ohio, serve them also to carry them from place to place. The French traders, having to carry their

5

trade-goods over the lakes have few horses but rely upon Canoes or Batteaux. The traders from the French are for the most part half-breeds, being the sons of Frenchmen and of Indian women from the tribes friendly to them.

III

OHIO is naturally gifted with all kinds of resources which are of vast advantage to an inland country, and well deserving the notice I take of them in the Map. It has the vastest forests I doubt not in the World with every kind of tree natural to the Temperate Zone the chiefest of which is Oak and Pine, but also divers Maples, Buttonwood, Hickory, Walnut, Chestnut and others too tedious to recount. There are also large drafts of Glades or natural Meadow without timber on which thousands of cattle may be supported from the natural clover and other grasses, and the soil is fit for the planting of Indian corn, Beans, Pumpkins and other Provitions. Ohio is naturally with Salt, Iron, Limestone, Grindstone, Millstone, Clay and Sand for Brick, Pottery and Glass-houses which are of vast advantage to an inland country and well deserving notice. Coal is also in abundance and may be picked up in the beds of the streams or from the sides of exposed hills. In 1748 a Coal Mine opposite Lamenshikola Mouth took Fire, and kept burning above a twelve-month, where great quantities are still left.

The Animals of the Ohio country are such as once were found in the now settled parts; those of Pray being the lyon, the wolf, and the wild cat; Those fit for food are the Buffaloe, the Elk, and the Deer, which last because of the inordinate draine of the skin Trade are becoming so scarce that nearly every Winter hath become a Starving Time for the Indian Nations. Prime furs of Beaver, Otter, Mink, &c., are now obtained for the most part beyond the Ohio River chiefly from the Mineami and Wabasha Rivers and from the country of the Outagamies and Otawas beyond Lake Michigan. In vermin the Ohio Country is surpassing abundant every rocky knoll bearing its Den of venomous Reptiles; so much so that in flood the voyager durst scarce set foot ashore. The stinging Flies and divers other

6

Insects but particularly Muskeetose in this country are like to rival the Seven Plagues of Egypt; but there are those who say that the spread of settlement will abate them, and in truth this is like to be the case. It is a peculiar Phaenomenon that Honey bees are not found far in the wilderness but go before the settlements a little distance and are called by the Indians the White Man's Flies: and here I must also mention a curious Indian superstition. A trader being up the Allegeni the Indians found a Rat and killed it, at which the antients seem'd concerned and told him that the French or English should get that land from them, the same prediction being made by their Grandfathers on finding a Rat on Delaware before the White People came.

IV

I HAVE not room here to enlarge on the state of the INDIANS, nor describe their several boundaries. But it must be observed, that they do not generally bound their countries by lines, but by considerable extents of land. As their numbers are not considerable in proportion of the lands they possess, they fix their Towns commonly on the edges of great rivers for the sake of the rich Lawns to sow their Corn in. The intermediate ground they reserve for their hunting, which equally serves for that purpose and a Frontier. The number of Nations is far less than is commonly imagined, and all their states are Republic in the strictest sense; and the Chiefs, as we call them, are only such in virtue of their credit, not their power. The number also of warriors is not great in proportion to the lands; They being greatly reduced by Starvation, Rum, and fowl Diseases carried in by the Traders.

The Country immediately beyond the Mountains belongs to the Six Confederate Nations by right of conquest and was by them kept devoid of inhabitants as a hunting preserve. It must be presumed, however, that the Six Nations are not as powerful as they once were, so that when the extension of cultivated lands into the Susquehanna Valley forced the Delawares and Shawanese to cross the Mountains, the Iroquois could not prevent this, but sent two Oneida chieftains to rule over them,

Scarouady over the Shawanese and Tanacharison (sometimes call'd the Half-King) over the Delawares. The Shawanese, upon first entering the West thirty years ago settled on the Allegeni at Chartier's Old Town, so called from their leader Peter Chartier, the son of the Frenchman under whom a part of the Nation had first come to Pensilvania from the Mississippi in the time of William Penn; Another branch, it is said, having been brought up the Ohio and across the Mountains about the same time by Arnold Viele, one of the Traders out of Albany. The two chief towns at present are Allaquippa's Town and Logstown: The former is at a great Rock a league below the Forks on the left bank of the Ohio (though in truth this village is on both sides the river) at the mouth of a creek call'd Allaquippa's (though of late known as Chartier's) and across two islands, marvellous Fertile; this name is from an old woman of so great credit among them that she was by the Traders call'd Queen, though now a chief Shingiss rules and Allaquippa has taken up her seat at the mouth of Youghiogani. Logstown is across the river and almost to the Beaver (and as its name signifies a collection of Miserable log Huts), and here is a mingling of the Indian Nations and a Parcel of reprobate Indian Traders, which is nevertheless the principall Mart of Trade in the Region and the beginning of all westward journeys. Besides the Delawares and Shawanese there are a few Wiandots upon Beaver, and sundry bastard Senecas who are known by their Neighbours as Mingos.

v

THERE are many British subjects scattered over the Ohio Country and to the Westward; but they cannot with any propriety be said to be *Settlers*, because they have not acquired Titles to the Soil under their King, nor cultivated their Land to any great extent by Husbandry; two things absolutely necessary to denominate a Settlement. The Traders of the Ohio are for the most part from Pensilvania (though of late years there have come a few from Winchester and other parts of Virginia) and rely upon the merchants of Philadelphia and Lancaster for trade-goods, obtaining them upon credit and recompensing with the Skins and Furs upon their return from the Indian country. They have few regular connexions but form temporary Concerns among themselves and with the merchants. And here it must be said that the French are at a great disadvantage in their commerce with the Indians, for the Strowds, Duffils, Blankets and other woollens which the Indians value are bought at a much cheaper rate in England than France. Rum is another article that the French want, by reason they have no commodities in Canada fit for the West India market, and Brandy, which is at a much dearer rate, is of no more value to the Indians. To this must be added the necessity of the long carriage from Montreal and the onerous taxes, for the French lay the whole charge of their Government on the Indian trade. To put the truth of this question out of all dispute, I need only to observe what is well known at Albany that almost all the Strowds carried by the French into the Indian Country, as well as large quantities of other goods for the use of the French themselves, are transported from Albany to Montreal where they are sold for twice their value at the English Posts.

The English manner of carrying on the Indian Trade is this: The regular Traders undertake twice or oftener each year journeys to the Indian villages, their Pack-horses laden with Strowds, match-coats, hats, looking-glasses, beads and bracelets of glass, knives, and all manner of Gawdy Toys and Knacks for children, as well as guns, flints, Powder and Lead, and cags of potent Rum to be watered when they arrive in the Indian Country. When there these Traders live with the Indians, selling them goods in prospect of the season's fur catch and often keeping one or more Squaws as wives and are trusted by their neighbours for they are content with a meer trifle of two or three hundred per centum profit above the cost of the Trade-goods and transport which it is said are nigh equall.

Other traders there are who frequently creep into the Woods with spirituous liquor and cheating trifles, after the Indian hunting camps, in the Winter season, and putting down severall Cags before them, make them drunk selling their liquor at ten times its value to the great injury of the Fair Trader who supplies them with all the conveniences for hunting; for as they will sell even their wearing shirt for inebriating liquors, they must be supplied anew in the Fall of the year by a Trader. These Traders are the most vicious and abandoned Wretches of our Nation and the Indians hold them in great contempt as a Set of Mean Dishonest mercenary Fellows and complain that they debauch their young women, and even their wives, when the husbands are from home or drunk. When your Indian has once got a smack of Rum he is never sober for ten days or untill there is no more left. Days and nights are passed in jovial, Amorous topers and in convival songs, dances, and sacrifices to Venus; for in these frolics both sexes take such liberties with each other, and act without constraint or shame such scenes as they would abhor when sober or in their senses. But, at last, their liquor running low, and being most of them sick through intoxication, they become more sober; and now the dejected, lifeless sots would pawn everything they own for a mouthful of spirits to settle their stomachs.

This is the time for the Wenches to make their market; for at these riots, every fellow has his own quart bottle of Rum, holding it by the neck; and with this, his beloved friend, he roves about continually, singing, roaring and reeling to an fro, presenting his bottle to every one, offering a drink; And is sure to meet his beloved Female whom he complacently begs to drink with him. She, being furnished with an empty Bottle, concealed in a mantle, at last consents and taking a good long draught, blushes, drops her pretty face on her bosom and artfully discharges the Rum into her Bottle. This she privately conveys to her secret store; and when the Comic Farce is over, the Wench retails this precious Cordial at her own price.

The most considerable of the Traders of whom there are about one hundred and of the greatest respectability are these: Thomas McKee who has traded across the mountains since the Shawanese left Minisink, John Fraser who hath a Store-house and Gun-smithy at Venango, Paul Pierce who roves Westward to the Wabasha, Hugh Crawford, Edward Ward, James and Alexander Lowery, and Alexander Maginty who gave me an

Account of the course of the Ohio, and William Trent and George Croghan who have lately been concerned together. This last is a Dublin Irishman who is a meer Idol among his countrymen, the Irish traders, and the Indians from whom he has taken a Squaw to wife, and is said to controul one-fourth the Trade of the Ohio Country and to have many servants and factors and associates and to have hundreds of Pack-horses for the hawling of his Trade-goods. He has Store-houses on Susquehanna fourteen days from the Ohio, at the Redstone, at the Forks of the Ohio, at Logstown, at Pickawillani and among the Sanduski Indians seated on Lake Erie and elsewhere and it is said has made ventures down the Ohio to the Kantucqui River and to the Wabasha. His most considerable Plantation in the Indian Country is at Pine Creek [*the site of Etna*] a league up the Allegeni where he has severall fields cleared and stockadoed, together with log-houses, batteaux and canoes, and a Factor in residence.

VI

I MUST not omit giving one caution to those in power. Hitherto we have apprehended no greater scheme of the French than making a Chain of Communication between Canada and the mouth of Mississippi. As this was remote, we thought ourselves but little interested in it. Now they are about to attempt it nigher us on Ohio as is daily witnessed by the talk of the French traders in that country and by the late progress of the Sieur de Céloron down the Ohio and the planting of leaden plates in the name of the French king; if this succeed, it is not Ohio only must fall under their Dominion, but the country thence Southward to the Bay of Mexico. We charge the Indians with fickleness, but with greater propriety we should charge ourselves with great want of sense or experience, in supposing any Nation is to be tied to another, by any thing other than interest. 'Tis a Custom, established with the English, to purchase the friendship of wavering Nations with many gifts, and to abandon their friends. Hence those who know this mixture of weakness and baseness that possesses us, keep members of

Council in the French interest as well as ours, to keep us under a perpetual contribution. In consequence we are like to lose both our Trade and our Domains to the French who daily court the Indian Nations with subtle blandishments and sumptuous presents.

Were there nothing at stake between the Crowns of Britain and France but the lands on that part of Ohio included in this Map, we may reckon it as great a prize, as has ever yet been contended for, between two Nations. The influence that a State will have in the world, when vested with all the wealth and power which will naturally arise from the Culture of so great an extent of good land and natural resources, in a happy climate, will make so great an addition to that Nation which wins it that the loser must inevitably sink under his rival. If his Majesty would be pleased to appoint a Colony to be made in Ohio, with a separate Governor, and an equitable form of Government, a full Liberty of Conscience, and the same secured by Charter; not all that the French could project would give it any impediment after a few years.

I

Virginia Takes a Hand in the West

HAD an observer been able to station himself with a spyglass on the hill now known as Mount Washington on a bleak day in late November, 1753, he would have been rewarded by a panoramic view of the region about the Forks of the Ohio that was soon to engross the attention of the world. The glory of autumn has passed and the leaves hang lifelessly upon the branches or carpet the ground beneath. Save for the very shores of the rivers and for the little fields of the Indians and traders, trees are everywhere, spreading over the plains and the hilltops and clinging to the sides of the steepest hills.

At the bottom of a sheer drop of three hundred feet, and so close underneath that one could throw a stone into its depths, rushes the yellow Monongahela in flood. Flowing in from the northeast to meet it comes the Allegheny, ordinarily clear and pure, but now scarcely to be distinguished in color from its sister stream. The waters, united into the Ohio, flow northwest between two lines of forest-clad hills—the hills on the southwest side rising abruptly from the river, those on the other sloping more gradually away from the edge of the water. In the distance a low island cleaves the current and just beyond a bold rock, around which rises the smoke from the cabins of

Shingas' Town, throws the side current back in the main stream. Three miles up the Allegheny River on the eastern shore huddle the cabins of Shannopin's Town, and across the river at the mouth of Pine Creek can be discerned the cleared fields and log houses of George Croghan's plantation and trading post. Traversing the line of low hills that bound the flood plain between the rivers, one's eyes rest again upon the Monongahela as it emerges from among the hills, rushing down from the direction of John Fraser's trading post at Turtle Creek and Queen Allaquippa's regal seat at the mouth of the Youghiogheny River.

There is the faint crack of a rifle shot below, and a deer bounds into sight near the Point and speeds upstream along the bank. A little group of horsemen debouches from the woods along the Allegheny River into the open space at the Point, where they tie their horses and dispose themselves for a wait. One of the number, however, leaves his companions and plunges into the woods. An hour later he reappears on the bank of the Monongahela a mile upstream and makes his way back through the tangled bushes and driftwood. He is a tall, athletic fellow, and, from the way in which he rips away the obstacles, young and vigorous. As he is nearing the forks a pirogue appears around the first bend of the Monongahela. When it reaches the junction of the rivers a line is thrown by the bowsman to the waiting men, and the boat is carefully towed and poled around the Point into the waters of the Allegheny. Some of the men clamber aboard with the reins of several horses in their hands; then the craft slowly fights its way across the river, with the horses following perforce. Another trip is made before the entire cavalcade is landed on the north shore, but once it is assembled and the pack horses laden no time is lost in taking up the trail to the north.

Late in the evening of the next day the tall young man seats himself before a rough table in one of the traders' houses in Logstown. A frugal stub of candle forced into the mouth of a bottle gutters in the cross drafts that find their way through the chinks of the rude cabin. Others are present—among them the Dutchman, Jacob Van Braam, who boasts that he speaks

French like a native, and the taciturn woodsman, Christopher Gist. They smoke and talk before the rude open fireplace whose dim light aids the candle in revealing the forms of several sleepers lying on the piles of bear and buffalo hides that cover the low bunks along the walls. From the next cabin there come the wild jovial shouts of several of Mother Nature's red-skinned sons gathered round the wassail bowl and bent on forgetting the high cost of strouds, gunpowder, and female gauds, as well as the vise that the French and English are rapidly closing upon them. The young man at the table opens a leather-bound journal and lingers lovingly over the first terse entry: *"Wednesday, 31st.* I was commissioned and appointed by the Honourable *Robert Dinwiddie,* Esq; Governor, &c., of *Virginia,* to visit and deliver a letter to the Commandant of the *French* forces on the *Ohio,* and set out on the Intended Journey the same day."

Musing on the importance of his mission, he hastily puts aside the thought that Governor Dinwiddie had sought diligently for an older and more responsible man before he had been forced to pitch upon one so young and inexperienced. He takes up a quill and dips it into the inkhorn. For the next few minutes he writes with complete absorption, and though his lines have the exactness of copperplate yet it is easy to see that ideas flow slowly. The young man is no master wordsmith.

"As I got down before the Canoe," he writes, "I spent some time in viewing the Rivers, and the Land in the Fork; which I think extremely well situated for a Fort, as it has the absolute Command of both Rivers. The Land at the Point is 20 or 25 Feet above the common Surface of the Water; and a considerable Bottome of flat, well-timbered land all around it, very convenient for Building."

He pauses to dip his pen and ponder a moment. The sounds of revelry in the Indian cabin are louder now, but no one heeds them. The experience is common in the lives of the men who haunt the wilderness. Only the Dutchman curses the revelers, half in protest, half in envy, as he knocks out his pipe on the hearth and gets ready for bed by the simple process of wrapping a buffalo robe about himself and tumbling into an interstice between the recumbent forms on one of the bunks. The young scribe, unperturbed by the caterwauling, bends to his journal. Half an hour later, with a sigh of relief, he closes the book and rises to prepare for bed. The candle is now very short indeed and the light it casts is dim but still sufficient to reveal, to anyone who has the learning and who will take the trouble to read, these words inked neatly into the fresh leather of the cover: "Maj^r. G. Washington. His Journal, Octr. 31st 1753——."

II

THE Virginia planter, if the old records are to be trusted, was a sociable person, always dining and wining his friends or being dined and wined. It is possible, therefore, to reconstruct a scene that had its setting in the sumptuous dining room of a Virginia mansion in 1747, a scene that led to young George Washington's journey to the Ohio country and that before long was to precipitate the Seven Years' War. The ladies, who had just been toasted in wine the cost of which was carried on the debit side of the ledger of some London merchant, retired with a vast swishing of silk ("10 yds. best fashionable brocade, lavender, 10£ 3sh.," also debited) to the withdrawing room, and their lords seated themselves to fill their pipes and their wineglasses and to discuss the serious business of the evening.

There is no way of knowing just who was there, but in all likelihood there were among those present Lawrence Washington, of Mount Vernon; his brother, Augustine; and his brother-in-law and neighbor, George William Fairfax; and then certainly there was the Honorable Thomas Lee, periwigged member of His Majesty's Council in Virginia, who had a scheme to propound. No record of the conversation was kept, but the circumstances that prompted the meeting and the results that came from it are so well known that we can easily conjecture what was said. Lee may have opened the discussion by reminding his friends that at the treaty of Lancaster in 1744 the Indians had surrendered to Virginia their claims to all the land within that dominion as far as "the setting sun." True, poor Lo had thought he was deeding away his hunting grounds only as far

as the crest of the Allegheny Mountains, but that was a matter of secondary importance. True, also, that the French, by some long-winded proclamation or other, had laid claim to all the vast country beyond the mountains, but that might also be rated as secondary. True, again, that Pennsylvania claimed a sizable portion of the transmontane region and her traders swarmed over the land like a plague of locusts, but then that, too, was secondary. An audible snicker must have passed around the table at the mere thought of Philadelphia's Quakers making an effective resistance to a movement on the part of Virginia to expand her settlements. "In fact, gentlemen," we can almost hear Lee say, "here is a golden opportunity beckoning us—indeed two golden opportunities, for there is a king's ransom in furs on those waters and the land is so marvelous fertile that thousands of backwoodsmen are already yearning to enter it. All we need is a slight outlay of cash and a little influence with the governor, or perchance with the King's councillors in London, to assure ourselves of an easy road to riches. Let us agree to bring in foreign Protestants as settlers, point out the easy land carriage between the headwaters of the Potomac and the Ohio, and stress the inevitable increase in the demand of both the Indian traders and the settlers for British manufactures. Part of the route will lie through Maryland and we can join with us some influential Marylander, probably Colonel Thomas Cresap, a fellow of rough exterior but with invaluable experience in the Indian trade. As to finances, perhaps John Hanbury, the London merchant, can be persuaded to back us, and perhaps," with a wry face, "in consideration of this opportunity he might grant some of us extensions on our unpaid balances. At any rate, gentlemen, this venture is worthy of trial and there is no reason to doubt but that the speculators will be amply recompensed."

The outcome of the consequent deliberations was the formation of an "association of gentlemen" under the name of the Ohio Company, and the drawing up of a petition, which in the course of events was acted upon favorably by the king's council. The king granted the company two hundred thousand acres in such parts of the West as should "be adjudged most proper" upon the condition that it settle a hundred families on the land within seven years; as soon as this was done and a fort built and garrisoned to protect the settlers an additional three hundred thousand acres was to be granted. The news of the grant was received in Virginia in July, 1749, and the company lost no time in beginning operations. An acquiescent Hanbury was instructed to send two shiploads of merchandise, a trading post was erected on the Virginia shore of the Potomac opposite the mouth of Wills Creek, and men were sent out to locate desirable lands.

The French were probably aware of the grant to the Ohio Company as soon as it was made. At any rate that very summer they dispatched an expedition under Céloron de Blainville to reassert French claims to sovereignty over the Ohio country, and with Céloron went several officers whose names were soon to become indelibly associated with the history of the French occupation of the region—among them Pierre de Contrecœur, Coulon de Jumonville, and the interpreters Philippe and Chabert Joncaire. The expedition entered the Allegheny River by way of Lake Chautauqua (the Jadághque of Lewis Evans) and Conewango Creek, floated down the Allegheny and Ohio rivers to the site of Cincinnati, and then went by the Miami-Maumee route to Lake Erie. Everywhere Céloron stopped he found the Indians unwilling to abandon the cheap and dependable trade goods of the English for the more expensive wares of the French; and, although he ordered the Pennsylvania traders that he encountered to retire across the mountains and not to return on pain of imprisonment and confiscation of their goods, yet the most solid achievement of his expedition was the burial at strategic points of leaden plates asserting the claim of the French king to the region. Céloron had scarcely disappeared around the bends of the Ohio before the traders were back at their posts, while the Ohio Company went on with its plans as calmly as though the French had never left the purlieus of Montreal.

In 1750 and again in 1751 the Ohio Company sent Christopher Gist to explore the western country, and in 1752 he and

Colonel Cresap headed a party that, with the assistance of Nemacolin, a Delaware Indian, cut a wagon road from Wills Creek to the Youghiogheny. The next summer Gist cleared a "plantation" on the site of Mount Braddock and brought in several families as settlers. Meanwhile the Quakers of Philadelphia, seeing their extensive interests in the fur trade jeopardized by the French and the Virginians, sent George Croghan in 1751 with a large present to meet the Indians in council at Logstown and promote the Pennsylvania interests. The Quaker assembly of the province, however, consistently refused to authorize or finance a fort to secure the Ohio Valley against the French, and the Indians and the traders began to turn to Virginia for protection. Consequently, when three Virginia commissioners appeared at Logstown the next year with a present from the king to the Indians they had the assistance of Croghan in inducing the tribes to allow the company to erect two forts on the Ohio and to begin settlement south of that river.

The French, however, under an enterprising new governor, the Marquis Duquesne, did not propose to let the Ohio Company entrench itself in the West without opposition. Duquesne spent his first winter in New France energetically reorganizing the military resources of the province and grandly planning a line of forts between Lake Erie and the Ohio. By late winter of 1752-53 he was ready to act. A series of attacks was launched upon the English traders at Sandusky and in the Miami and Kentucky countries that sent them scampering for the East. In April a French force under the cantankerous Chevalier Pierre Paul Marin appeared at Presque Isle and began the construction of a fort, and a little later work was begun on a second fort at Lake Le Bœuf (Waterford) on French Creek, at the end of a fifteen mile portage from Presque Isle. While these tasks were in progress a French detachment appeared at John Fraser's log blacksmith shop and trading post at the mouth of French Creek and captured two of his employees. Fraser discreetly moved his business to the mouth of Turtle Creek, and the captors ran up their flag over his abandoned establishment and named it Fort Machault.

By May of 1753 the English traders, riding their useless pack horses or paddling their empty batteaux up the crooked Ohio, had streamed in from the West and were gathered at Croghan's plantation at the mouth of Pine Creek, dreading the next move of the French. Then one day a letter came from John Fraser containing the news that the French had landed on the shore of Lake Erie. The consternation of the traders must have been reflected in their faces. What would the harassed red men do, now that the French were at the doors of their wigwams, while the English still dallied in coming to the relief of their friends? Croghan and his associates called the Indians into council and put the question to them. The reply was, in effect, that circumstances compelled the red men to be neutral unless the English were prepared to give active assistance against the French. The issue and the magnitude of the emergency were clear. A mere "association of gentlemen" was no match for the might of France.

III

YOUNG Major Washington's chance had indeed come, for before many months his name was to ring through the courts of Europe as well as the cabins of America. He was accompanied from Logstown by an Indian escort including Tanacharison, the Half-King, and on the fourth of December he and his companions were received by one of the half-Indian Joncaires at the whilom bower of Mr. Fraser at Venango. "He invited us to sup with them; and treated us with the greatest Complaisance," wrote George, with an anticipatory thrill at the stir his news would make at the palace in Williamsburg. "The Wine, as they dosed themselves pretty plentifully with it, soon banished the Restraint which at first appeared in their Conversation; and gave licence to the Tongues to reveal their Sentiments more freely. They told me, That it was their absolute Design to take Possession of the *Ohio*, and by G—— they would do it; For that altho' they were sensible the *English* could raise two Men for their one; yet they knew their Motions were too slow and dilatory to prevent any Undertaking of theirs."

A week later, after a gruelling journey through the snow and

rain and hampered by the grumbling Half-King and his Indians who had parted reluctantly from Joncaire's brandied blandishments, Emissary Washington appeared before the log walls of Fort Le Bœuf. He was presently received by the new French commander, oldish, one-eyed Legardeur de St. Pierre, who recently, upon his return from an unsuccessful search for the Rocky Mountains, had been appointed to succeed the deceased General Marin. St. Pierre and his officers retired to translate the letter from Dinwiddie and to hold a council of war, while the Virginian, stilling his conscience with the reflection that the French were mere interlopers on His Britannic Majesty's domains, seized the "Opportunity of taking the Dimensions of the Fort, and making what Observations I could."

It was four days before St. Pierre had ready his reply ("I am here by Virtue of the Order of my General; and I intreat you, Sir, not to doubt one Moment, but I am determined to conform myself to them") and another day before Washington was able to pry his Indians loose from French brandy and presents. Fortunately the horses had been sent ahead to Venango, but when Washington arrived there he found them too weak to carry the baggage and to make any speed, so he was eventually forced to leave them in charge of Van Braam while he and Gist set out alone to walk overland to the Forks of the Ohio. Escaping by sheer good fortune the attempt of a French Indian to murder one of them, they arrived three bitter days later at the Allegheny River, a mass of grinding ice.

That day, Saturday, was spent in putting together a raft, doubtless using some of Mr. Croghan's fence rails or perhaps the logs from an outhouse. About sunset they started to cross the river. Washington, in attempting to maneuver his setting pole, was thrown out into ten feet of water and barely managed to clamber back on the raft. Even at the price of this involuntary Saturday night bath, the two were unable to make the shore but were forced to entrust themselves to the slippery crust of ice that had formed along the bank of an island, the major desperately clutching the knapsack that bore his precious papers. The night was passed on the island. By morning Gist had had his fingers frozen, but the ice had closed over the current and they were able to walk ashore near Shannopin's Town and then to make their way to John Fraser's trading post.

While they were waiting for Fraser to find horses for them Washington and Gist took the occasion to visit Queen Allaquippa at the "Mouth of *Youghyaughane*." "I made her a Present of a Matchcoat and a Bottle of Rum," wrote Washington, "which latter was thought much the best Present of the Two." The next day the two travelers set out across the mountains, and met on the way "17 Horses loaded with Materials and Stores, for a Fort at the Forks of Ohio, and the Day after some Families going out to settle." On January 16 Washington arrived in Williamsburg. How proudly he must have ridden down Duke of Gloucester Street and across the magnificent plaza to the pretentious palace of the governor; and with what elation he must have handed to that dignitary the letter he had brought all the way from Fort Le Bœuf, and that by way of dedication had been christened in the icy spray of the Allegheny.

IV

THE report that Washington, at Dinwiddie's bidding, threw together in one day was speedily printed and hawked about the streets, first of Williamsburg, then of London. Recruiting of soldiers began at once, and the able Colonel Joshua Fry, professor of mathematics at William and Mary College, and a cartographer and land speculator of might, was placed in command. Washington himself was set to raising and drilling a company of two hundred men, though where in all the broad expanse of Virginia this green commander was to find clothing and weapons for his soldiers Dinwiddie failed to say. The governor did comfort the harassed young officer, however, by approving his promotion to a lieutenant-colonelcy and by ordering him to prepare his men to march to the Forks of the Ohio to "finish and compleat in the best manner and as soon as You possibly can, the Fort w'ch I expect is already begun by the Ohio Comp'a."

His Excellency was probably singing in the rain when he expressed such faith in the fort having been begun by the

"Comp'a." True enough, he had sent a captain's commission to William Trent, the Pennsylvania trader, and had directed him to enlist a hundred men to build and garrison the fort. Trent had done some fighting in northern New York during King George's War and was an excellent choice for the task, but he was not properly backed up by Dinwiddie, who was having troubles of his own with the House of Burgesses. Trent, who knew on which side his bread was buttered, began his service by building for the company a storehouse at Redstone Old Fort (Brownsville) for the reception of trade goods and military supplies to be shipped to the Forks. About February 17 he reached the Point and began to erect a log fort that he grandiloquently named Fort Prince George in honor of the future George III. Croghan, who had a faculty of being in the thick of interesting events, appeared on the scene and occupied himself in winning Indian consent to the erection of the fort, and he succeeded so well that the Half-King, probably with an eye on the rum keg, aided in laying the first log.

The work on the fort had been under way perhaps three weeks when Trent, warned that the French projected an immediate attack on the post, departed for the East to hurry the delivery of provisions and equipment. John Fraser, now Trent's lieutenant, who should have assumed the responsibility for the continuance of the work, seems to have spent his time at his trading post and to have left Ensign Edward Ward, Croghan's half brother, in actual charge. About April 13 Ward was shown a letter written by a trader, John Davison, that stated that the French were on the way to the Forks. Ward, who had only forty-one men, four small cannon, and no provisions save Indian corn, hastened to the mouth of the Youghiogheny to consult Fraser. The lieutenant gave him scant comfort, merely saying that there was nothing that could be done and that if he abandoned his business and went to defend the fort he would "loose" a shilling for a penny. Ward, thus thrown upon his own resources, hastened back to the fort and succeeded in having the last gate of the stockade put in place.

On April 16 the French under Contrecœur, to the number of

23

five hundred, arrived at Shannopin's Town; to the anxious Ward their flotilla must have seemed to cover the Allegheny. Through a nervous night the little English garrison waited, watching the glare of the enemy campfires and listening to the roll of the drums. The next day the French marched down toward the Point and drew up at about gunshot distance from the fort, while four cannon were landed and trained on the defenses. The French engineer, Le Mercier, was designated to deliver the summons to surrender, and he approached the fort with an interpreter and two drummers. The drums beat the parley with all the punctilio so dear to the military heart, and then Le Mercier through the interpreter delivered the summons to Ward, "looked at his watch which was about two, and gave him an hour to fix his Resolution, telling him he must come to the French Camp with his Determination in Writeing."

The harassed Ward went into a huddle with the Half-King, "who advised him to acquaint the French he was no Officer of Rank or invested with powers to answer their Demands and requested them to Wait the Arrival of the principal Commander." Ward accordingly entered the French lines with the Half-King and two or three other companions and delivered this astonishing answer to the French commander. Contrecœur snorted at the naïveté of this erstwhile trader and gave him the choice between immediate surrender and bombardment. Ward looked down the mouths of the French cannon and at the long ranks of the enemy, whom he hastily estimated as at least a thousand in number, and chose surrender.

Contrecœur considerately gave him until the next day at noon to evacuate the fort and allowed him to carry off all the property belonging to the garrison and to the workmen. When the Union Jack had been slowly lowered from its place over the stockade, Ward marched out without benefit of drum or fife. He was forced to camp near by in order to complete his preparations for the return to the East. Contrecœur invited Ward to dine with him that evening, probably at the table that had only recently belonged to the Englishman. During the meal the ensign was plied with questions "concerning the English Governments," but side-stepped them by professing ignorance. When however, Contrecœur offered to buy some of the defeated garrison's carpentering tools, Ward drew himself up in offended patriotism and answered that "he loved his King and Country too well to part with any of them And then retired."

The next morning Ward's company set out for Redstone on the first lap of the long march back to Virginia.

v

THE Virginia expeditionary forces, with Washington as field commander, though scarce 160 in number and clothed in rags and armed with antiquated muskets and rusty cutlasses, reached Wills Creek in good time to meet Ward and his returning veterans and to hearken to their tale of woe. A council of war resolved to advance to Redstone and to supplement the company's storehouse with a fort, hoping to use that point as a base for an attack on Fort Duquesne—the new French stronghold at the forks of the Ohio. As the first step the troops were ordered to "amend the Road," which had fallen into disrepair. Washington, meanwhile, with uncharacteristic lack of tact, had tried to improve the chances of success not only by vilifying poor Croghan (who was now working ardently to promote Virginian success) but by seizing his pack horses and leaving his furs and trade goods in the West to the mercy of the French.

But the little army made progress and by the end of May had reached the Great Meadows, a few miles east of Chestnut Ridge, "and by clearing ye Bushes out of these Meadows, prepar'd a charming field for an Encounter." Perhaps, after all, the young commander was a wordsmith. On May 28 Washington met and conquered a scouting party of Frenchmen under Coulon de Jumonville, and this victory was soon followed by the news that the untimely death of Colonel Fry had made him commander of the Virginia troops. Washington caught the torch from the fallen hand and carried on; doubtless there were many times during the succeeding weeks when he was to wonder if he had not seized the wrong end of the torch. The little expedition was now raised to about three hundred men by reinforcements, part of them from Virginia and part of them from South Carolina, under a young Scotchman, Captain Aeneas Mackay, who as the bearer of the king's commission was not disposed to give precedence to a mere Virginia colonel. In spite of this and other jurisdictional squabbles the army pushed on to Gist's Plantation, hewing its way through thirteen miles of forest in thirteen days. Here it was learned that the French were advancing in force, so a council of war decided upon a retreat to the Great Meadows; the wagons and artillery were painfully dragged back across the Chestnut Ridge, and the intrenchments at the old camp were strengthened and christened Fort Necessity. Here in damp and dysenteric misery the half-starved, half-armed colonials waited for the attack.

It was not long in coming. The French, taking advantage of Washington's laboriously cut road over the mountain, appeared five hundred strong before Fort Necessity on July 3 and opened fire. Their commander, who took a grim pleasure in his duty, was Coulon de Villiers, the brother of the fallen Jumonville. All through that long rainy day the firing continued, until the ammunition of both sides was nearly expended. About eight o'clock in the evening the French commander proposed a parley, which soon led to a surrender. The next day the Virginians marched away, leaving Captain Robert Stobo and Van Braam with the French as hostages. It served Van Braam right, for in spite of his boasted gift of tongues, in his ignorance of the French language he had allowed Washington to sign articles of capitulation that included an acknowledgment that Jumonville had been "assassinated."

The French returned to Fort Duquesne by way of Gist's Plantation and Redstone, destroying the cabins at those and intermediate points. They had demonstrated that the proud dominion of Virginia was no match for the might of France.

II

How Are the Mighty Fallen!

JUNE 18, 1755. General Edward Braddock—a red-faced, stout-hearted Irishman, slightly stupid when military routine did not prescribe an easy course of action, an elderly libertine and rakehelly if you wish, and a crusty martinet, but not the super-cilious cad of American tradition—watched the long wagon trains of his army toil up the rocky heights of Meadow Mountain, as infantrymen tugged at the ropes or strained at the wheels, their scarlet coats gleaming in the cursed, unnaturally bright, American sun. There had been ten eternal days of this crawling up and down the sides of inhospitable mountains, of decrepit wagons breaking down and overworked horses founder-ing. Ten eternal days—two thousand men crazed by heat, thirst, fever, dysentery, and chiggers; constant fear of stealthy death in the shape of Red Indians or scarcely less savage Frenchmen, a fear only too often realized by careless detach-ments or lone stragglers.

Two fantastically painted Indians appeared in the road as though by magic. One of them spoke in English to an aide and Braddock recognized beneath the war paint the features of George Croghan, a fellow Irishman from Dublin, now thor-oughly metamorphosed into one of the half-Indian provincials.

27

Well, at any rate the fellow was of some use, since the Indian scouts, antagonized because the officers had been so "scandalously fond of their squaws," had packed up their families and departed into the forest. Demn these provincials, anyhow. How could one be expected to gain victories with regiments rounded out by raw American country jakes, who revenged themselves for the contempt of the regulars by holding forth on the terrors of the forest and its redskinned savages. Not a thimbleful of discipline in the lot. The Coldstream Guards, now—there was discipline for you. How well he remembered that day at Fontenoy in '45 and the hopeless charge against the French Guards which was carried on as calmly and with as much precision as though they were on parade, every man in his best suit of scarlet and gold, the officers armed only with light rattans. As the English approached the French, Lord Charles Hay doffed his gold-laced hat and the French officers returned the courtesy as punctiliously as though they were saluting royalty. "Gentlemen," cried Lord Charles, "fire, if you please." "Pardon, monsieur," the enemy replied, "the French Guards never fire first: pray, fire yourselves."

Nothing like that would ever be seen in this country of prison-sweepings, German bumpkins, and cast-off younger sons. Confound this Ohio Company whose Hanbury had possessed the influence at court to have the army ordered to take this steep and dangerous road leading out of provisionless Virginia, instead of the Raystown Path that led out of fruitful Pennsylvania. And confound their puny, weak-kneed, contentious little governments. Why was it that neither people nor governments could be depended on? Braddock, who possessed all the Irishman's facility with picturesque profanity, had found plenty of use for the talent in his relations with the colonists. He chuckled at a sudden humorous thought. That scientific fellow from Philadelphia, now—what was his name? Franklin, Benjamin Franklin. The only instance of ability and honesty in these provinces. The general almost burst into laughter at the recollection of how Franklin had gone among the tight-fisted Pennsylvania Germans and warned them against the possibility of reprisals at the hands of Sir John St. Clair, "the Hussar," if they refused to let him have their wagons for the use of the army. The Germans evidently had come into contact with hussars in the old country, for they had turned in their horses and wagons with amazing speed.

A horse bearing a tall young man in scarlet coat slowly edged by the foremost wagon train and picked its way on up the boulder-strewn highway. He would be that cocky young aide, Washington, out of his hospital wagon against orders; personable enough chap and with some knowledge of the country and its outlandish denizens, but, like the rest of his countrymen, ignorant of discipline and tactics and fractious as the devil. You'd never think he'd recently ended a bad campaign with a worse surrender. Lay a half joe he's coming now to plague me again with his pet scheme that we push on to Fort Duquesne with ten or twelve hundred light troops. Not a bad idea, even if it is his. Sound head on his shoulders, sometimes, though he'll never make a general. Let me see, we're perhaps ninety miles from Duquesne—come twenty-some miles in ten days. We'll do it, by Gad, get this demnable campaign over, and get back to civilization—well, at least to Alexandria.

A rush of memories blotted out the ocean of mountain and forest and the struggling supply train below. The general was back in England again—amid the blaze of the lamps at Vauxhall, watching the court of Comus at Ranelagh, making the circuit of the ballrooms and gambling parlors of Bath. And George Anne Bellamy, dear little Pop. Would he ever see her again! He was conscious again of his surroundings, of the oppressive loneliness of the great brooding American forest with its endless green canopy, hiding God alone knew what mysteries and terrors. Gad! it was uncanny. For the first time he understood why the faces of his oldest veterans wore that strained, haunted look that no European campaign had ever yet laid there. The pit of the stout old Irishman's stomach seemed to him to be caving in. Strange, it had never been given to that, even on the hardest fought battlefields. Only once before—that night when he had kissed little Pop good-by in London, and whispered to her that he and his men were being sent like sacrifices to the altar. Perhaps his premonition that night was more than a premonition. Perhaps it was a prophecy.

II

BRADDOCK did push on with his best troops as Washington had suggested, though even at that his progress through the forest was painfully slow. Gist's Plantation was reached on June 27, 1755, and from thence the army marched to the vicinity of the present town of Irwin. In order to avoid ambush in the deep gorge of Turtle Creek the army forded the Monongahela six miles above the mouth of that creek and recrossed it below. These crossings, completed by early afternoon of July 9, were to Braddock's surprise accomplished without any sign of opposition; the way seemed clear for a rapid march covering the last ten miles of the distance to Fort Duquesne. On the banks of the Monongahela, in John Fraser's clearing, where the Edgar Thomson Works of the Carnegie-Illinois Steel Corporation now stand, the British regiments halted for a spot of late breakfast and a bit of heartening drill, this last partly to impress the French and Indians who the general felt sure were watching from covert. Years later a survivor of the battle described the passages of the river and the drill: "A fairer sight could not have been beheld, the shining barrels of the muskets, the excellent order of the men, the cleanliness of their appearance, the joy depicted on every face at being so near Fort Duquesne, the highest object of their wishes—the music re-echoed through the mountains. How brilliant the morning—how melancholy the evening!"

The garrison of Fort Duquesne, meanwhile, was in panic at the approach of Braddock, and Contrecœur, it is supposed, planned a retreat by water. Captain Daniel Lienard de Beaujeu and Captain Jean Daniel Dumas, however, had a different plan, and the former begged Contrecœur to allow them to attack the British during the last miles of their march, while they were still entangled in the forest. Contrecœur finally consented, being almost obliged to do so because De Beaujeu had been sent out as his successor; and he gave the captain between 200 and 250 French and as many Indians as could be persuaded to accompany him. De Beaujeu repaired posthaste to the Indian encampment outside the fort and, calling the chiefs into council, threw a tomahawk at their feet as a summons to battle. The Indians, doubtless impressed by the might of the mad Irishman and his redcoats and perhaps also secretly pleased at the thought of letting the French and British slaughter each other, wrapped their blankets of good English strouding about them and impassively refused to budge.

In the morning De Beaujeu and his band attended mass in the little log chapel of the Assumption of the Blessed Virgin at the Beautiful River and received the Communion from the black-robed Father Baron. De Beaujeu then went again to the Indian encampment and besought the chiefs to follow him. The tale goes that the chiefs were still firm in their decision; but when a runner appeared with word that the British were on their way to the second ford of the Monongahela, De Beaujeu seized that electric moment to declare, "I am determined to go out against the enemy. I am certain of victory. What! Will you suffer your father to go alone?" The savages, fired by this appeal to their loyalty, sprang to their feet and shouted their determination to accompany him.

Young James Smith, a provincial lad who had been captured and forced to run the gantlet by the Indians, and who was then in the French fort convalescing from his bruises, heard the stir without, clambered upon the wall, and looked down upon a strange scene. Kegs of bullets and gunpowder had been broached before the gate, and the Indians "in a huddle" were helping themselves, "everyone taking what suited." Each tribe in the French alliance for hundreds of miles around was represented. There were, of course, the newly won over Delawares, Shawnee, and Mingo; the Chippewa were there from beyond Lake Michigan, the Ottawa under the soon-to-be famous Pontiac, and the Huron under the ferocious mission-named Athanase of Lorette. There were probably about six hundred savage allies who fell into line with De Beaujeu and his French and Canadians

31

as they took the well-trod path that led through the field of knee-high corn and up the winding course of the Monongahela.

III

THE British advance party under Lieutenant-Colonel Thomas Gage (destined to hold the British command in America at the beginning of the Revolution) angled away from the river toward the gently rising hill; following the advance with two little cannon came the pioneers who, under Sir John St. Clair, busied themselves in clearing a wagon road through the forest; and all too close came the main body of troops, split into parallel columns by the wagon train and without room between the platoons to maneuver in case of attack. The line of march extended from the river shore at the present upper end of the Edgar Thomson Steel Works, through the present junction of Jones and Bell Avenues just north of Braddock Station on the Pennsylvania Railroad, and to about the place where Penn Street meets the same railroad; most of the line was in the southern part of what is now the borough of North Braddock. The woods on every side were so open that "Carridges could have been drove in any part of them." The advance party had crossed one deep ravine that ran at a right angle to their course and were just emerging from the second such ravine, about a thousand yards from the ford, when, through the forest, they saw De Beaujeu with his French and Indians coming on the run—too late to dispute the passage of the river, but not too late to win an overwhelming victory in the woods.

The British fired promptly, and a hundred untried young Canadians took to their heels and stopped not until they had reached Fort Duquesne; the Indians stood undecided. De Beaujeu and Dumas waved their hats as a signal to their men to form a skirmish line and charge. The British, seeing the flight of the Canadians, fired another volley and cried "God save the King!" They might better have forgotten the king, snug in his English palace, and spoken for themselves. By this time the two cannon had been brought into play and De Beaujeu fell dead at the head of the French charge, while the Indians,

32

dismayed by the artillery fire, fled. Dumas, however, directed his platoon of regulars so effectively that the British advance was stopped; and the savages, seeing this, obeyed Dumas' orders to spread out along the enemy's flanks. Trees, bushes, and inequalities in the ground were put to use by the savages, and a hill to the right of the British was used as a vantage point from which to fire down on the enemy.

Braddock and his staff, napkins tucked under chins, were at dinner when the cannonading began, but at the sound of the firing they sprang up and hurried to their posts, some of them not even bothering to remove their napkins. Among the officers was Washington, just off a sick pallet in a provision wagon, and still so weak and gaunt that he had to have a pillow placed in his saddle. Braddock ineptly ordered up the main body, then plunged into the forest and hurried to the head of the line where the firing was heaviest. The advance party had been crumpled and thrown back about 250 yards on the line of march to the vicinity of the point where Jones and Bell Avenues now meet in North Braddock; the two cannon had been abandoned to the French. The troops were crowded into the twelve-foot wide road or crouched behind the prostrate trees that had been felled a few hours beforehand; they could not retreat along the road because it was jammed with confused masses of reinforcements, and they did not dare to get very far out on the flanks for fear of the Indians, who sporadically charged the line and, after taking a few scalps, melted back into the forest. The British soldiers, European and colonial, lost their wits completely and spent their ammunition firing uselessly into the tops of trees.

Braddock rode into this turmoil and probably decided in his muddled way that if he could whip his men into line and march them forward out of range of the hill that the savages were using as a citadel the French and Indians would be caught as in a vise and would have to flee or be annihilated by musketry and shell fire; even a retreat would have enabled the artillery to get in its deadly work and have cleared the way for a victorious advance. Before the troops could advance or retreat it was essential that they form on the road in some regular order. The soldiers, however, terrified by this new kind of warfare and hopelessly out of touch with their platoons, refused to stand up and be shot at. When commands and entreaties failed Braddock rode about beating his men with the flat of his sword, trying to force them into line. He was a conspicuous figure in scarlet coat and brilliant sash, his hat bound on with his dinner napkin, urging his horse from tree to tree, commanding, cajoling, pleading, and cursing, his bright sword gleaming in the spotty sunlight as it rose and fell on the shoulders of the recalcitrant soldiers; but all to no avail. General Braddock had come a long way from Fontenoy.

The standards were raised from the stumps and bushes where they had fallen in the first panic and were thrust deeply into the soft wood's mold to furnish rallying points, while the officers, as terrified as the common soldiers, joined half-heartedly in urging the men into line. Suddenly Braddock's horse, struck by a bullet, sank under him, but in another moment he had ordered an officer from his horse and was up again. Washington, who had been following Braddock meanwhile, also found his horse crumpling to the ground and for a moment he must have been uncertain whether it had been he or the horse that had given way. Braddock's servant Bishop lifted the buckskin-clad Virginian onto another horse. But now the young aide-de-camp had an idea. If he could only bring up the company of Virginia troops and flank the French and Indians the day might be saved. Braddock's consent was given with a sulphurous aside, and Washington fought his way back down the seething forest aisle.

Presently some of the calmer British soldiers, looking into the woods on the right, saw a party of buckskinned men whom they took for Frenchmen advancing on a parallel. The watchers delivered one of the few effective volleys of the day upon the buckskins and about two-thirds of them fell. They had fired on Washington's Virginians. Another flanking party under Captain Waggoner received similar treatment, thus effectually discouraging any attempts at easing the pressure of the French and

Indians. Washington's men joined the British line and he, his second horse dead and his clothes riddled with bullets, walked about among them exhorting them to "Draw your sights for the honour of old Virginia!" Sir Peter Halkett was shot and his son, bending over to lift his father's body, fell dead across it. Years later another Halkett was to recognize his father's and brother's remains by the positions of their bodies. Of the men who were later to become famous, Thomas Gage, Henry Gladwin, and Horatio Gates were wounded; characteristically enough, Charles Lee came out unscathed. Providence, of course, saw to it that Washington was unharmed; he certainly could not have been credited with looking out for his own safety.

IV

By now Braddock was on his fifth horse and so infuriated that he was running his men through. One of the men he killed, so runs the legend, was a Pennsylvanian named Fawcett; the man's brother, Tom Fawcett, thereupon drew a bead on the general and brought him off his horse, mortally wounded. Whether or not the fatal shot was fired in this manner, Braddock was down and all pretense of discipline was over. This was probably between four and five o'clock. Apparently the press at the lower end of the road had eased, for the dammed stream of humanity above was now able to move its thinning current. As soon as they realized that they could get away the soldiers ran, throwing away their weapons and knapsacks and even some of their garments in their terrified haste. Braddock would probably have been trampled to death had not one of his aides, Captain Robert Orme, stood over him while Bishop tried to stanch the wound. Orme, wounded himself, tried in vain to get help in moving the fallen general; the maddened fugitives pressed on, flinging a curse at him and doubtless adding that they hoped the general would roast in hell before night. Braddock was not popular, then or since.

Washington and Croghan finally came by and lifted the dying man to the back of a horse and then into a wagon, in spite of his protests that he wished to be left on the field of his dis-

35

grace. Washington turned back and joined the surviving officers and a handful of the men in holding the ford; a rear action so well fought that the Indians had no stomach for further combat but occupied themselves with the spoils of the battle field. During the night Braddock sent Washington, Croghan, and a few light-horsemen to Colonel Dunbar, who had led the remainder of the army as far as Gist's Plantation, with orders to hurry food and wagons on to the army. Braddock followed in a litter.

Dunbar, had he possessed the resolution, might yet have retrieved victory, but, almost as terrified as the rank and file, he hastily destroyed most of the wagons and stores and began the retreat that ended in Philadelphia—winter quarters in August, with each of his men rewarded for his haste by the gift of a flannel jacket and an apple-pie dinner from the Quakers. Braddock died four days after the battle and was buried in the road near Great Meadows. George Washington, it is said, read the burial service in lieu of the chaplain, who had been badly wounded. The remaining wagons, two of them piloted by Daniel Morgan and Daniel Boone, were then driven over the grave to keep the Indians from locating the spot. Of the eighty-three commissioned officers with Braddock, sixty-three were killed or wounded, and over four hundred and fifty enlisted men were killed. French and Indians together had only thirty dead.

v

THE news of Braddock's defeat spread consternation throughout the colonies, especially on the frontier, where it was realized that the victorious Indians would soon be on the warpath, bound for the outlying settlements. The Quakers considered the disaster a judgment for having made war on the Indians. In far off Newport the Reverend William Vinal, taking for a text the words "Sanctify Yourselves against To-morrow," preached a sermon on "The Accursed Thing That Hinders Success and Victory in War." The "Accursed Thing," it developed, was self-confidence, which had led not only Braddock's soldiers but the British nation to *discharge Vollies* of profane Oaths and Curses against the *Battlements* of Heaven."

"How are the mighty fallen," he cried, "and the Weapons of War perished! Tell it not at *Quebec*, publish it not in the Streets of *Paris*, lest the Daughters of *France* rejoice, and the Sons of *Anti-christ* triumph. Ye Mountains of *Apalachea*, and ye plains of *Ohio*, let there be no Dew, neither let there be rain upon you—and thou *Monongahela*, let not thy Waters, stain'd with the Blood of British Warriors, henceforth flow, to regale and fertilise thy fatal Banks." Vinal closed with the exhortation "as therefore we have taken the *Sword* in one Hand, we ought to take *Prayer* in the other"; from which, perhaps, his hearers understood that war was a sanctified institution as long as the warrior trusted in the Lord and refrained from enjoying his work.

III

Robbers' Roost

FOR more than a year after Ward's surrender of Fort Prince George in April, 1754, the axes of the French woodsmen rang across the low plain between the rivers, and when they ceased the primeval forest had vanished forever from what is now the Golden Triangle. In its place a small, compact fort had risen at the Point, while between the fort and the forest remaining on the higher ground stretched from river to river an immense field of waving corn that in wet seasons was partially inundated by ponds about which mosquitos and ducks loved to congregate.

The rude palisade that constituted Fort Prince George had been destroyed by the invaders, who had then spent several days in exploration before deciding to utilize the site for the new structure. The fort, which appropriately enough was named for the Marquis Duquesne, was placed directly at the Point, one corner, the northwestern, being perhaps ten yards from the junction of the rivers. The main structure of the fort was about fifty yards square, with the sides, or curtains, almost facing the points of the compass. There was an arrowhead shaped bastion placed at each corner to enable the garrison to control with its fire the approaches to the curtains; these bastions were formed of two walls of squared logs filled with earth, and were said to have been twelve feet thick and eight feet high. Each bastion was defended by cannon. The curtains on the landward sides were four or five feet thick at the top and with platforms inside where riflemen could stand; these curtains were also formed of dirt and logs. The curtains toward the rivers and the northwestern bastion between them were simple log stockades about twelve feet high. Two lunettes, or supplementary earthen bastions, were placed on the landward sides, the east and south. A moat, subject to overflow from the river, enclosed the entire fort and there probably was at one time a seven-foot stockade in addition. The land entrance was by means of a passage through the eastern lunette and a drawbridge over the moat; the water entrance was through the western curtain. The interior of the fort, though constricted, contained a kitchen, smithy, storehouse, magazine, commandant's house, and doubtless other buildings used from time to time for various purposes. The garrison, which varied in size at different years and seasons, was apparently never small enough to be housed in the limited quarters within the fort. At first it was lodged in bark huts outside the fort on the landward side, but later barracks were erected on the bank of the Allegheny. Other houses or cabins were built outside the fort during the latter years of the French occupation. Vegetable gardens occupied parts of the banks of the rivers, and there, where railroads and warehouses now vie for possession, many a homesick Frenchman did fatigue among the onions and radishes and dreamed of the little gardens along the Seine or the Loire.

II

SOMEWHERE on the cornfield edge of the parade ground outside the fort there was probably located a village of bark wigwams used by the Indian allies who appeared at Fort Duquesne from time to time. The proverbial schoolboy knows that in the French and Indian War the British, having the triple advantages of being agricultural, of ruling the sea, and of holding the shorter inner line with a compact colonial population of a million and a quarter, were destined to conquer the wood-ranging Frenchmen, who were weak at sea, and who, with a scanty colonial population of eighty thousand, were forced to defend a long frontier extending from Nova Scotia to the Gulf of Mexico. What the proverbial schoolboy does not know, however, is that every night the Ohio Indian prayed to the Great Manitou that the two Great White Fathers might devour each other.

The Indian, who was no fool at diplomacy, was little impressed by either side's protestations of friendship. At the moment the French, having won the first round, were to be preferred, but the Indian never forgot that English trade goods were cheaper and better. On the other hand, there were those ubiquitous English settlers who persisted in clearing the land and driving out the game. The French were not much given to that, but then had not one of their commanders taunted the native sons of the Ohio country that not so much as the dirt under their finger nails was theirs? It was not any wonder that one puzzled Indian, viewing the struggle between the two great powers, "desired to know where the Indians' Land lay, for that the French claimed all the Land on one side the River Ohio & the English on the other Side."

The commandants of Fort Duquesne, though they were ostensibly in control of the Ohio Valley, looked over the ramparts at the circle of Indian fires in the clearing, fully aware they they were being watched by thousands of distrustful eyes. The Indians openly jeered at the white man's story that the war was simply for the control of the fur trade; with all the cunning that Mother Nature gives to her sons they astutely played the French and English against each other, while the squaws in their smoky wigwams strung their gayest wampum and cured their choicest tobacco against the day of the peace treaty with the winner.

III

LATE on the afternoon of Braddock's defeat young James Smith, who had been prowling restlessly about Fort Duquesne hoping for the best but fearing the worst, heard a number of halloos and saw a company of French and Indians arrive laden with British canteens, bayonets, grenadier's hats, and scalps. This was only the first of a long procession. The sun sank blood red over the towering height beyond the Monongahela, and still the victors continued to come in with spoils from the battlefield. Savages from beyond the lakes, who had never known anything better than buckskin and the woolen trade blankets called strouds, strutted about the plaza in scarlet coats (some of them with blood-stained bullet holes), silver gorgets, and gold-laced hats; a dozen prisoners stripped and blackened shivered at one side, not so much because of the evening chill as in antici-pation of the coming torture; Delawares and Shawnee, drunk on captured rum, reeled about flourishing raw scalps on bloody swords; hideously painted savages from the prairies of Iowa and Illinois danced and yelled in an ecstasy of blood drunkenness; over all rose the sharp reports of muskets as the Indians, revel-ing in the possession of a superabundance of powder, spent it in a frenzy of jubilation. The scene was not one of mere victory over the English; it was essentially the unleashing of primitive passions and their slaking in an orgy of blood. If the French ac-counts are to be believed, the Indians even resorted to cannibal-ism on that dreadful day, drinking broth made from the flesh of their victims. There were scalps, hundreds of blond, brown, or black British scalps, still dripping blood as the savages stretched them on hoops to cure.

The street of the little village along the Allegheny was prob-ably the scene on this day of numerous gantlet-runnings. The Indians, men and women, gathered in two long files facing each other, all armed with knives, tomahawks, or clubs. The prisoners were then forced to run between the lines while the Indians each tried to get in as many effective blows as they could on the naked bodies of the runners. This was the mildest part of the Indian's greeting to the visitors—as one old Delaware explained to James Smith, it was just "like how do you do." The warmest part of the welcome came about sundown, when the prisoners were fer-ried over the Allegheny to Smoky Island, a low bar on the north shore directly across from the Point. There they were tied to stakes or saplings and put to the most fiendish tortures that the savages could devise. Coals of fire were heaped about their feet; the women thrust red-hot ramrods through their nostrils and ears and seared their bodies with blazing sticks; even the children stood around with their half-sized bows and shot arrows into the legs of the victims. Young Smith, watching from the ramparts of the fort, was so sickened by the sight and by the piteous screams of the dying men that he retreated to his quarters, where a Frenchman essayed to comfort him with a copy of Russel's *Seven Sermons*, which had been salvaged from the battlefield.

The torture scene after Braddock's defeat was only one of many such that occurred near the fort during its occupation by the French. The commandants of Fort Duquesne were merciful men and did all they could to prevent the torture of prisoners, but unless the Indians would sell their captives there was little the French officers could do. Under garrisoned and under supplied, the French were largely dependent upon the Indians both for defense and for carrying the war into the English settlements, and they could not afford to antagonize their allies.

IV

THE Indian, far from being the lofty stoic of fiction, possessed a lively curiosity about the world, and his wiry arms would wield the paddle across thousands of miles of northern lakes and rivers or his supple legs would pad at a tireless lope across prairie, through forest, and over hill or mountain to satisfy that curiosity. Just as the young Englishman of the sixteen-hundreds went to blood his sword on the Turks as an excuse for travel and excitement, or the wealthy sportsman of today goes to Africa to shoot elephants or to India to shoot tigers, so the young red man in the seventeen-fifties went to western Pennsylvania to indulge in the satisfying and profitable but not too dangerous sport of hunting Englishmen. Around the fort at the Point gathered not only the local Shawnee and Delawares and the mission Indians from the St. Lawrence, but also wheat-raising Indians from Kaskaskia and tattooed Miami from the Maumee River Valley, where the maize was whiter and sweeter than elsewhere and where the buffalo defied nature by eating clay. Then there were vermilioned Ouaitenon from the Wabash, the land of plenty, who loved games and dances, and who were so cleanly that they kept the ground in their villages sanded like the Tuileries and went to great trouble to village-break their dogs. But allies came from even greater distances. The Ottawa from the shores of Lake Superior crouched about their fires and played a curious game with a bowl and parti-colored pebbles, or matched themselves against the visiting Foxes of Wisconsin at brutal games of lacrosse upon the parade of the fort; Chippewa threw the last of their wild rice into the cooking pot and after they had eaten it lay down to dream of their bark huts on the shores of the Minnesota lakes. When some of the young men of the tribes from the lower Mississippi, perhaps Chickasaw or Osage, who had been traditional enemies of the French and allies of the English traders from Carolina, appeared to join in the hunt, the suspicious commandant held a council with them under the grapeshotted guns of the fort.

The Point must have been a colorful spot during the French occupation. Not only were there Indians there from every tribe in the French alliance, but fleets of bateaux from Canada and the Illinois were arriving with provisions and munitions and were tied to the banks while the voluble red-capped boatmen went off in search of brandy and Indian women. Bovine Canadian militia or spruce soldiers of the marine (for New France was governed through the navy), arriving to serve their stint at this far outpost, flirted with the wives and daughters of the villagers. They gazed with fascinated horror at the blood-stained scalps of incoming war parties and at the gaunt linsey-woolsey clad men and women from the English settlements undergoing the cruel ordeal of running the gantlet or dying slowly at the stake. It would not be long, however, before the new arrivals would become hardened to blood and suffering and would be traversing the steep trails that led to the English forts, whose crowded denizens were destined to become prey to tomahawk, scalping knife, and stake.

Dumas succeeded to the command of Fort Duquesne, probably in September, 1755, and vigorously pushed the war against the English settlements. The havoc that the French and Indian bands, under the leadership of young cadets, wrought upon the

Pennsylvania, Maryland, and Virginia borders during the years from 1755 to 1758 is written in letters of blood in the annals of the frontier. Hundreds of captives were taken to Fort Duquesne, and night after night the agonized screams of the tortured captives on Smoky Island must have made the French soldiers and citizens at the Point bury their heads under the blankets. The haughty Indian allies were a continual problem to the French commandants, especially when they were in liquor, and matters finally reached the point where a military order was issued forbidding the sale or gift of brandy to the savages.

v

Not all the life at Fort Duquesne was concerned with war and torture. The Recollect priest, Father Denys Baron, was busy with the affairs of his parish, baptizing the children of the French families housed around the fort, saying mass in the little chapel of the Assumption of the Virgin Mary at the Beautiful River, listening to the confessions of homesick soldier boys, or blessing, perhaps with a tug of remorse in his gentle heart, the departure of stripling cadets upon raids on the English settlements.

Perhaps it was Father Denys of whom it was whispered that he had once been a cavalry officer and had become a priest after the death of the girl whom he was to marry. If this was true he must have taken a melancholy interest in the love story of an American girl known only as Rachel. Like the other prisoners, she had been forced to run the gantlet when she was brought in and had been so seriously injured that the commandant of the fort had placed her in the hospital. During the following weeks of convalescence she picked up some knowledge of French and in the process, since she was pretty and possessed of a sweet disposition, won the heart of a romantic young Canadian, who finally summoned the courage to ask the commandant's consent to their marriage. The permission was given readily on the condition that Father Denys instruct her in the principles of Catholicism and baptize her. This was soon done and the marriage ceremony was performed—perhaps the first white marriage on the site of Pittsburgh.

The marital bliss of the young couple was, however, soon interrupted. The Indians who had captured Rachel, and who had probably taken it for granted that she was dead, recognized their captive and demanded her of the commandant. When it became apparent that the savages would cause trouble if the girl was not surrendered, the commandant secretly sent the young couple down river to New Orleans in a bateau with guides and provisions, then, when a week had elapsed, informed the Indians that he had sent her to the governor and that the case was out of his hands.

The little village of about sixty cabins at the Forks was not solely a military post, though it is difficult to say just what civil pursuits were carried on. The military storekeeper seems to have done some bartering with the Indians, and there was at least one civilian trader, John Gasper Norment. His son, John Daniel, born to his wife, Mary Joseph Chainier, on September 18, 1755, and who lived only a week, was probably the first white child born in what is now Pittsburgh. There was at least one other birth during the French occupation, that of the child of an unnamed captive mother in May, 1756. The child was baptized Denise Louisa. The distance of Fort Duquesne from the source of supplies made it necessary for the garrison and the villagers to raise as much of their food supply as they could, and they took advantage of every fertile open space. It was probably the French who first cultivated the site of Hazelwood, which during the later British occupation came to be known as Scotch Flats. The regular business of the village was occasionally interrupted by floods, and one of these, in the fall of 1757, carried away fifteen cabins; not very serious losses, however, as they were easily replaced in a few days. Father Denys sometimes had the joy of welcoming to his chapel and confessional families that had fled from the English settlements and made their way to "join the Catholics of these parts." Among them was a French family that had made its way from North Carolina; the father had been killed on the journey by the Indians, who had brought in the mother. Runaway Irish servants also came in, and so many of them left

45

the settlements that the English accused French agents of having bribed them to join the Indians and to use their influence in the French cause.

VI

THE French owed their long occupation of Fort Duquesne, not to the strength of the position, but to the ineffectual prosecution of the Seven Years' War by the English. The accession of William Pitt the Elder to power in the British cabinet checked the tide of British defeats in America. Louisburg, Fort Duquesne, Quebec, and Montreal in turn fell before Pitt's victorious armies, and the French power was swept from North America never to return.

As the British succeeded in hampering French shipment of supplies to Canada and in capturing the French fleet on Lake Ontario, Fort Duquesne suffered in increasing measure for lack of munitions and trade goods, and the situation of the garrison, surrounded by potentially hostile savages, became more precarious from week to week. The officers of the fort were speculating with the pitifully inadequate supplies: the assistant storekeeper alone cleared over thirty-two thousand francs, probably in part by selling government property to the Indians. Hostile Indians and scouts haunted the woods outside the fort and occasionally picked off an unwary hunter or woodcutter for the sake of his hair. François Marchand de Ligneris, who had succeeded Dumas as commandant of the fort as early as December, 1756, had been abandoned by the Detroit Indians and the Illinois and Louisiana militia, and shortage of provisions had forced him to send away part of the men left. When his appeals to Governor-General Vaudreuil had failed to bring results De Ligneris morosely gave up and sought to drown his troubles in drink.

The safety of Fort Duquesne under its drunken commandant was further jeopardized by the diplomatic activities of that man of peace, Christian Frederick Post. As a Moravian missionary with fifteen years experience among the Indians, Post had, at the request of the government of Pennsylvania, undertaken the task of weaning the Indians away from the French alliance and smoothing the way for the military expedition that was already making its way through the defiles of the mountains. Guarded by friendly Shawnee and Mingo who had promised to "carry me in their bosoms," Post reached the bank of the Allegheny across from Fort Duquesne on August 24, 1758. Here, perhaps on the torture ground of Smoky Island, a council that lasted for three days was held with the chiefs of the tribes gathered at Fort Duquesne. French officers took over a table and writing materials and made notes on Post's speeches to the Indians. "I spoke in the middle of them with a free conscience," said Post, "and perceived, by the look of the French, they were not pleased with what I said." The French made an attempt to imprison the emissary by trying to persuade the Indians that he should be blindfolded according to the white custom and confined in the fort, but the Indians understood the French intent and refused; when the French insisted, "the Indians desired them to let them hear no more about it; but to send them one hundred loaves of bread, for they were hungry." The French then offered a reward for Post's scalp, but the missionary, warned of his danger, stayed close to the fires of his friends.

When Post left Fort Duquesne his mission had been accomplished to all practical purposes. Further negotiation and military measures would be necessary before the British control over the Ohio could be consolidated, but De Ligneris in his dipsomaniacal nightmares could read on the wall the handwriting that foretold the doom of French ambitions in the Ohio country.

IV

The Head of Iron

THE British campaign of 1758 in Pennsylvania was under the direction of the doughty, dourly handsome General John Forbes, known in western legend as the "Head of Iron," who, since he was already in the last stages of the malady that was to cause his death the next year, had to do his marching in a litter. His right hand was a Swiss lieutenant-colonel of the Royal American Regiment, Henry Bouquet, a soldier who had been trained in the wars of the European continent, but who was probably the first to develop the open order of battle that was to prove so effective against the Indians and that has become a basic principle of modern warfare. The summer of 1758 was spent by Forbes in mobilizing his six thousand motley troops, drawn from the regular army and colonial militia, and in hewing a road over the Raystown Path—a route selected in spite of the protests of Washington, who accompanied the army as one of the colonels of the Virginia troops. Evidently the interests of the Ohio Company still figured in the thoughts of loyal Virginians.

The advance, which was extremely cautious—Forbes, be it recorded, was a Scotsman—was well protected by fortified camps; and a screen of scouts so effectively veiled the movement that for several months the French, perhaps grown lax under the leader-

ship of the drunken De Ligneris, were half convinced that the
main English force, when it got ready to march, would come by
Braddock's old road. Only the peculiar fatality that seemed to
dog the footsteps of the British armies in western Pennsylvania
prevented Fort Duquesne from falling an easy prey to a recon-
noitering party, when on September 14, 1758, eight hundred
Highlanders and provincials under blustering, hot-headed Major
James Grant appeared early in the morning on the hill that overlooked the fort at the Point and the ripening corn between—the
hill that now bears the major's name and on which stand Pittsburgh's municipal buildings and tallest skyscrapers.

In his greed to snatch the prospective laurels from Forbes's
brow, Grant had developed an unwieldy plan whereby he hoped
to draw the French and Indians from the fort and into an ambush. When the little army, probably marching near the line of
what is now Penn Avenue, arrived at the hill above the fort about
two o'clock in the morning, the Adonis-like Virginia frontiersman, Major Andrew Lewis, was sent forward with four hundred
men, each with a white shirt over his uniform "to prevent mis-
takes," and ordered to bayonet the sentries and attack the Indians around their campfires. Toward dawn Lewis returned with
the complaint that his men were hopelessly lost in the fog and
darkness and were wandering around among fences, cornfields,
and fallen logs. It was not long before the white shirts began to
loom out of the fog as Lewis' Virginians straggled back to the hill.

Grant, who was furious at what he took to be Lewis' disobe-
dience, immediately sent out another party of fifty men to attack
a cabin that scouts the day before had reported as surrounded
by Indians. The Indians were gone, so the party set fire to the
cabin—thus exposing themselves to the French—and returned
to Grant about daylight. By seven o'clock the mist that obscured
the ground between the rivers had cleared away and Grant sent
a party of a hundred men to make a reconnaissance of the fort.
The nightshirt brigade of provincials was sent back to the pack-
horse train to form the ambuscade that Grant planned, and
Lewis, his classic profile still awry and cursing under his breath
all British martinets, departed at their head.

II

WORD WAS now brought to Grant that some Indians had discovered his left flank near the Monongahela and he, thinking that there was no further chance of surprising the Indians, had his drums beat the reveille "to put on a good countenance and to convince our men they had no reason to be afraid," as he expressed it. The sound of the drums was a deliberate challenge to attack, and presently the French and Indians in unexpected numbers swarmed out of the fort and its adjacent huts and barracks. While several hundred of them attacked the Highlanders in Grant's center, two other parties quietly made their way up the Monongahela and Allegheny rivers under the concealment of the banks and fell suddenly upon the British flanks. Before long Grant's entire line was in confusion and the men were retreating. Lewis, hearing the firing, came to Grant's support but missed the main line of retreat, and his men became scattered among the scores of melees that stretched from the Monongahela to the Allegheny. The soldiers, most of them either veterans of a different sort of warfare or else raw farmer boys from the seaboard, because of the tales they had heard of Braddock's defeat, were conditioned to flee before the firing began, and it is said that a hundred provincials on Grant's right actually ran at first sight of the Indians. Grant wrote later that he hoped that he would "never see again such a pannick among troops." The woods and its tangle of paths between the Allegheny and what is now known as Herron Hill were full of British and Americans, tripping over grapevines and discarded rifles and knapsacks or running into trees as they looked behind them for the descending tomahawk. Their only thought was to reach the safety of the camp at Loyalhanna fifty miles away. About 270 men were killed or captured by the French and Indians before the slaughter was over, and Major Lewis was among the captured.

Grant rallied what men he could and, turning at intervals to contest the pursuit, slowly retired to the place, probably not far from Arsenal Park, where Captain Bullett had been left with fifty Virginians in charge of the baggage. Here the fugitives gathered behind a slight barricade and withstood the French and

Indian onslaught. When all seemed lost Bullett hoisted a white flag, and he and his men emerged with their rifles held above their heads in token of surrender. Silently they advanced to within a few yards of the enemy, who had by now clustered in the open, then suddenly poured a volley into the close ranks of the bewildered victors and charged with fixed bayonets. The Indians fled helter-skelter and Bullett and his men made their escape.

Bullett, before his escape, stumbled over Grant sitting on the bank of the Allegheny with his head in his hands and his feet in the water moaning like a disconsolate Scotch Cassandra: "My heart is broke; I shall never outlive this day." When Bullett urged him to forget about military honor and join the retreat he refused and swore that he would not quit the field of battle as long as there was a man who would fight. The prosaic Virginian shrugged his buckskinned shoulders and left, while Grant and a dozen men made a last stand at the edge of the river. At first the French and Indians held their fire, desiring to take Grant prisoner, but upon his refusal to surrender they fired and drove the band into the stream. A few probably managed to swim across in spite of the plopping bullets, for the red men were notoriously poor marksmen, but Grant himself was surrounded and captured.

III

Soon afterward Major Grant, who had been placed on parole to the extent of being allowed the freedom of the fort, wrote a letter to Bouquet in which he laid the onus for the defeat on Lewis. He managed to smuggle the letter out of the fort, but it was intercepted by Indians who took it to De Ligneris; the latter, just tipsy enough to be imbued with a spirit of good clean fun, immediately read it to Andrew Lewis, who was glooming about the fort. Lewis promptly sought out Grant and challenged him to a duel, which Grant contemptuously refused. Lewis, summoning the rheum of his anger, thereupon deliberately spat in the Highlander's face. Apparently nothing more happened; at least the Virginian lived to become a well-known general during the Revolution and was even urged for the post of commander in chief of the Continental army. Grant was a British brigadier general during the Revolution and died at an advanced age, fat and full of honors.

With the preliminary comedy out of the way, De Ligneris' Indians turned to serious business. Five prisoners were burned on the parade ground before the fort. Several of the "petticoat warriors," as the fun-loving children of the forest dubbed the Highlanders, were decapitated and their heads placed on peeled stakes driven into the ground along the Indian race track. Their kilts were draped derisively around the stakes. It is said that one canny Highlander, seeing the tortures to which his fellows were subjected, persuaded the Indians that he knew the secret of an herb concoction that would make any part of the human anatomy invulnerable. When given a chance to prove his claim he smeared his neck with plant juices and, stretching it over a log, confidently gave the signal to swing the ax. The result was inevitable; perhaps the Scotsman was rewarded by having his head added to the tartan portrait gallery along the race track.

IV

NIBBLE their turkey quills as they might, neither Forbes nor Bouquet was able to give the prime minister a sufficiently exculpatory account of the defeat. De Ligneris, however, did afford them the opportunity to transmit more cheerful news a month later when he sent out a French force in an ineffectual attempt to capture the camp at Loyalhanna. Meanwhile Forbes's main army was advancing through the red and gold glory of autumn in the Pennsylvania mountains, though he, poor fellow, probably had no spirit to do more than worry about delayed provision trains and curse the jolting litter in which his pain-racked form reclined. Bouquet at the advance camp had the slightly more cheerful duties of hunting stray horses and hanging the scores of half-wild dogs that had joined the army on a vendetta of their own with the French poodles.

Finally, on November 24, the British army encamped ten or twelve miles from the fort. During the evening Indian scouts reported that Fort Duquesne had been abandoned by the French and set on fire. A troop of horse was sent on immediately to save the fort if they could. About midnight Forbes's sentries, pacing their leaf-strewn, starlit beats beneath the bare trees, heard a dull boom out of the West. The French were indeed gone. Some of them had launched their bateaux in the flickering glare of the burning fort and departed down the river to the Illinois; the others went across country or up the Allegheny to Venango.

The next morning dawned clear and crisp and the men huddled around the fires as they bolted their rations. Every heart was lifted up as the army glimpsed the end of the arduous campaign, but Forbes, remembering past tragedies and vigilant against possible surprise, threw out a strong advance guard and formed his troops into three columns. Thus marshaled, and with its hasty feet checked by the slow tap of the drum, the army advanced through the forest upon the long-sought goal. Night was just beginning to fall, however, when the army came down from the wooded hills above the Allegheny and advanced along the road that Grant had trodden so confidently a few weeks before and that was now strewn with the decayed, half-devoured bodies of his fallen comrades. The race path along which the Indians had erected their horrible trophies of Grant's defeat was near the army's route to the fort. The colonials who led passed by the spot with earnest imprecations upon the red devils and their work, but otherwise in good order. The Highlanders were next in the line of march. Presently the provincials heard a slow buzz in the rear, a buzz that rapidly swelled to an angry roar, as the enraged Highlanders, their muskets cast aside and only their deadly, naked claymores in their hands, rushed by the provincials swearing vengeance upon the French and Indian miscreants. The enemy was gone, however, and only the sodden, smoldering logs of the fort remained for the Highlanders to glut their wrath upon.

v

The Union Jack was run up over the half-fallen earth and log bastions of Fort Duquesne by the hand of the Pennsylvanian, Colonel John Armstrong of Kittanning fame, and the next two days were devoted to rest and jubilation. On November 26 a sermon of thanksgiving was delivered by the Reverend Charles Beatty, the Presbyterian chaplain; and thus early was established the priority of the Presbyterian claim on Pittsburgh. The same day the Forks of the Ohio was rechristened in honor of England's great statesman, William Pitt the Elder. With all of a Scotsman's honest glow at a task well done, Forbes took his pen in hand, headed his letter "Pittsbourgh. 27th Novem^r. 1758," and in neat, old-fashioned characters went on: "Sir, I do myself the Honour of acquainting you that it has pleased God to crown His Majesty's Arms with Success over all His Enemies upon the Ohio . . . I have used the freedom of giving your name to Fort Du Quesne, as I hope it was in some measure the being actuated by your spirits that now makes us Masters of the place. . . . I hope the name Fathers will take [it] under their Protection, In which case these dreary deserts will soon be the richest and most fertile of any possest by the British in N^o. America."

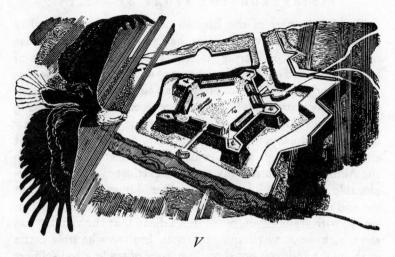

V

Britannia Rules the Ohio

WHEN Forbes and Bouquet left the Point less than two weeks
after its capture, Colonel Hugh Mercer, a Scotch medico who
had marched with Bonnie Prince Charlie and was later to lay
down his life at the battle of Princeton, was left in command
with two hundred green-coated Pennsylvanians, about eighty
Marylanders and Virginians, and a scattering of kilted Highlanders and scarlet-clad Royal Americans. Mercer and his soldiers worked frantically to erect a stockade as a protection both
against the approaching winter and against any surprise move
on the part of the half-pacified savages. The new fort, which was
located on the Monongahela River between the ends of the present West Street and Liberty Avenue, was a square structure of
earthworks and logs with four bastions; its erection progressed
so rapidly that in the early part of January, 1759, Mercer was
able to write that "the Works are now capable of some Defence,
tho' huddled up in a very hasty manner, the Weather being Extremely Severe." A line of log cabins and bark huts had meanwhile been built along the bank of the Monongahela to provide
temporary shelters for the soldiers, but as the work progressed
and the garrison was able to move into the fort, the houses were
filled by traders and their families.

The first winter of the English occupation seemed endless to the little garrison at the Point, half starved as it was because of the necessity of sharing its scanty rations with swarms of savage allies and harassed by rumors of an impending French invasion. Spring and summer brought no surcease from worry; instead it was learned that French forces were actually gathering on the upper Allegheny and expected to descend within a few days. John Ormsby, Mercer's commissary and later a prominent citizen of Pittsburgh, tells how he made "sincere application to the Almighty, to pardon my sins and extricate us from this deplorable situation." The young Quaker, James Kenny, who at the end of June had reached Pittsburgh with a pack-horse train loaded with trade goods, noted in his diary that the vicinity was alive with scouting parties of French Indians who stole cattle in the night and took pot shots at parties of traders and soldiers —not always missing their aim. Colonel Mercer and George Croghan worked overtime in their endeavor to keep the friendship of the local Indians, and dealt out rum and barbecued ox with lavish hands. James Kenny, with the egotism of the mystic, tried to pass off the worst of the rumors as attempts to frighten him from business, the while he dosed his flux-ridden partners, George Allen and Samuel Lightfoot, with "Dr Paschal's Arcanam" and "six bouleses of Specifick Vegitable" and encouraged himself by cheerful dreams.

The number as well as the success of the attacks upon isolated parties increased during the summer; a Frenchman swam over the Allegheny and viewed the fort from Grant's Hill; several large bateaux stole down the Allegheny past the fort late one July night and remained silent in spite of the fire of the English sentries; Ligonier was sorely beset by French Indians for three days, and Mercer, anticipating an attack on Pittsburgh, pulled down the huts on the bank of the Monongahela and moved the traders with their goods and families into the already cramped quarters within the fort. The Indians that infested the Point moved across the Allegheny to Smoky Island to await the outcome of the battle in ostentatious neutrality, though they beguiled the weary wait by slipping back through the English sentries and stealing horses. On July 30 Kenny wrote, perhaps in all seriousness, "Samuel Lightfoot departed this life, being somewhat light headed towards ye last." Kenny himself then came down with the flux, "occasioned by ye smell in tending on him," but was up and "worming" skins when the news came that the French had abandoned their forts at Presque Isle and Venango and had met with a disastrous defeat at Niagara. That battle broke the power of the French in the West; Pittsburgh was safe, at least for a time.

II

IN AUGUST, 1759, came Forbes's successor, General John Stanwix, who, though he entered Pittsburgh to the sound of music, was appraised by the critical Quaker eyes of Kenny as "very plainly dressed & seems not proud." The general lost no time in beginning the erection of a permanent stronghold at the Point. Two army engineers, Bernard Ratzer and Harry Gordon, were responsible for the plans. Artificers came out from Philadelphia and the soldiers provided an abundance of unskilled labor, so that before the end of August the mounded ruins of Fort Duquesne had become the center of a busy collection of forges, saw pits, and brick kilns, and a water-powered sawmill was being erected on what has ever since been known as Sawmill Run on the south side of the Ohio about a mile below the Point. The stone was probably quarried from Herron Hill, and the clay for brick, so says tradition, was dug from the hill on which Duquesne University now stands, then known as Ayres's Hill from the commander of a British battery posted there. There were a million and a quarter of these bricks, a dirty white in color; when the fort was abandoned years later they were valued as building material by the townsmen. The noble savage who drifted in from the forest to exchange wampum with the big white chief and to eat his bread saw with dismay and resentment that every sign pointed to a permanent occupation by the whites. The slovenly aggregation of log cabins and bark huts on the bank of the Monongahela had reappeared and even spread to Grant's Hill and the bank of the Allegheny. A census taken

57

in July, 1760, listed 201 houses and "hutts." There were in the village, besides soldiers, 90 men, 29 women, 14 boys, and 18 girls, a total population of 151. Convenient flats along the rivers were being cleared and planted, and tavern-keepers were being encouraged to settle along Forbes's road.

By March, 1760, the troops were able to move into the new fort, though a year's work was yet to be done upon it. Stanwix departed for the East and left Major John Tulleken in command of a greatly augmented garrison. During the summer Pittsburgh was visited by Stanwix' successor, General Robert Monckton, who sent Bouquet north to occupy Venango and Presque Isle and held a long and amicable powwow with the chiefs of the Six Nations. Tulleken was succeeded by Colonel James Burd, a Scotch-Pennsylvanian who had earned his spurs under Forbes, and Burd was succeeded by Major Vaughn. Bouquet was, under Monckton, the commander in the West.

James Kenny, who had returned East in 1759, came back to Pittsburgh in April, 1761, as a clerk in the store established there by the province of Pennsylvania. As he approached the Point from the east the young Quaker must have halted in open-mouthed wonder before the frowning battlements that formed such a contrast to the log stockade he had left. The outer work was a formidable serrated embankment stretching from the Monongahela River to the Allegheny River across the lower end of the point. When the clerk entered the fort to present his pass to Colonel Bouquet he passed through a narrow slit in the embankment and crossed a drawbridge that led to what was literally an island in a moat; the muddy water of the swollen Allegheny flowed in and completely encircled the inner fortifications. A second drawbridge led from the island in the moat through a gateway in the massive fifteen-foot brick and earth wall of the inner fort. Upon entering the trader could see that he was in an irregular pentagon with five bastions. The two sides to landward were of brick and earth reënforced with stone, and the other three were of earth surmounted with stockades. The longest side of the pentagon was about sixty yards in length.

Built into the steep brick walls or jammed against the stockades were long casemates, or bombproof shelters for the garrison's guns, and near them snuggled the barracks and storehouses, with their roofs peeping over the top of the fort. Flights of steps led up to the firing parapet that extended around part of the interior.

A tour of the fort showed that each of the bastions had its complement of cannon. These bastions were all named. The one on the southwest was known as the Monongahela; the one on the southeast was appropriately called the Flag, because it held "a High Poal like a Mast & top Mast to Hoist ye flag on which is Hoisted on every first Day of ye Week from about Eleven to One o'clock & on State Days." Just north of the Flag was the largest bastion, the Grenadier, which guarded the main entrance to the fort and which held two stone magazines heavily covered with earth. Near by were the entrances to the dark underground dungeons where prisoners were confined. Kenny probably looked into the dank depths with a shudder and then hastily ascended the steps to the ramparts where he could breathe pure air and continue his tour. The next bastion was called the Music, per-haps because the garrison's buglers blew their signals at this point or because Pittsburgh's first band concerts were played there. Certainly a good view might be had from there of the King's Artillery Gardens along the Allegheny River, where walks and vegetable plots had been laid out and where the tender green of pear and apple trees had just unfolded for the first time in Pitts-burgh. The spot was already the favorite strolling place of officers and townsmen in the cool of the evening. The remaining bastion, the Ohio, overlooked the Allegheny River, which was still con-sidered as part of the Ohio River. From the Ohio Kenny could look across the moat toward the Point and see that the glacis on that side was sodded carefully, and that several overall-clad soldiers were swishing their sickles through the grass. Beyond the glacis, along the river banks, and following in part the con-tour of old Fort Duquesne, ran a log stockade intended to prevent an enemy from gaining access to the glacis. The paci-fistic Quaker as he turned away from this new Gibraltar of the

West must have agreed with the red men that it looked as though British military might had come to the Ohio Valley to stay, and perhaps, as a thrifty trader, he was not ill-pleased with these signs of the march of progress.

III

PITTSBURGH was completely under military rule during the first years of the English occupation. Traders could build houses only by permission, and selling or renting was strictly prohibited; only small quantities of powder and lead could be sold to the Indians, and no liquor; trade ceased automatically upon the firing of the sunset gun at the fort. Bouquet, to prove that he was not fooling, even banished several traders who had been guilty of breaking the regulations and had their houses pulled down. George Croghan was the crown representative in the regulation of the trade, and there were those who claimed that he did not hesitate to turn his position to personal advantage by favoring certain traders with whom he was secretly in partnership. Kenny had brought a consignment of wampum with him when he came West in 1759, but Croghan, apparently seeing a chance to turn a penny, had appropriated half of it for "yᵉ kings use." The Quaker had no recourse, but a little later he noted with satisfaction that the king's man had a black eye given him by the Indian, Tedyuscung, in a brawl.

There were probably never less than a score of traders in Pittsburgh and these with their clerks, their packers, and their families made a populous community. Since the Indians usually came in from the north the traders at first built on the bank of the Allegheny; when an Indian with a bundle of peltry on his back appeared at the edge of the woods and hallooed across the river, there was considerable rivalry as to who should ferry him across and gain his business. The competition among the traders was bitter. The Jewish firm of Levy and Franks, with which William Trent and Croghan were affiliated, dismayed its competitors by allowing liberal credit. The provincial store under the management of Josiah Davenport, with James Kenny as one of his clerks, did not flourish at first, but as its business picked up it became the target for its rivals' venom. Kenny found melancholy satisfaction in being an "Obstruction to ye Progress of Satan's Govinen^t or Kingdom at this place." He did, however, oblige Satan in one respect; since the traders made a practice of doing business on the Sabbath, he would occasionally open the store on that day for the accommodation of the Indians. The fact that Kenny was a Quaker made him more or less popular with the Indians, and he smugly noted in his diary that of all the traders in Pittsburgh they trusted only him and John Hart. The latter was the dean of the English traders; he had been among the first to follow the Shawnee across the mountains and could speak to every customer in his own tongue and reminisce about the days when neither English nor French soldiers had infested the western wilderness.

The Indians were as temperamental as children in their trade relations. On Christmas day, 1761, an Indian sold four turkeys to Kenny and lingered for Christmas dinner. Later in the day the Indian heard of a better market so came and took back his turkeys. For some reason he was not pleased with the second offer and took his turkeys back to Kenny. "But," recorded the Quaker quaintly, "he said Dam it several times at ye Second Chap." Upon another occasion, when the squeamish Kenny refused to allow some of his customers to spend the night in the store with their squaws, the Indians vented their spleen by throwing stones at the house. Indians had to be watched every moment that they were in the store, and robberies were so frequent at night in the village that between the "fleeas" and the apprehension caused by every noise Kenny got little sleep. In spite of these drawbacks and the fact that the Indians would "grummle much" and threaten to carry their goods to other traders, Kenny found them quite reasonable and so naïve that "scarcely any of them but may be easily Cheat'd."

IV

LIFE in Pittsburgh during the summer of 1761 had its recompenses, even for a suspicious young Quaker set down in the midst of the sons of Belial. Work was still under way upon the fort, and Kenny, when he applied to Bouquet to detail a green-coat from the Pennsylvania troops to aid in the provincial store, was assured that not a man could be spared. Kenny noted with characteristic approval that the garrison was very "deligent" in their work. "Y^e Drum beats as its light in ye morning to set all to Work & holds it untill ye Gun fires late after sun Down." Kenny himself, since trade was dull in the store, engaged in what innocent amusements the place afforded: he went with Dr. James Miller, the military surgeon, to "Vissit ye Sick & see him Dress sores," or botanized with John Bartram, the father of American botanical science, and brought back from the old battlefield on Grant's Hill a sackful of bones to fit together during quiet evenings with pipe and slippers by the fireside; he crossed the Monongahela and climbed up a precipitous path to a mine where he could watch sacks of coal being heaved down the hill to the water's edge; he fished industriously, hoping for one of the hundred-pound catfish that were known to exist in the rivers, but had to be content with a few nine-pounders and a multitude of mosquito bites; William Ramsey occasioned nine days of wonder by navigating a swivel boat made by fastening together two square-stern boats at the after ends and rigging up two paddle wheels that were turned by a "Traddle." In September Kenny made a trip down the Ohio to "ye Oyle Spring," but failed to find it; about the same time Dr. Miller "Cut his own throat at Night in his Room with two Rayzors, which affect'd ye People very much in General; he had been at times Hipt or Lunatick."

Summer and autumn wore away. In November what was probably Pittsburgh's first school was organized and held in Colonel Burd's house on the slopes of Grant's Hill. Kenny, who evidently considered himself above the need of schoolmaster or church service, recorded: "Many of ye Inhabitants here have hired a School Master & Subscrib'd above Sixty Pounds for this Year to him, he has about Twenty Schollars, likewise ye Soberer sort of People seems to Long for some publick way of Worship, so ye School Master Reads ye Littany & Common Prayer on ye first Days to a Congregation of different Principels (he being a Prisbiterant) where they behave very Grave (as I hear), on y^e

occasion ye Children also are brought to Church as they Call it."

The routine of Pittsburgh life was interrupted early in January, 1762, by a sudden rise in the rivers. The water boiled up into the fort through the drains and sally-ports and flooded the magazines and casemates. Bouquet brought the king's bateaux into the fort and had them loaded with provisions in the event that the fort had to be abandoned, and he sent part of his men to the safety of Grant's Hill. The colonel remained on the ramparts throughout one night; even in the darkness he could tell that the currents of the two rivers, covered with ice and trees, had joined above the fort. About one o'clock, when the water had reached the top of the ramparts and the men of the garrison were about to take to their overladen bateaux, the rising waters were stopped by a cold snap. The damage done to the fort was considerable, but the traders suffered even more. Most of their houses on the bank of the Allegheny were swept away and some of them were smashed on the present Neville Island; most of their stock in trade was lost and what was left decorated the bushes on Grant's Hill for a week, as the owners attempted to dry it out.

The villagers, however, were soon living their normal lives again. Several soldiers who had been convicted of forgery were given a thousand lashes each; with the coming of spring the inhabitants "sow'd Sallad & Red Beets & Cabbage"; John Hart made the error of favoring his red friends with rum and at Croghan's complaint had his liquor carried into the king's storehouse; Pittsburgh's first recorded epidemic of flu was noted by Kenny in April, 1762; an Indian chief was buried with military honors, and all through the night the Indians shot off guns to scare away the evil spirit; Bouquet departed in May for a short visit in the East, leaving Captain Thomas Barnsley in command; a plague of grasshoppers fell upon the cabbage patches of the villagers and devoured the vegetables; twenty or more bateaux were built; the Indians surrendered about fifty white captives, but many of the latter were so enamored with the savage life that they slipped back to the Indian villages; Croghan's scheme of trusting the Indians for payment did not turn out so well and had to be abandoned; John Ormsby, the king's commissary, was appointed by his good friend Bouquet to read the Book of Common Prayer in public on Sundays. Traders and officers who came in from visits to the Indian villages went into long sessions with the commandants and reported invariably that the French were stirring up the Indians to confederate under the great Ottawa chieftain, Pontiac, and that they planned to drive the English back across the mountains, if not into the ocean. The cautious Bouquet took his informants so seriously that the cannon of the fort were kept loaded while artillerymen with lighted fuses stood by them day and night to guard against surprise.

The summer and the next winter passed peaceably enough, however. Every Monday the officers held a "club"—a new euphemism for "drinking bout"—and every Saturday there was a ball, probably in the commandant's brick dwelling house within the fort, to which the village beauties waded through the mud and where they flirted and drank punch with the redcoats. Doubtless more than one of the girls was able to wangle for herself a marital interest in a king's commission. Kenny, who was still fighting the devil on the frontier, and who never failed to hear scandal about Croghan, whispered to his diary that the Irishman in his cups on St. Patrick's night had proposed a toast to the Old Pretender, King James, and two days later Captain Simon Ecuyer, a Swiss mercenary who had been made commandant, wrote that Croghan had not yet recovered sufficiently to write a report on his Indian affairs. The missionary, Christian Frederick Post, was frequently in Pittsburgh mixing provincial duties with church business and occasionally stopped off at the Pennsylvania store to indulge in theological dispute with Kenny. The Quaker noted with gloomy satisfaction that the missionary "Sallutes men by ye Hat & bowing & Cringing drink Healths & be their Humble Servant"; one night he dreamed that the devil with the "ficognomy & Dress" of Post appeared to him. Post was probably disturbed neither by Kenny's arguments nor his dreams, but went on holding divine services "in his manner." When Ecuyer's waiting man applied to Post to marry him to a village girl, the missionary, to the discomfiture of the soldier, had the banns published for thirty days "in three sundry places, which makes ye people here Stair, it being so Strange a thing here."

March, 1763, brought a flood that rose even higher than that of the year before, but did not do as much damage to the village, though it undermined three sides of the fort and tumbled part of the ramparts into the moat. Ecuyer reported to Bouquet that the flood did not prevent the celebration of St. Patrick's day in every manner.

VI

Pioneer Village in War and Peace

THE storm that Pontiac and his conspirators had been conjuring up in the Northwest during the winter burst in May, 1763, and of the frontier posts only Detroit, Niagara, Pitt, Ligonier, and Bedford held out. There had been a number of murders of whites by Indians in the vicinity of Fort Pitt during May, and Ecuyer had done everything he could to put the fort into a state of defense, not a very easy matter, because of the damage caused by the late flood. Ecuyer, however, filled the gap in the ramparts with a palisade strengthened by a fraise with the sharpened stakes pointing outward, and erected firing parapets. The townsmen, less than a hundred in number, were at first organized into two companies of militia under William Trent but soon afterward were distributed among the regular troops. The first warning Pittsburgh had that an attack in force was imminent came on May 27 when a certain Turtle's Heart, after trading with a group of friends at the provincial store, sought out Alexander McKee, Croghan's deputy in the management of Indian affairs, and besought him to leave at once for the East. On the twenty-ninth word came that William Clapham and most of his family and servants had been killed on the Youghiogheny near the site of West Newton.

James Kenny had for a month been planning to leave for home on the first of June, and this "Alarm sot his Hair upright" so effectually that he insisted on leaving at once lest he be unable to get away before winter. In reply to Davenport's threats and sneers Kenny frankly confessed that he had never had any illusions about his own courage so had no shame in leaving; whereupon he mounted his pack horse and disappeared from Pittsburgh history, much to the regret of later generations, who would have found invaluable a continuance of his day to day record of village life.

Meanwhile Ecuyer ordered the houses on Grant's Hill to be burned; those on the Monongahela and the few remaining on the Allegheny, with one or two exceptions, were pulled down and the lumber taken into the fort and used to build shelters for the villagers, who with their goods had taken refuge there. The cattle and horses of the soldiers and townsmen were collected and fenced in a field just outside the fort. When everyone was in, Ecuyer found that he had 330 men, 104 women, and 196 children, most of whom had to be fed from the fort's supplies. Even while the preparations for defense were going on the Indians set fire to a house half a mile from the fort. Refugees appeared daily with harrowing tales of slaughter and rapine. George Croghan's house went up in a telltale pillar of smoke; militiamen putting up a fence were fired upon but reached the fort safely. On the night of June 11 Indians set fire to a house that had escaped destruction in the upper town, and though a shell was thrown among them their eerie halloos were soon echoing among the ruins of the lower town near the fort. On the fifteenth a party that went out to cut spelts (a kind of loose-eared wheat) ventured to Grant's Hill and one of the number was killed. The next day four Shawnee appeared across the Allegheny and at their request Alexander McKee went over to make powwow with them. He was assured that the traders captured by the Indians were being taken care of. It appeared later that the besiegers numbered well over four hundred, drawn chiefly from the Delawares, Shawnee, Wyandot, and Mingo, and so confident were they of victory that they had brought their wom-

en and children to aid in carrying away the loot. The great
Mingo chief, Guyasuta, is generally supposed to have been the
leader.

II

THE days that followed were creeping horrors. The Indians
mocked the calls of the sentinels or stalked them at night and
shot them down; the enemy appeared suddenly in the fields
and managed to get away with some of the horses and cattle;
solitary men who ventured from the fort were killed and scalped
in sight of their comrades; an express from Bedford got into
the fort through a hail of Indian bullets and brought word that
Bouquet was marching with strong reinforcements; several sur-
vivors came in from Forts Le Bœuf and Presque Isle and told
harrowing tales of battle and sudden death; Indians crept into
the dry moat, and it was only the Lord's mercy that prevented
them from potting the sentinels. To top it all off, smallpox
broke out in the fort. One day Turtle's Heart appeared with a
friend, and when McKee went out to him the Indians made
many protestations of friendship and urged the garrison to abandon the fort and set out for the East. Ecuyer, through McKee,
thanked them profusely, told them many lies about the succour
that was soon expected, and out of the largeness of his heart
gave them two blankets and a handkerchief from the smallpox
hospital, hoping, no doubt, for the best.

On the morning of July 3 four Indians, naked and painted in
different colors, appeared on the opposite side of the Allegheny
singing and waving two small British flags. McKee went outside the fort, and they announced that they were Ottawa come
to treat for peace. The next morning ten Ottawa appeared on
the opposite side of the Allegheny and finally persuaded Ecuyer
to send two soldiers with a canoe to them. The soldiers had no
sooner touched the shore than they were seized by the Indians
and were only released when their captors scattered in terror
before a charge of grapeshot. Several days of quiet followed,
and the people grew careless as they went out into the fields
to tend their cattle and to cut spelts. After about ten days Trent

records that he ventured for the first time in a month to take off his clothes before going to bed. The interval of peace was too good to last, however, and was ended by a sudden attack and the mortal wounding of one of the militia. The Indians then began boldly to show themselves on the rivers, and one party even waded across the Allegheny to beg for provisions; Ecuyer finally forbade them to pass near the fort, and when a canoe load persisted in passing up the Monongahela he punctuated the order with grapeshot. The Indians abandoned the canoe and made their escape but returned in the evening and brazenly inquired why the white brothers were angry at them. A parley followed during which both sides did some plain speaking, then they all went back to their guns. During the following days the Indians, from the shelter of the river banks, killed two of the garrison and wounded several others, including Captain Ecuyer. They also shot fire arrows at the buildings in the fort but did not succeed in setting them afire, though the whole garrison had to be on the watch all one night.

About the first of August most of the Indians disappeared and the beleaguered garrison was disturbed only by an occasional shot or an eerie death halloo. Provisions were almost gone, all the liquor had been used up, and Ecuyer complained that there was no "cabbage" to mix with what little tobacco was left.

On the tenth, expresses arrived with word from Colonel Bouquet of a victory at Bushy Run. A few hours later, as they bent over their tasks in garrison or field, the members of the little garrison heard the sounds of Bouquet's bagpipes and drums as he marched across the scene of Grant's defeat to raise the ten weeks' siege of Pittsburgh. All work was dropped as the people streamed across the stubble fields to meet their saviors. Children jumped and shouted, men fired off the last precious rounds of powder in a wild urge to make a noise, while women laughed even as they dabbed with soiled and ragged aprons at the tears in their eyes. From their vantage points on the heights across the Monongahela and the Allegheny the late besiegers watched the demonstration with heavy hearts. Their supreme effort had failed. Slowly and silently they gathered up their scanty belongings and set their faces toward the west. Though the Indians fought on desperately during many a year to come, yet from that day they must have realized that nothing they could do would turn aside the tide of white conquest. Their old hunting grounds would never belong to them again.

III

THE first task before the people of Pittsburgh at the close of the siege of 1763 was the reconstruction of their homes—the third village that had risen on the site since the English conquest. The second village had been widely scattered over the territory between the rivers, but the third seems to have been centered about the bank of the Monongahela in four blocks surveyed by Colonel John Campbell in 1764 at the instance of the military authorities and now included within Ferry, Water, and Market Streets and the Boulevard of the Allies. The growth of the town was slow; in 1770, when Washington visited it on one of his land-hunting expeditions, he found only about twenty log houses in the place (perhaps there were huts in addition), though two years later another visitor claimed that there were twice as many.

Colonel Bouquet in 1764 built a pentagonal brick blockhouse midway between the Monongahela and Ohio bastions from which sharpshooters could fire upon attackers approaching by way of the moat. This is the only part of Fort Pitt that survives. There were at one time several other redoubts, or perhaps they were merely houses, that in later years were moved from the fort to convenient positions near by and utilized as residences. The fort itself seems never to have been reconstructed on the original plan after the disastrous flood of 1763. The two brick incased curtains to landward remained as first built and the other three curtains, originally composed of earthen embankments, were supplanted by stockades; the moat, perennially in need of cleaning, still surrounded the fort. From 1765 to 1768 Fort Pitt was under the command of Major William Murray, a shrewd, good-humored Scotsman who resigned from the army to become agent for a Philadelphia trading firm in the Illinois. Murray and his Royal Americans were succeeded at the fort by Major Charles Edmondstone and two companies of Royal Irish.

During 1764 Fort Pitt was an important base of operations for Bouquet on his expeditions against the Indians in Ohio, but with the cessation of the Indian troubles Fort Pitt was no longer important. There may, also, have been an idea in the minds of the British ministers that the Americans, since they were proving so fractious, should be left to defend their own frontiers. At any rate in October, 1772, Captain Charles Edmondstone sold the materials in Fort Pitt to Edward Hand, the military surgeon of the garrison, Alexander Ross, and William Thompson for the sum of fifty pounds, New York currency. Only a corporal and three privates were left to care for the boats used in keeping up the communication with Fort Chartres in the Illinois. Edward Ward, the same man who had given up the Point to the French eighteen years before, was placed in charge of the property and sold part of the materials or used them in building for Ross several houses that he inclosed with a picket fence and a brick wall. The fort was not completely dismantled, however, and was yet to play an important role in the history of Pittsburgh and the nation during the Revolution.

IV

THE years between the end of Pontiac's War and the beginning of the Revolution saw the settlement of all the desirable lands in southwestern Pennsylvania. The British policy at first was to restrict the right to settle to those who had been given permits to keep taverns or whose presence was necessary for a successful military occupation. In spite of repeated warnings and a number of evictions settlers came to the Monongahela country literally by the thousands. The inevitable result was a purchase from the Indians by the Penns at Fort Stanwix in 1768, and the lands were thrown open to settlement after the proprietors had reserved for themselves two "manors," one at Pittsburgh and the other at Kittanning. Land could be bought from the Penns for about twenty cents an acre, while Virginia allowed fifty acres free to each immigrant, and he could purchase additional acreage for negligible sums. Virginia's more liberal terms led to the immigration of great numbers from that province and it is safe to say that of the fifty thousand inhabitants of the Monongahela country at the opening of the Revolution the majority of those settled just west of Laurel Hill were Virginian in origin or in sympathy.

Probably half the western population in 1775 was English in blood, perhaps one or more generations removed from England, while the other half was composed of Irish, Scotch, or Scotch-Irish, three elements among which it is not always easy to make a distinction. The frontier had already placed its stamp upon all these national stocks, so that there were more similarities among them than dissimilarities. In general, however, the Scotch-Irish were distinguished for their political ability; their democracy; their shrewdness in money matters; their possession of a certain mental hardness, or rigidity, and a lack of imaginativeness; their contempt for many of the social amenities; and their close adherence to their Presbyterian kirks and ministers. The English, on the other hand, perhaps influenced by the "cavalier" society of Virginia, were freer handed and more luxury loving, sometimes less democratic, and certainly possessed of fewer of the intellectual and religious inhibitions that characterized the Scotch-Irish.

v

THE Pittsburgh of about 1770, while not thriving industrially, gave promise of commercial importance. The army was continually moving supplies by water to the Illinois country or by way of the Allegheny River, French Creek, and Lake Erie to Detroit. The Philadelphia firm of Baynton, Wharton, and Morgan had engaged in trade with the Illinois country for several years, and its coin had fattened the purses of Pittsburgh's boatwrights, bateau men, and pack-horse men. George Morgan, one of the partners, had spent some time in the town before his departure to Illinois and had erected at the northeast corner of Ferry and Water Streets a two-story house of squared logs to serve as a store and warehouse. The house, so it was said, had the first nailed-on shingle roof in town. Baynton, Wharton, and Morgan had finally failed and had sold out to Franks and Company of Lancaster, who carried on the Illinois trade with Major Murray, the former commander of Fort Pitt, as their agent.

The older generation of traders had pretty well disappeared, and younger men had taken their places. George Croghan lingered on but was preoccupied with the management of his estates and with the embellishment of his home, "Croghan's Castle," four miles up the Allegheny near the foot of modern McCandless Street. Alexander McKee, son of the trader, Thomas McKee, was a deputy Indian superintendent. John Gibson, known to the Indians as "Horseface," was an up and coming youngster who was often seen in town on business for his trading post across the river from Logstown, where, to make himself solid with his Indian customers, he had taken unto himself in marriage a sister of the great Mingo chief, Logan. Richard and William Butler were prospering in trade with the Shawnee and were considering bringing into partnership three promising younger brothers who were growing up on the old home place back in Lancaster County. James O'Hara, a young Irish descendant of a line of Jacobite soldiers of fortune, was just entering the Indian trade, and those who took the trouble to note his complete absorption in the task at hand prophesied success for him. Devereaux Smith, an Englishman who had come to America as a soldier and whose name was later given to Smithfield Street, was one of the most solid and respected traders. Matthew Elliott and Simon Girty were two other traders, not yet so well known, who were to play important roles in the American Revolution in the West. Most important of all, however, was the firm of Joseph Simon and John Campbell (the surveyor) which, perhaps because of its generous financial backing from the Franks and Gratz families of Lancaster and Philadelphia, had engrossed an unreasonable share of the business of the upper Ohio and was casting about for ways and means to absorb more.

Most of these traders kept stores in Pittsburgh, small, square, log structures crammed full of unbelievably complete assortments of goods, but affording room for the owner and his clerks

and family (if any) to live in. Goods calculated to please townsmen were slowly but inexorably crowding out the cheaper and
coarser strouds and gewgaws preferred by the Indians; still poor
Lo, when he appeared with the odorous spoil of a winter's labor,
found a warm welcome and could choose from an ample supply
of gauds and wilderness necessities, though in doing so he might
have to rub elbows with the scented wife of the village doctor
or lawyer.

VI

IF LIFE in Pittsburgh was rude or vulgar, there were few to
complain. Those who may have known better had become ac-
climated or found adequate recompense in freedom from restraint. It was easy enough for visiting ministers to turn up
their noses between the pages of their diaries at this "frontier
of depravity"—one expected that of gentlemen of the cloth.
The red-blooded packer or boatman enjoyed himself in his own
zestful way. Those concerned with moral uplift, if no peripatetic
theological neophyte from the eastern presbyteries was passing
through, might go to the garrison and listen to the Reverend
Maclagan preach a red-hot Protestant sermon to the Catholic
soldiers—however, if one hit the wrong Sunday he would be but
little edified, for the sermon would be in Erse. There was the
possibility also that one could scare up a partner for a game of
billards in the great room of Samuel Semple's tavern in the building that once had served George Morgan as a warehouse. One
was almost certain to meet there the personable Dr. John Connolly, a nephew of George Croghan, who had married Semple's
daughter Susanna and who needed no urging to recount with
embellishments the sights he had witnessed and the adventures
he had experienced. If nothing better offered one could sit in a
great chair by mine host's cheery fireplace with a hot glass in
one hand and a Philadelphia paper in the other until other gentlemen came in, as they were sure to do—only if one leaned to
the popular side in politics it was best to avoid the sharp tongue
of Mistress Semple, who made no secret of her admiration for
His Majesty.

74

On clear, warm, summer days one could play at handball with the officers of the garrison in the dry moat where the towering brick wall of the curtain formed an excellent court; or perhaps an excursion by ferry could be arranged with a party of ladies and gentlemen to the lofty green hill across the Monongahela, where the coals in the bowels of the earth had become ignited and which some wiseacre had observed was like to become a volcano. Always there was something doing—boats arriving from Le Bœuf or the Illinois, express riders dashing in with dispatches from the East and likely to spatter the pedestrian from head to foot if he didn't look lively, old trappers half in their cups and anxious to tell about the good old days before the cussed ploughboys ruined the hunting, Indians in the stores chaffering with grunts and signs, or perhaps even a rousing fight between a packer and a wagoner.

If all these amusements failed there were still the oldest and most utilitarian amusements known to man—hunting and fishing. It was no fable that hundred-pound catfish lay buried in the mud at the bottoms of the rivers—one of them when caught and opened had yielded a cavalry boot with the leg of the unfortunate owner in it. There were so many squirrels in the woods immediately around the town that they were a nuisance to the farmers, and it was uncommon to walk for two hours without crossing the trail of a deer or a bear—not as plentiful as they once had been but numerous enough for diversion. Yes, life in Pittsburgh had its recompenses. After all, those who saw only the seamy side of the town were to be more pitied than censured. They found what they looked for.

VII

"Intestin Broyls"

Squire George Washington, late colonel in the provincial forces of Virginia and now gentleman farmer and speculator in western lands, looked gravely across the table at the handsome young medico who was recounting tales of his adventures at the siege of Martinico in 1762. They were in the taproom of that "very good house of entertainment" kept by Samuel Semple at the corner of Water and Ferry Streets in Pittsburgh, and the company included a dozen gentlemen of town and garrison who were being wined and dined by Colonel Washington in return for their attentions to him. The Virginian's eyes slowly traveled about the circle of guests. Colonel Aeneas Mackay (stouter and less fiery than at Fort Necessity) wore on his ruddy Scots countenance an expression half amused, half cynical; Devereux Smith was striving to conceal distaste; the seamed features of Washington's oldtime enemy, George Croghan, softened with something akin to pride in the ready flow of anecdote falling from the lips of the speaker; and the puffy features of mine host bore an expression that was almost adoration. Young Dr. Connolly was a gentleman of native distinction, reflected Washington, and old Croghan was right in being proud of his nephew and Mr. Semple of his son-in-law.

76

The doctor glided easily from Martinico to the wind-swept prairies of the Illinois and then by degrees down the Mississippi and up the Ohio. When he had passed the mouth of the Tennessee River he paused for a moment, but before any one could interrupt went on: "This land between the Ohio and the Tennessee, or as some call it, Kaintuckee, is rolling but not rough —a country of alternate forests and canebrakes and grassy savannas, marvelous fertile, and abounding in game of every description. The French boatmen have been known to float in high water from there to New Orleans in a week and seldom does it require more than six weeks to row upstream—an excellent location, gentlemen, for a new government."

There was a slight shift of the doctor's eyes to meet those of his host, then he went on. That glance, however, was enough to tell Washington that Dr. Connolly purposely had been leading up to this point, and he would be willing to swear himself a Dutchman if he were not about to be sounded out by the engaging doctor concerning his willingness to find financial backers for a colony in this Kaintuckee. A pleasant glow pervaded the Virginian at the recognition of his hard-won but undoubted importance, and his mind wandered back seventeen years to that first venture in the world of affairs, when he had passed over this very spot on his way to the French forts. By this time Dr. Connolly, excellent diplomat that he was, had left the subject of Kaintuckee and had launched into some extended remarks upon the undoubted preference of the Monongahela countrymen for the suzerainty of Virginia.

"There can be no doubt, gentlemen," said he, "that the country west of Laurel Hill is in that part of His Majesty's dominion of Virginia known as Augusta, and that Pennsylvania, limited to the land five degrees west of the Delaware River, cannot justly claim it. The enormous price levied by the Penns for the purchase of lands, when contrasted with the fifty acres headright allowed by Virginia to each settler, makes it no wonder that we, even though we may have been bred in Pennsylvania, prefer to dwell under the mild and equitable jurisdiction of Virginia. And that is not all. The expensive administration of justice in Pennsylvania is oppressive to the poor and burdensome to all, particularly in trying titles to land and in the recovery of small debts, wherein their officers' fees are so disproportioned that they seem rather calculated for enriching individuals than the public good; add to these a heavy Provincial tax, a great part thereof being swallowed up by the officers who lay and collect the same, to the great grievance of the subject, and this without any attempt at a system of defense against the faithless and barbarous natives nor even a law for the mustering of militia upon certain days.

"It is well known, moreover, that Virginia, unlike Pennsylvania, has never been slack in extending its frontiers, both for the benefit of those who would cultivate lands and of those who would venture their capital. It is the difference between a government of gentlemen and one of tradesmen. Though I say it, who am a Pennsylvanian born, yet there is a prejudice among the Scotch-Irish for the Virginia gentlemen as against the puling tradesmen of the Quaker city, so that they would gladly support the extension of the Virginia government over these lands to the west of the mountains."

At this juncture Colonel Mackay, who had for some time been fidgeting in his chair, broke out in his broadest Scots: "Faith, doctor-r-r, it wad be gude business to awsk the Vir-r-ginians in. As I aften tell ma frien' Andra Leevy, the Jew is muckle over-r-rated as a business mon, for the Scoatch-Eerishmon can beat him fi' days oot o' seven—that is, allowin' for their respective Sawbaths—but the Quaker-r wi' the halp o' the Laird an' Jock Penn hae squeezed the Scoatch-Eerishmon 'til he wad sell oot to Auld Hornie himsel' wad he but whustle a psalm tune."

There was a shout of laughter at the colonel's blunt analysis of the political situation, and the tide of conversation passed on, leaving the brash young medico stranded. There was a glint of amusement in Washington's eyes, as he comprehended the townsmen's estimate of Dr. Connolly. A man of intelligence was he, and indeed of sensibility, but like those who strut before mirrors he was apt to overreach himself.

As Washington had conjectured, the doctor waited upon him

at the first opportunity and spread before him on the rough pine table a neat map of Kaintuckee (albeit with many vacant spots and with mountain ranges running at cross purposes), together with an elaborately segmented plan for the formation of a "new government." The future father of his country, interested in spite of himself, promised to lay the scheme before those with money and influence; but though an extensive correspondence followed, nothing important ever came of it.

II

THE ambitious doctor was not wrong in his diagnosis of the state of mind in the Monongahela country. In 1771, the very next year after the meeting in Semple's tavern, when the tax collectors for the new Pennsylvania county of Bedford appeared in Pittsburgh they gathered more insults than currency. Colonel George Wilson, a Bedford County justice resident on Georges Creek, wrote to Arthur St. Clair, a fellow justice, a long description of the "intestin Broyls" that ensued when a mob "Ware assembled as Was seposed to Resque" a prisoner who had been "ordered into Custotey." George Croghan, who for years had teetered between Pennsylvania and Virginia, finally decided that his vast landholdings, which had been purchased from the Indians, would be invalidated if Pennsylvania acquired the western country—a result that actually came to pass and that led to his death in poverty—and threw his influence to the side of Virginia, as did by far the greater part of the landholders west of the mountains, even including many who had purchased their lands from the Penns. Early in 1773 the assembly of Pennsylvania erected Westmoreland County and the seat of justice was set at Hannastown, about three miles north of present Greensburg. Aeneas Mackay, Andrew McFarlane, and Devereux Smith, all of Pittsburgh, and George Wilson, Arthur St. Clair, and William Crawford were appointed justices.

In the summer of 1773 John Murray, Earl of Dunmore, the new governor of Virginia, made a progress through his realm during which he appeared at Pittsburgh. In him Dr. Connolly found an "Auld Hornie" not only willing but anxious to "whustle a psalm tune" to charm the Scotch-Irishmen away from the Penns. Connolly and the merchant John Campbell, one of his cronies, were given patents to the land on which Louisville, Kentucky, now stands, and it is safe to presume that this was the *quid pro quo* for which Connolly agreed to play the role of Moses to the Scotch-Irish. On January 1, 1774, Connolly, all out of breath from a hasty journey from Williamsburg, nailed up in Pittsburgh a poster that announced his appointment by Dunmore as captain commandant of the militia of Pittsburgh and its "Dependencies" and that ordered a muster of the militia on the twenty-fifth of the month. The imminent formation of a new county was also announced, and John Campbell, John Gibson, and Dorsey Pentecost, among others, were appointed justices.

Arthur St. Clair, not yet old and dilatory, countered with a surprise. Connolly was caught off his guard, seized, and lodged in the draughty Hannastown jail. On the day named for the muster about eighty Virginia adherents gathered, chiefly from the neighborhood of George Croghan's plantation on Pine Creek ("See!" exulted the Pennsylvanians, "the King of the Traders is up to his old tricks!"), and thundered into Pittsburgh yelling and firing their guns. Presently they made their way within the crumbling walls of Fort Pitt, knocked out the head of a cask of rum, and proceeded to get as drunk as the limited amount of liquor would allow. St. Clair and his fellow magistrates summoned their courage, read a long disquisition upon the rights of Pennsylvania, and ordered the mob to disperse. That was before the rum began to work. A few hours later St. Clair "thought prudent to keep out of their way"—which probably meant that he left town on the swiftest horse he could find.

A few days after his imprisonment Connolly was released by Sheriff John Proctor on condition that he appear before the next court, in April. The doctor gathered a guard of about twenty men and departed for Williamsburg to consult with Dunmore. It was during this stay in the capital that Dunmore produced a dignified letter from John Penn protesting against Virginia's usurpation of authority on the Monongahela, and doubtless he and Connolly, with many a gleeful chuckle, composed between them the smart alec answer that demanded St. Clair's dismissal for his interference with the due process of Virginia laws "unless he can prevail, by proper submission, on Mr. Connolly to demand his pardon of me." On March 28 Connolly was back in Pittsburgh, where he was joined by a party of his adherents from the settlements on Chartiers Creek; they occupied Fort Pitt and constituted themselves a garrison pledged to support the civil and military authority of Virginia. Sheriff Proctor was arrested, and the deputy sheriff and the constables were forced to go into hiding to avoid the same fate. One of Connolly's henchmen who "grossly insulted" Aeneas Mackay was arrested by that justice and placed in confinement. The man's companions soon heard of the affair; in rescuing him they apparently broke into Mackay's house, and in the scuffle one of Connolly's captains, George Aston, wounded Mrs. Mackay in the arm with his cutlass.

III

CONNOLLY had promised to appear before the Westmoreland County Court, and he kept his word like a man of the strictest honor, when, on April 6, with a fine instinct for the dramatic, he suddenly rode into Hannastown followed by nearly two hundred buckskinned horsemen. Court was not at the moment in session, so Connolly, placing guards at the door of the courthouse, entered the building and sent a sardonic message to the justices saying that he had come in fulfillment of his promise and would wait upon them. The bench and bar gathered in Robert Hanna's house, and Connolly read to them a statement asserting that himself was not amenable to their jurisdiction, but, to prevent confusion, he would allow them to try such cases as were brought before them until he was instructed otherwise by Dunmore. The Westmoreland justices, fearing that Connolly was seeking some "colorable reason" for a quarrel, answered with a pacific note that they were forced to deliver, like suppliants, at the courthouse door. A few minutes later the Virginians, with derisory yells at the humiliated Pennsylvanians, rode out of town.

The Westmoreland Court adjourned immediately and the justices departed for their homes. The next day Mackay, McFarlane, and Smith were arrested in Pittsburgh on the ground that their answer to Connolly the day before had been insolent. All three refused to give bail, so McFarlane and Smith were sent prisoners to Staunton, while Mackay was allowed to go to Williamsburg to lay their case before Dunmore. Dunmore heard him out and answered tartly that so far as their imprisonment was concerned, what was sauce for the goose was sauce for the gander. More merciful than Connolly, however, and perhaps with a clearer vision of the possible consequences of holding them, he permitted the three justices to go home. When an official embassy appeared from the Pennsylvania council a few weeks later Dunmore refused to give it a reasonable answer.

The amiable doctor was meanwhile riding high in the Monongahela country. Pittsburgh and its fort were re-christened Fort Dunmore, and from this center detachments under Simon Girty, George Aston, and others were sent to patrol the roads and river, and furs and skins belonging to the Pennsylvania traders were seized and confiscated. At the same time such favors were shown to the firm of Joseph Simon and John Campbell that it practically held the monopoly of the fur trade. Those who were known to be Pennsylvania partisans were subjected to numerous petty annoyances. Sometimes their cattle, sheep, or hogs were slaughtered or their horses were seized, though if the owner were present Connolly's men would give him a bill on Lord Dunmore—"downright mockery," complained St. Clair. Upon one occasion, when lumber was needed at the fort, Mackay's outbuildings were torn down and carted off, and the owner was knocked unconscious while attempting to protect his property. When Mrs. Mackay, her arm still in a sling from Aston's cutlass slash, remonstrated, Connolly shouted "Damn me, Madam, I will pull down the very house you live in if I have occasion for it." William Amberson, a clerk in Joseph Spear's store, was arrested without explanation, and the store was left open and unprotected. William Butler made the mistake of forcibly preventing Connolly's men from seizing some of Devereux Smith's property, while the latter was in Staunton, and was hounded until he was caught and confined in the fort. Smith's house was stoned for several hours one evening just to "shew him what Virginia Boys could do." Two raids were made upon the Hannastown jail to release prisoners; one of the raids, it was claimed, was made at the instigation of William Crawford, the president justice of Westmoreland County, who had joined the Virginia cause.

IV

AMONG their other statesmanlike policies, Dunmore and Connolly planned an Indian war—a move likely to prove popular among the Scotch-Irish and the land-hungry speculators and pioneers of Virginia, who were avariciously eying the rich lands of the "Kaintuckee" that Connolly had praised so warmly. The war was begun, quite in the approved style for the precipitation of international conflicts, by a series of "incidents" along the Ohio River that culminated in the massacre of a band of Mingo that included the family of the famous Logan, who had been one of the staunchest friends of the whites. Within a week after the massacre the inhabitants of the country between the Ohio and the Monongahela were fleeing in panic, and it was said that a thousand of them crossed the latter river in one day at three ferries not a mile apart. Unperturbed by this tragic exodus, Connolly proceeded to make war inevitable by ordering the arrest of a party of peaceful Shawnee that had accompanied some white traders to Pittsburgh to protect them from the vengeance of the Mingo. The traders managed to spirit the Indians out of town just in the nick of time, and sped them on their way home with liberal gifts. Unfortunately Connolly's militia overtook the Indians at Beaver Creek, fired upon them, wounded one, and then retreated "in the most dastardly manner." Connolly and Dunmore got their war.

Dunmore's War was fought by the Mingo and Shawnee on one side and the Virginians on the other; the Indians, with an admirable sense of justice, left the settlements closest to the mountains strictly alone, presuming them to be under Pennsylvania jurisdiction. The Pennsylvania partisans, aided by

Croghan, who did not approve of his nephew's Indian policy, raised a company of a hundred men to patrol the frontier along the Allegheny River and to prevent Indian invasions, and though the step was not aimed at Connolly it had the value of halting the worst of his outrages. The war dragged on until October, when Lord Dunmore and Andrew Lewis, the former marching by way of Fort Dunmore and Wheeling, and the latter by way of the Kanawha River Valley (he won the battle of Point Pleasant en route), imposed a peace upon the belligerent red men. The chief provision of this peace, significantly enough, was that the Indians should abandon Kentucky to the whites. At last Connolly was free to undertake his "new government," though not on as pretentious a scale as he had planned.

Virginia next adjourned the Augusta County Court from Staunton to Fort Dunmore, where it was opened on February 21, 1775, as the court of the District of West Augusta, with Connolly, Croghan, Campbell, and Gibson among the justices. The next day two Westmoreland justices, Robert Hanna and James Caveat, were arrested and imprisoned. During the next three months the opening events of the Revolution were occuring and Connolly, who espoused the British cause, found his power weakening. Sometime in June the Pennsylvanians made a nocturnal raid on Pittsburgh, released their two justices, and carried off Connolly; but they soon released him upon the demand of the West Augusta Revolutionary committee. Within a few days the doctor departed for the East to mature plans for holding the western waters for the king. Upon the return journey he was captured and imprisoned in Maryland, and the Monongahela country saw him no more, unless he accompanied the British and Indians who attacked Hannastown in 1782. Violence ended with the departure of Connolly. An address of July 25, 1775, signed by the delegates of both provinces to the Continental Congress, called upon the two factions to unite in defense of the common liberty and marked the transition of the boundary dispute from the violent into the diplomatic phase.

VIII

Revolt in the West

IT MUST have been about the first of May, 1775, that a weary man, riding a no less weary nag, slowly descended the Laurel Ridge into the Monongahela country and spread the news from Ligonier to Pittsburgh that the farmers of Massachusetts had taken down their squirrel rifles from over their sooty fireplaces and had penned the redcoats into the narrow confines of Boston town. The Pittsburghers had already been represented by John Harvie in the provincial convention that had met at Richmond to protest against parliamentary usurpation and to formulate measures for resistance, so now the decisive action of the Bay Province met with an instant response. A meeting to express West Augusta's approbation of Massachusetts' course and to prepare for a similar exigency in the West was called for May 16. The man of affairs in town to see his lawyer received the news, and upon the return journey his halloo before each squalid forest cabin brought about his horse the settler and his wife and tousle-headed brood, to listen in open-mouthed wonder to the broadclothed gentleman expatiate on the "liberties of the subject"; the substantial citizen in the double cabin at the crossroads, perhaps a justice, or a militia captain, or an innkeeper, quietly rearranged his daily routine so that he could ride to Pittsburgh on the sixteenth; the farmer who carried his grain to the mill returned home with something to think about beside the high cost of milling; the trader shouted the news to men working in the fields as he paddled down the broad Ohio, and at night while he smoked his pipe by the campfire his troubled thoughts dwelt upon the effect revolution would have on his trade and whether the canny red man could be prevented from playing both ends against the middle in this family quarrel.

May 16 was a day long to be remembered by the patriots of the Monongahela country, but particularly by the tavern-keepers of Pittsburgh, for every taproom was crowded with earnest patriots who spent freely. Because the boundary controversy was at its height (one wonders what Doctor Connolly was doing that day) most of those who met at Pittsburgh were Virginia partisans, though along with George Croghan, William Crawford, John Campbell, and John Gibson were Devereux Smith and George Wilson, Westmoreland justices and Pennsylvania adherents. The meeting was probably held in the open, most likely in one of the fields just outside the village, so that everyone could attend, but the wheels had been well oiled beforehand by the substantial men of the community. A chairman was speedily elected, and a slate of members for a resolutions committee was proposed and elected. The meeting then recessed while the committee retired to a quiet upper chamber of Semple's tavern to do their composing. Doubtless Mistress Semple puffed up the stairs many times during the next two hours bearing mental lubricants foaming in brassbound tankards or glowing rosily in glass decanters, the while, as a loyal subject of His Majesty, she cursed rebellion but did not scruple to reap the rewards thereof.

Presently the word sped through the town that the resolutions committee had finished its labors and was returning to the meeting place. The citizens gathered quickly, the meeting was called to order, and a stump served as a rostrum while in the hush the solemn periods of the resolutions fell upon the receptive ears of the listening Pittsburghers.

"*Resolved*, That John Campbell, John Ormsby, Edward Ward, Thomas Smallman, Samuel Semple, John Anderson, and Devereux Smith, or any four of them be a Standing Committee, and have full power to meet at such times as they shall judge necessary . . .

"*Resolved unanimously*, That this committee have the highest sense of the spirited behavior of their brethren in New England, and do most cordially approve of their opposing the invaders of American rights and privileges to the utmost extreme . . .

"The imminent danger that threatens America in general, . . . as well as the danger to be apprehended to this colony in particular from a domestic enemy, said to be prompted by the wicked minions of power to execute our ruin, added to the menaces of an Indian war, likewise said to be in contemplation, thereby think to engage our attention, and divert it from that still more interesting object of liberty and freedom, that deeply, and with so much justice hath called forth the attention of all America; for the prevention of all, or any of those impending evils, it is

"*Resolved*, That the recommendation of the Richmond Convention, relative to the embodying, arming, and disciplining the militia be immediately carried into execution . . .

"*Resolved*, That this committee do approve of the resolution of the committee of the other part of this county, relative to the cultivating a friendship with the Indians . . .

"Ordered, That the standing committee be directed to secure such arms and ammunition as are not employed in actual service, or private property, and that they get the same repaired, and deliver them to such Captains of Independent Companies as may make application for the same."

The Revolution had come to Pittsburgh.

II

With the fall of night there began a scene that for wild jubilation had not been equalled since the days when the Indians had lined up before Fort Duquesne to welcome their prisoners from Braddock's Field with the ordeal of the gantlet. No beer or wine for the honest citizenry of Pittsburgh, but rich, full-bodied whiskey, just rolled around the hill by a black boy from the distillery at Suke's Run (Try Street). There was a cry of "make way" and a dozen stalwart mechanics appeared bearing a thirty-foot pine tree newly stripped of its boughs. The village was about to witness the revival of an old custom, the origin of which is lost in the mists of Teutonic legend; that is, the planting of the war pole, renamed the liberty pole to suit the current issues of 1775. The pine was carried to a place where a hole had already been dug (not even tradition marks the spot) and there set up amid the huzzas and libations of the crowd. A huge bonfire was lighted and more kegs were rolled in. As the effect of the Monongahela rye began to be felt, the glare of the bonfire lit up a scene such as only the frontier could furnish. Long hunters in town on a frolic after their winter's toil, Connolly's wild militia from the thickets of Chartiers Creek, grimy mechanics from the forges and boat yards, dandified clerks from the trading houses sowing their wild oats in the West, and the red-shirted boatmen from the Illinois and the red-skirted companions of their leisure hours, joined hands in a dance about the liberty pole. Hunters and militia saluted the dawn of liberty with rifle shots, and since, following the Indian fashion, they used bullets with their charges, life and limb were prematurely put at peril in liberty's cause.

That night the "gentlemen of respectability" met at Semple's and joined in a rousing toast to "Liberty, the birthright of Englishmen," and then, after mine host had unctuously refilled the glasses, in another to "His Majesty, King George the Third, God bless him. Confusion to all his enemies, not forgetting Parliament and its ministers." It was all very polite and genteel in Samuel Semple's "Assembly Room," for there ordered liberty and its responsibilities were well understood. A late comer opened the door and as the faint shouts of the merrymakers around the liberty pole drifted in someone remarked that there was a vast difference between liberty and license. Already there were visible the differences between the two forces within the American Revolution.

The sober citizens of the town did well to remain indoors with their ladies, or at most to go no farther than Semple's to drink a social glass with their cronies. They would have been shocked at the boldness with which the celebrants around the liberty pole avowed leveling sentiments, for the democratic leaven of the frontier had done its work well. The commoners envisioned their enemies as closer to home than were Parliament or ministry: they thought of them as the placid, scheming Quaker financiers of Philadelphia, the slave-driving gentry of the Virginia tidewater, and the unscrupulous land speculators and extortionate lawyers who, they believed, lived extravagantly on the sweat of the poor.

III

NOT even all the revolutionary committee, as a matter of fact, were trusted by their humbler followers, as was amply proved a few months later. By July the precious hoards of tea in Pittsburgh had been used and, since it was an article interdicted by the Continental Congress everywhere, there was no possibility of obtaining more, much to the grief of the village housewives. Finally Simon and Campbell—Connolly's pets—let it be known that they had obtained, by means best known to themselves, some tea and would sell it to those who were not too steeped in patriotism to have no need of the beverage. Before long, however, it became known in the country that Simon and Campbell's store was selling tea, and certain earnest and intolerant patriots resolved to put a stop to it. On the night of August 24 more than a score of Westmorelanders headed by Colonel Archibald Lochry rode into town. Just what followed is obscure, but at any rate the next morning John Campbell was summoned to appear before the combined West Augusta and Westmoreland committees. He acknowledged that he had the tea and upon demand delivered up all that remained unsold— two ten-gallon kegs, one box, and one bag—and this was carried to the liberty pole and there burned as an example to noncoöperators, while behind closed shutters those ladies of Pittsburgh who placed tea above patriotism sniffed the pungent odor and wept tears of helpless rage at being deprived of their favorite beverage.

IV

ONE day in July, 1775, a traveler near Old Town, Maryland, met "Capt. Michael Cresap marching at the head of a formidable company of upwards of one hundred and thirty men from the mountains and backwoods, painted like Indians, armed with tomahawks and rifles, dressed in hunting-shirts and moccasins, and though some of them had traveled near eight hundred miles from the banks of the Ohio, they seemed to walk light and easy, and not with less spirit than on the first hour of their march." The company was composed of the same men who had followed Cresap in Dunmore's War the year before and who had gathered from as far away as Kentucky at the call of their old leader and were now on their way to join the besiegers of Boston—probably the first men from the West to march to the scene of war in the East.

Many other such companies were raised in the West during the course of the war, but the chief military organizations furnished by the Monongahela country were the Seventh and Thirteenth Virginia Regiments and the Eighth Pennsylvania Regiment. The first two were raised by William Crawford, respectively in the winter of 1775-76 and in the following summer. The Seventh Virginia was commanded in succession by William Dangerfield, William Crawford, and Alexander McClanachan. It served in the East during the first part of its existence, then returned to the West and performed garrison duty until it was mustered out. The Thirteenth Virginia, or as it was usually known, the West Augusta Regiment, was commanded by Colonel William Russell and Lieutenant-colonel John Gibson and it did garrison duty in its home section until it was mustered out. The third western regiment, the Eighth Regiment of the Pennsylvania Line, was raised for garrison duty at the western posts and was mustered into service in July, 1776, at Kittanning. Aeneas Mackay was its first colonel and George Wilson the lieutenant-colonel. In January, 1777, in the midst of one of the most severe winters the West had experienced, it obeyed orders to join the Continental army in New Jersey and made one of the most heroic marches in American history. The result was a great deal of sickness from the sufferings endured on the march and many of the men died, among them Mackay and Wilson. The regiment was commanded in turn by Daniel Brodhead and Stephen Bayard. It was on duty in the East until March, 1778, when it was returned to western Pennsylvania to serve until mustered out at the close of the war. Daniel Morgan drew upon the best shots in the regiments recruited in the Monongahela country when he formed his famous Rifles, taking among others the erstwhile trader, Richard Butler, as his second in command.

v

THE danger of conflict with the Indians had been accentuated by the outbreak of the Revolution (no frontiersman could be convinced that the British were not ready to offer the Indians generous bounties for the service of lifting his hair), and it was essential that a regular military guard be stationed in the West. With this in mind the Virginia Provincial Convention ordered Captain John Neville of Winchester to occupy Fort Pitt with a body of a hundred militia. Neville reached the fort on September 11, 1775, much to the discomfiture of a Congressional commission that had arrived to hold a treaty with the Indians. Neville fortunately did nothing to aggravate the quarrel between Virginia and Pennsylvania but conducted himself with discretion. He had served both in the French and Indian War and in Dunmore's War and had been about to move to certain lands that he had patented on Chartiers Creek when he received his marching orders. His occupation of Fort Pitt was the beginning of a public career of considerable importance.

Congress was fully aware that the country was open to British attack in the West, an attack that might prove fatal to American interests if the Indians joined in. Therefore, in an attempt to keep the Indians out of the "family quarrel," an Indian Department was organized, and Richard Butler of Pittsburgh was made its agent in that vicinity. A conference was held with the Delawares, Wyandot, and Iroquois in September and October. Each delegation arrived in Pittsburgh with a tribal standard borne before it and attendants firing salutes. The conference was held in a rude tabernacle or council house, open at the sides, that had been especially erected for the occasion. The powwow continued for over three weeks and from the standpoint of the Americans was completely successful. The dramatic climax of the occasion came when the great Delaware leader, White Eyes, encouraged by the colonial rebellion, seized the opportunity to break the age-long bondage of his people to the Iroquois. In one of the most eloquent and dramatic speeches ever heard in Pittsburgh this noble and patriotic red man issued his declaration of independence. "You say that you had conquered me, that you had cut off my legs—had put a petticoat on me, giving me a hoe and corn pounder, saying:'now woman! your business hence forward shall be to plant and hoe corn, and pound the same for bread, for us men and warriors!' Look at my legs! if, as you say, you had cut them off, they have grown again to their proper size! the petticoat I have thrown away, and have put on my proper dress!—the corn hoe and pounder I have exchanged for these fire arms, and I declare that I am a man!" He raised his right hand and, pointing northward over the heads of the scowling Iroquois to the dark foilage that marked the virgin wilderness beyond the Allegheny, cried, "And all the country on the other side of that river is *mine.*"

Alas for the patriotic hopes of White Eyes and his tribesmen! The faithless American applauded—and left the Delawares to their fate. Already the Americans were learning the rule, "Divide and conquer" that has made possible the formation of more empires than theirs. But in the meantime White Eyes's warm friend, George Morgan, the erstwhile Illinois trader who succeeded Richard Butler in the spring of 1776, labored hard to merit the good will of the Delawares and to extend this good will to other tribes. For a year he seemed to be successful, but in reality all the Indians save the Delawares were simply awaiting the issue of the struggle and accepting presents from both sides. Unfortunately for the continuance of peace, the traditional land hunger of the frontiersmen was an incentive towards war, and the incursions of Chief Pluggy's Mingo tribesmen who remained unreconstructed from Dunmore's War furnished a ready excuse. At this juncture it seemed best to Congress to end Virginia's military control of the region, so in June, 1777, Brigadier-General Edward Hand appeared before the fort at which a few years before he had acted as surgeon to the Royal Irish. Robert Campbell, who with a body of local militia had taken over the care of Fort Pitt from Neville in the previous February, turned over the command. Hand favored a policy of active defense against the savages, so that before the end of the year, in spite of Morgan's heroic efforts, a virtual state of war existed between whites and Indians. Only the Delawares remained neutral.

VI

GEORGE MORGAN, still faithful to his pacific policy, earned the universal hatred of the frontier and was even accused of treason —a charge that was investigated by a Congressional committee and found groundless. His position was not improved, however, when in the fall of 1777 three of his agents, Alexander McKee, Matthew Elliot, and Simon Girty, were arrested on suspicion of being in British service. McKee's parole was accepted, but as the net of evidence against him tightened he decided to flee to Detroit; the escape was accomplished in March, 1778, together with that of Elliot and Girty, and the British gained three recruits who were to become the mainstays of the Indian resistance to American conquest during the next twenty years. The British had been endeavoring to induce Tories and military deserters to go to Detroit, and the flight of McKee and his friends was the signal for others to depart. In one case several deserters were captured, brought back to Fort Pitt, and executed.

McKee was possessed of considerable influence over the Delawares, and his flight alienated some of them from Morgan. Hand undertook to improve the situation by going on an expedition with some Westmoreland militia to destroy British stores at Cuyahoga, probably near modern Cleveland. The troops became lost in the flooded woods and were so disgruntled that when they came across some Delaware women engaged in boiling salt water at a lick they murdered them. From this circumstance the fiasco was dubbed the Squaw Campaign. The Americans tried to put the best face they could on the affair. George Clymer, who was in Pittsburgh on congressional business, wrote "if our Heroes here can sing Tedeum over the scalps of a few Squaws they think they have done great Matters, but their tedeum is unhappily turned to Miserere." Apparently the bands of soldiers that Hand had painted and dressed as savages and set to guard the frontier were not preventing all the marauders from slipping through; for the general wrote that the country was much exposed to the "Insults of the Savages." Oppressed by a growing conviction that nothing could save the situation and that the western side of the mountains should be abandoned, Hand finally resigned in the spring of 1778.

One of Hand's accomplishments was the erection of a military hospital on Chartiers Creek not far from the place where the Steubenville Pike crosses it today. The hospital, according to tradition, was a two-story log structure about thirty by one hundred feet, with two doors, no windows, and a broad veranda extending all the way around it. Several small blockhouses stood near by for defense and for the accommodation of the guard and attendants.

The next general to command in the West was the Georgian Scot, Lachlan McIntosh, fresh from the duel in which he had slain Button Gwinnett—he of the rare autographs. It had become evident by this time that only the capture of the British stronghold at Detroit could bring peace to the frontier, and McIntosh brought orders to organize an expedition against that place. At a treaty held in Pittsburgh in September, 1778, during Morgan's absence in the East the Delawares were persuaded to sign a document that later they found to their surprise put them into alliance with the United States. This treaty ended Morgan's policy of Indian neutrality. Soon afterwards White Eyes was murdered, but even McIntosh was able to understand what consequences might ensue if the truth got out, so he announced that the chief had died of smallpox. The expedition against Detroit was abandoned, but McIntosh undertook to defend the frontier more efficiently by pushing outposts into the Indian country, and he built Fort McIntosh at the mouth of Beaver River and Fort Laurens on the Tuscarawas River, in the present state of Ohio. A few weeks later a cabal that Daniel Brodhead had organized against his commander was successful in having McIntosh recalled in February, 1779, and Brodhead succeeded him. Upon his return from Philadelphia Morgan found that John Gibson was, by military command, performing the functions of Indian agent. When Morgan undertook to expose the deceit practiced upon the Delawares at the last treaty he found himself threatened with another Congressional inquiry. He resigned in disgust in May and a few months later the Delawares, no longer restrained by their friend, went to war against the United States. Only a few of them under Chief Killbuck refused to join the war and moved to Smoky Island at the mouth of the Allegheny to be under the protection of the guns of Fort Pitt.

VII

McINTOSH had moved his headquarters from Pittsburgh to Fort McIntosh, and Brodhead seems to have continued the arrangement. Brodhead's regime turned out to be as fruitless as that of his predecessors. The Indians "visited" the settlements as usual, and as usual they took away numerous scalps. The chronic shortage of food, clothing, and munitions, as well as men—for the settlers hesitated to leave their families unprotected while they gallivanted off on military excursions—prevented the efficient defense of the settlements either by patrolling the countryside with bands of rangers or by adequately manning the string of forts that had sprung up from Kittanning to the mouth of the Kanawha. Brodhead did, however, undertake an expedition against the Seneca on the upper Allegheny in August, 1779, at the time that Sullivan was pillaging and burning the Iroquois towns in New York. Another expedition against the Delaware towns near Coshocton, Ohio, in April, 1781, though successful, was stained by several useless murders of prisoners. Brodhead's arbitrary methods—perhaps circumstances warranted them—led to his recall in May, 1781. John Gibson, who was distrusted by the ignorant and unthinking whites because of his Indian wife, took over command in the West. The massacre in

August of a force under Archibald Lochry, of Westmoreland County, on the way down the Ohio to join George Rogers Clark's projected expedition against Detroit threw the whole frontier into a panic and led to serious consideration of the advisability of the settlers' abandoning the West to the Indians

The arrival of General William Irvine at the end of September to assume command put another face on the situation, for he proved to be the best commander yet assigned to the troublesome task of holding together the shreds of order in the West. He arrived at Fort Pitt in good time to aid in the celebration over the surrender of Cornwallis at Yorktown. The troops were drawn up in their ragged best, with their colors displayed, while thirteen cannon thunderously wasted powder that might have been saved to use on the Indians. Each man also drew "a gill of liquor extraordinary . . . on this joyful occasion."

Irvine found his time well occupied in trying to drill some discipline into the rebellious, half-starved soldiers under his command, but he accomplished his end and stamped out a mutiny at Fort McIntosh with the execution of one of the leaders. He also spent a great deal of time and labor in repairing Fort Pitt, his headquarters, which his predecessors had allowed to fall into a disgracefully ruinous state. Men were sent to work the coal mines across the river, and new energy was infused into the lazy commissary department. All this activity had at least one benefit. A force of British, Tories, and Indians that had gathered on Lake Chautauqua under Dr. John Connolly for a descent on Fort Pitt gave up the attempt, though they did attack and burn Hannastown in July, 1782. One is entitled to wonder if Connolly wasn't mixing a personal grudge against his former Westmoreland rivals with his military duty.

Meanwhile, early in March, the frenzy of fear and rage on the frontier had led to the cold-blooded murder of ninety Moravian Delaware Indians at Gnadenhütten. This example was what probably inspired some militia from Chartiers Creek to add one more episode to the bloody history of Smoky Island, when they fell upon Killbuck's friendly Delawares encamped there and killed all but a few who managed to escape to the woods or to the fort. The murderers even sent word to Gibson, who was commanding during Irvine's absence at Fort McIntosh, that they would scalp him next. So general was the approbation of the murder of the Moravians that Irvine had to request his wife not to express any opinion on the subject lest it be attributed to him. With these crimes on their consciences one can scarcely avoid the thought that Colonel William Crawford's men deserved their defeat in June while on an expedition against the British and Indians of Sandusky.

The spring of 1783 opened with the usual Indian raids, but they slackened in May and finally ceased almost altogether. Irvine was forced to furlough permanently most of his troops because of lack of provisions, those at Fort Pitt being mustered out by Major William Croghan. Irvine himself waited until September, when a Maryland detachment under Captain Joseph Marbury took over Fort Pitt, then departed for his home in Carlisle.

VIII

IMMIGRATION into the Monongahela country received a decided stimulus from the Revolution, for the West offered the most convenient asylum for Tories fleeing from Whiggish tar and feathers, and for those who were either genuine pacifists or who were cynically doubtful as to the desirability of exchanging the yoke of a parliament across the Atlantic for that of a congress close to home. The development of Kentucky drained away many of the older Monongahela settlers, and the movement was accelerated when, after the settlement of the boundary dispute, Pennsylvania's law for the gradual emancipation of slaves came into effect in the West and caused slaveholders to move out. It was easy, therefore, for refugees from the East to purchase land in a country where few questions would be asked as to their antecedents, provided they were willing to offer lip service to the Revolutionary cause. This immigration finally became so marked that in 1780 General Brodhead could complain that "The King of Great Britain's health is often drunk in companies; & I believe those wish to see the Regular Troops removed from this department, & a favorable opportunity to submit to British Government."

While there is no reason for stigmatizing all the inhabitants of the West with the epithets of Tories or neutrals, yet a number of circumstances inexorably led to a degree of non-coöperation on the part of the people that handicapped the progress of the war almost as much as they could have hindered it had they been disloyal. The renewal each spring of the "visits" of the Indians in search of hirsute souvenirs made men hesitate to leave their homes for extended military service and led to considerable complaint because the regular regiments raised for the defense of the region had been ordered to the East. It was true that the county courts allowed a pittance in paper money to the destitute families of soldiers, but the amount was so little in comparison with the need that the most earnest patriots in the ranks were sorely tempted to desert and return home to provide for their families as well as to protect them from the raids of the savages. Officers sometimes found themselves obliged to engage in trade on the side in order to provide the scantest necessities for themselves, their families, and even for the men under them—a measure that often called down the wrath of the slacking civilians with whom they competed.

The typical Revolutionary soldier in the West was, if possible, even more ragged and hunger bitten than his eastern comrade, and it was unusual for him to have enough powder and lead to carry him through a skirmish with the Indians. There was, of course, plenty of paper money, but the farmers and army contractors could scarcely be blamed for refusing to accept it. Before 1779 Colonel George Morgan did succeed fairly well in collecting food for both the state and continental garrisons, but he had to overcome tremendous obstacles. He had to buy wheat, contract for the milling, buy or make kegs in which to put the flour, purchase or hire pack horses, and purchase or construct bateaux to transport it from post to post. Cattle and hogs, fortunately, could be driven on the hoof to Pittsburgh, and there slaughtered and salted, or if salt could not be obtained, smoked. The price of salt naturally followed other prices skyward until finally, when it could not be obtained at any price, it had to be seized. Pittsburgh, as the headquarters of the service of supply, was the location of many of the military stores, of the slaughtering pens, and of a government boat yard where freight bateaux and convoy boats armed with swivel guns were built. The successful journey of George Gibson and William Linn to New Orleans in 1776 to buy powder led to at least one other such expedition, that of David Rogers in 1778, which terminated in a disastrous Indian attack on the upward journey. James Willing's raid on West Florida in 1778 was outfitted by Morgan's efforts, as was also the more famous expedition of George Rogers Clark to Illinois the same year.

With Morgan's departure from the West the service of supply became demoralized. Brodhead was reduced to such an extremity for food in 1780 that he sent foraging parties out to seize cattle and grain, but when the inhabitants removed their stock to the mountains the general, as a last desperate measure, sent hunters to the Little Kanawha. When the hunters returned empty handed the soldiers in the rickety stockades dignified with the names of forts either resigned themselves to starvation or descended to beg of the Indians. In the spring of 1782 the noncommissioned officers and soldiers of the Seventh Virginia stationed at Fort Pitt addressed to Irvine a pathetic appeal that stated that they had been without pay for two years and three months and were naked, hungry, and without fuel. "Though we have been upbraided by the country inhabitants for our fidelity —" read the address, "they calling us fools, cowards and a set of mean fellows for staying without our pay and just dues—yet we think more of our honor than to listen to any advice than what is given to us by our officers."

The rise in the price of food was caused primarily by the inflation of the currency, but it also resulted because farmers failed to plant grain lest it be burned by the Indians and because they held their wheat, corn, and cattle for speculation. The county courts made efforts to set the prices that tavern-keepers could ask for entertainment, but when one dollar of specie was worth forty-five in Pennsylvania currency such efforts probably meant little. The army officers of Fort Pitt, blaming the rise of prices upon speculators, attempted in 1779 to regulate all prices west of the mountains. There is no evidence to show that the attempt did not end in a dismal failure. Trade really seems to have flourished; in the early years of the Revolution all available food supplies were purchased by immigrants or by the army, and in the later years a flatboat trade was begun with New Orleans, a trade that increased year after year in spite of Indian hazards and the technical restrictions placed by the Spanish upon entry into their territory.

IX

DURING the greater part of the Revolution Virginia was in actual control of the Monongahela country; Pennsylvania's Westmoreland County exercised jurisdiction only over the eastern two-thirds of the present county of that name and some sparsely inhabited country farther north. In October, 1776, the District of West Augusta was divided into the counties of Yohogania, Monongalia, and Ohio. Pittsburgh was in Yohogania County, but the courthouse was located on the plantation of Andrew Heath on a hill above the Monongahela River not far from modern West Elizabeth. It was not until 1779 that commissioners from Pennsylvania and Virginia met in Baltimore and agreed to extend Mason and Dixon's line due west to a point five degrees west of the Delaware and thence to run the boundary north. The boundary agreement received its final approval by both states in 1780, and the next year Pennsylvania erected Washington County, embracing the territory west of the Monongahela and south of the Ohio, though the boundary line between the states was not accurately run until 1784. Meanwhile a movement was begun by the disappointed Virginians to set up a new state in the Monongahela country. So great was the danger from the advocates of the measure that in September, 1782, Irvine, who was planning to leave the region for a few weeks, warned Major Isaac Craig, who was to become the temporary commandant of Fort Pitt, against calling in volunteers who might seize the fort to promote the new state. In December the Pennsylvania General

Assembly passed an act declaring it treason to attempt to set up a new state, and the Supreme Executive Council, with a touching faith in the efficacy of the printed word, struck off a hundred copies of the act and sent the Reverend James Finley to the Monongahela to distribute them to the inhabitants. Whether or not the act was responsible, the new state talk gradually died out.

George Clymer, during his sojourn in Pittsburgh in 1778, wrote to his wife that the town was "excellent to do pennance in." Nevertheless, even in wartime, there was social life of a kind. The soldiers of the garrison occasionally held Masonic meetings, and sometimes plays were staged, doubtless by officers and townsmen together. The courts of West Augusta for a time sat regularly in the town, and it must have afforded the citizens much amusement to listen as Peter Nesewanger was formally charged "for wilfully exhibiting a melitious and Scandalous Lybell," or to watch James Johnston's face empurple as he paid a fine of twenty shillings because he "did this day swear two profane oaths and two profane Cusses." A ducking stool was erected in 1775 at the "Confluence of OHio with the Monongohale" but there is no record that it was ever used. Jacob Bausman in 1775 was licensed to keep a ferry over the Monongahela at the foot of Wood Street, and four years later John Ormsby was authorized to keep one at the foot of Ferry Street in connection with his tavern, once Samuel Semple's. There were at least a half dozen ordinaries, or taverns, in the town, one of them kept by a "David Dunking." A familiar charge that has appeared many times since on police blotters was first introduced in 1777 when one of the ordinary proprietors was hailed before the Yohogania court for "keeping a disorderly House." The rates that ordinaries could charge were carefully specified by the court in 1778. "Whiskie by the half pint" cost two shillings sixpence, "a hot Breakfast" three shillings, "a Cold ditto" two shillings sixpence, a dinner four shillings, and a supper three. "Lodging with Clean Sheats" came to one shilling sixpence, and "Stablage with good hay or fodder" five shillings.

As late as 1782 Edward Ward was still living at the Point as the agent of Ross and Thompson, who claimed to own the fort. There must have been three redoubts connected with the fort, for in 1778 James McGoldrick was fined for having pulled one down; and Ward sued Brodhead in 1779 for quartering some troops in an old redoubt that had been moved away, and Irvine inherited the trouble. In 1781 John Irwin lived in a third redoubt, probably the one at the entrance to Redoubt Alley. The brick redoubt, which still stands, was probably used by the garrison. General Irvine opened himself to more trouble with Ward when he fenced in thirty-four acres of the King's Artillery Gardens as pasture for the army horses. There were at the time about a hundred apple trees on the tract. Irvine wrote to his wife that between his arduous military duties he rode, walked, hunted or gardened. "I assure you we have a pretty good garden," he wrote, "such as would pass with you as tolerable. How elegant our peas are—thick and fine! and we have wild tongue-grass, asparagus, and a variety of fine greens in great abundance."

IX
Between Revolts

IN 1784, when Colonel George Woods of Bedford, with a surveyor's rod that by some oversight was too long by an eighth of an inch in ten feet, laid out the familiar plan of the Triangle for the Penns, he was so accommodating as to make Market Street only forty feet wide instead of sixty because the owners of the log cabins that extended out over the proposed thoroughfare begged him to save their property. Supremely unconscious of the traffic problems he was posing for future generations, Woods continued John Campbell's plan of 1764 to Grant Street, then laid out Liberty and Penn Avenues parallel to the Allegheny and at acute angles to the streets that were parallel to the Monongahela. A public square, the Diamond, was laid out on Market Street not far from Liberty and near this place the civic life of Pittsburgh was destined to center for nearly half a century. The streets close to the Monongahela were given the names that, with a few exceptions, they still bear; Grant Street was named for Major James Grant, Smithfield for Devereux Smith, and Wood for the surveyor. The streets at right angles to the Allegheny, now distinguished by a hodgepodge of modern names or numbers, were in order, Marbury, Hay, Pitt, St. Clair, Irwin, Hand, Wayne, and Washington.

The Pittsburgh of the decade after the Revolution was a gangling, growing, pioneer village, with its business houses facing the muddy, irregular bank of the Monongahela; in some places the bank encroached so close on Water Street that a wagon could barely pass. The land upon which the town was built was uneven, and when the river reached a moderate height the water rushed into Wood Street and rendered it impassable. There were several ponds back of the town, one of them sprawled across the present site of Kaufmann's store (the ground level has since been raised, probably for the most part with the parings of Grant's Hill); another was west of the Diamond; and a third, probably near the old moat between the fort and the Allegheny River, was a favorite resort of wild ducks.

There were in the town, at the close of the Revolution, perhaps fifty or more houses, nearly all of them of logs, and one might guess that there were five hundred inhabitants. The complaint of one traveler that the place was infested by a "Combination of pensioned Scoundrels" who made a business of cheating and overcharging strangers was echoed too often by newcomers; and John Wilkins, Sr., a prominent citizen who had arrived at the end of 1783, later admitted that "all sorts of wickedness were carried on to excess, and there was no appearance of morality or regular order. . . . it seemed to me that the Presbyterian ministers were afraid to come to the place lest they should be mocked or mistreated." The streets were muddy and filthy, the houses were ramshackle and unpainted log structures (though it must have been during this period that John Gibson built a brick house near the northeast corner of Second Avenue and Chancery Lane), too often with makeshift, ugly furnishings. Wash day was an occasion, sanitary provisions were primitive, the dogs made night hideous with their howls, and drunken Indians and whites snored beside the hogs in the mud puddles. There were even those so ignorant, it was claimed, that when they entered the house of Captain O'Hara and his bride in the King's Artillery Gardens they hestitated to walk on the carpets because they mistook them for bed covers. But perhaps their diffidence was a sign of dawning culture.

II

IN LATER life one citizen was to remember the closing years of the century with nostalgia, and write of the "lonely, mournful sound of the cowbells in the little valley of Suke's Run"; the "smell of coal smoke in coming down Coal Hill"; and the sycamores growing along the bank of the Monongahela. Life among the commoners possessed a simplicity and spontaneity that at least lacked the boredom of sophistication. When one Frederick Moseman was drowned in the Monongahela the "wagglopers," to locate the dead man's body, tied a loaf of bread into his other shirt and set them afloat, the belief being that they would float till they came over the man's body and then sink. The bread and shirt sank as expected, but when the body could not be found the "experiment could not be repeated," for poor Frederick, alas! had but one extra shirt. The Scots celebrated St. Andrew's day with copious libations, the Irish celebrated St. Patrick's day in like fashion, everyone celebrated the Fourth of July with a salute of thirteen cannon shots, and all who could get into the "Green Tree" tavern topped off with "an elegant entertainment" and thirteen toasts, ending with "Success to Pittsburgh, and a Free Navigation of the Western Country."

The celebration longest remembered by the people of Pittsburgh was that held in June, 1788, upon the ratification of the federal constitution by New Hampshire, the ninth state, whose action made certain the setting up of a new national government. The citizens gathered upon the slopes of Grant's Hill, then well outside the town, and listened to an oration by the lawyer, Hugh Henry Brackenridge. Afterwards nine of thirteen piles of wood were ignited to represent the nine states that had ratified the constitution; it was considered a good omen when the fire leaped across to the unlighted piles and set them ablaze.

Though the town boasted two physicians, Nathaniel Bedford and Thomas Parker, the more simple citizens doctored the rheumatism with willow-bark tea, the ague with an infusion of brimstone, lemon juice, and rum, and treated their children's worms by the application of angleworms first to the stomach and then successively lower down until, presto! the worms were gone. Henry Chapese, who sold medicines and paints, advertised an infallible cure for snakebite; but only the gullible bought, for it was well known that the best antidote for snakebite was a skinful of whiskey. One observer was so inconsiderate as to propose to improve the health of the village by draining the ponds, a measure that would have ruined the sport of the duck hunters; it is to be hoped that his suggestion was properly scorned.

Those who were ailing and could afford the treatment journeyed to the "Federal Springs" on Tom's Run ten miles away from Pittsburgh and not far from modern Bridgeville. There the enterprising owners had erected "a very convenient Bathing House, in which there are two plunging and two shower Baths, and a dressing room annexed to each bathing room; also a common Bath, and a number of houses, with chimnies, for taverns, private lodgings, and the accomodation of private families." Prospective patients were assured that the water "is so very pure and light that any person may drink a gallon of it without feeling his stomach in the least oppressed." It was recommended for those afflicted with rheumatism, scurvy, gravel, "white swellings, catahrs, incomes on the knees, &c." Doubtless the ladies of Pittsburgh found it also an excellent cure for ennui.

III

PITTSBURGH remained a garrison town until after the War of 1812, though during the decade after the Revolution Fort Pitt was being literally carried away piecemeal. In 1784 Major Isaac Craig, who had been stationed there during the Revolution, and his business partner, Colonel Stephen Bayard, bought the fort and the land on which it stood from the Penns for themselves and their financial associates in a Philadelphia firm headed by William Turnbull; and though years of litigation followed among the various claimants to the property, they were finally awarded possession. The dismantling of the fort had begun before the Revolution; it was resumed afterwards, and by the late nineties nothing remained save the brick redoubt, a stone magazine, and the mounds of earth and debris that marked the lines of the walls. The bricks taken from the fort were distinguishable by their whitish color and for many years they were pointed out in the buildings of the town, especially in a row of houses erected in 1791 on Market Street between Second (Boulevard of the Allies) and Third Avenues. Part of Fort Pitt was occupied by a garrison until 1792; the known commandants after the Revolution were Captain Joseph Marbury, Captain Lucket, Lieutenant Matthew Ernest, and Captain Hughes. Major Craig and his family lived in the brick redoubt for a while, and another redoubt at the mouth of Redoubt Alley was occupied by John Irwin, who had been prominent in Pittsburgh during the Revolution and who was the owner of a ropewalk. The fort was inevitably a social center and in 1790 the *Gazette* advertised that "a Theatrical Representation of the TRAGEDY of CATO, with the FARCE of *All the World's a Stage*," would be given in the theater of the garrison.

The renewal of the Indian wars after the Revolution placed Pittsburgh in unpleasant peril, and whenever there was a rumor of the approach of savages there was a great "running to and fro in the night," and upon one occasion the citizenry demanded and obtained arms from Major Craig who was in charge of the federal arsenal. There was considerable resentment that Guyasuta, who had commanded the Indians during the siege of Pittsburgh in 1763 and at the burning of Hannastown, should dare to live on a fertile bottom across the Allegheny, just above present-day Sharpsburg. A writer in the *Gazette* sarcastically wrote: "We are happy to have an opportunity of congratulating our fellow citizens on the arrival in this town of the great, the mighty, and the warlike GIOSOTA the first, king of the Seneca nation; defender of Hannah's-town; protector of the widow and orphan, &c. &c." Arthur Lee reported, less maliciously, that Guyasuta was "a very provident Indian . . . having two wives . . . one well stricken in years who paid great attention to his food and his clothes, the other a handsome young squaw." The average Pittsburgher's contempt for Indians was well expressed by one who wrote: "I have seen Indian princes in Pittsburgh, as plenty as in the time of Adonibezek, who had three score and ten kings under his table. Many a chief I have seen driven out of a kitchen by a maid with a broomstick, lest he should steal a tin cup or a table spoon."

The situation finally became so alarming that in 1791, immediately after St. Clair's disastrous defeat, Major Craig was instructed to erect a new fort to take the place of the rapidly disintegrating Fort Pitt. As a consequence Captain Hughes on May 5, 1792, moved his men to Fort Fayette, a square stockade located across Penn Avenue, probably between Ninth and Tenth Streets. The fort was a stockade, inclosing about an acre or so, with four bastions, containing blockhouses, a brick arsenal, and a barracks with thirty rooms. Victor Collot, a French soldier who visited the fort in 1796, ridiculed the place and asserted that on "a dark night four grenadiers, with a dozen faggots of dry wood, might burn the fort and all the garrison, and not a single individual escape." When "Mad Anthony" Wayne appeared in Pittsburgh during 1792 with his "Legion" of Indian-*strafers* his headquarters was located at the southeast corner of Liberty and West Streets; his army was encamped on Suke's Run and across the Allegheny River until he was ready to leave for his "winter ground" at Legionville on the site of old Logstown. During the years of Indian warfare Pittsburgh was the point at which army supplies brought by pack horse or wagon from the East were loaded upon boats to be carried forward to the army at Legionville or in Ohio. James O'Hara as quartermaster general and Craig as his deputy were kept busy buying flour, meat, forage, and other supplies, and contracting for boats for the use of the army. This demand for the products of the Monongahela country did much to promote prosperity and attract farmers and mechanics as settlers. Fort Fayette remained a center of military activity until its abandonment sometime in the winter of 1815.

IV

By 1788 Pittsburgh had become such a center of population that it was made the seat of a new county, Allegheny, which at first included all the land northwest of the Allegheny River; but most of that area was lost with the wholesale creation of new counties in 1800. The legislature had planned to put the county seat in a new town that was to be erected across the Allegheny on a tract of land reserved by the state from public sale, but the Supreme Executive Council was finally so obliging as to have an act passed authorizing the county trustees to erect a courthouse and jail in Pittsburgh. For many years courts seem to have been held in the second story of Andrew Watson's log tavern near the corner of First and Market Streets. The first courthouse, completed in 1799, was located on the western half of the Diamond. It was a brick structure with a two-story central building surmounted by a belfry and steeple and with two wings for offices.

Pittsburgh became a borough on April 22, 1794, and the first borough elections, held on May 19, resulted in the choice of George Robinson and Josiah Tannehill as chief burgesses; Nathaniel Irish, John Johnston, George Adams, and Nathaniel Bedford as assistant burgesses; Samuel Morrison, high constable; and James Clow, town clerk. One of the first acts of the burgesses was to post an ordinance prohibiting hogs from running at large. But, inasmuch as the hogs could not read, they continued to wallow luxuriantly in the rich mire that was everywhere on Pittsburgh's streets. Another ordinance that forbade anyone to disturb the peace by galloping his horse and firing his gun in the town was just as blandly ignored. The burgesses did succeed, however, in erecting a market house at the foot of Market Street, in addition to one put up in 1787 at Second Avenue and Market.

Among its other improvements Pittsburgh could boast a post office, and the inhabitants kept their ears cocked on certain days for the blast of the postrider's tin horn, which announced the arrival of the mail. The first regular mail service had been started in 1788 after the personable young politician, James Brison, had made a trip to New York to lobby for it with Congress. The first postmaster seems to have been William Tilton, who served from July 7, 1788, to January 5, 1789. John Scull, the local printer, succeeded Tilton and for eight years kept post office in connection with his print shop. George Adams became postmaster in 1797, Dr. Hugh Scott in 1803, and John Johnston in 1804.

The Pittsburgh Fire Company dated from 1793 and its volunteer members were the proud possessors of a hand engine brought over the mountains from Philadelphia. Like most fire companies of the day, this one was as much for social as for fire-fighting purposes. There were two other organizations in Pittsburgh that provided refuge for henpecked males. The Freemasons, chartered in 1785 as "Lodge No. 45 of Ancient York Masons," included on its roll the names of the town's leading citizens and was the chief social organization in the community. Its meetings were usually held at the "Sign of the Green Tree" tavern on Water Street, and certain religious holidays were observed with a pomp that delighted the hearts of Pittsburgh's small boys. The lodge left its hall in full regalia—cocked hats, knee breeches, craft aprons, and embroidered collars; the officers carried truncheons and staves, the sword-bearer led the procession, and the Bible, with compass and square, was borne aloft on a velvet cushion. A sermon was delivered in the Presbyterian meetinghouse, after which the lodge sat down to a heavy but eminently satisfactory dinner at the "Green Tree." The workingmen had their own social and educational organization, the "Mechanical Society," a local branch of which was founded in Pittsburgh in 1788. It met in Andrew Watson's tavern and devoted itself to the betterment of the workingmen and, besides endeavoring to attract industries to the town, sought to build up a library and museum.

By 1790 there were two churches in Pittsburgh. The first one was the German Evangelical Church, organized in 1782 with the Reverend Johann Wilhelm Weber as pastor. The congregation occupied a log cabin at Wood and Diamond Streets until the early nineties, when it built another cabin at Smithfield Street and Sixth Avenue on land donated by the Penns. The Presbyterian congregation of Pittsburgh was incorporated by a legislative act in 1787 and, probably in the same year, built a church of squared logs east of Wood Street between Sixth and Oliver Avenues, also on land donated by the Penns. The Reverend Samuel Barr was the first pastor, and the chief pillar of the church was Jonathan Plumer, a New Englander, whose son George, born December 5, 1762, is reputed to have been the first white child born in Pittsburgh after the British occupation.

Property adjacent to the Presbyterian church was reserved for a prospective Episcopal church.

Until 1789 Pittsburgh youth depended for instruction upon fly-by-night teachers who set up school wherever they could rent a room and who charged as much tuition as the parents of the pupils would pay. In November, 1786, a Mrs. Pride started "a boarding and day school for young ladies" and advertised that she would teach needlework and "Reading English, and knitting if required." About the same time the "inhabitants of Pittsburgh" advertised for "a man who understands Vocal Music, and who can teach it with propriety." In January, 1788, a Thomas Tonsey opened a school in which were taught "the Latin Language, Reading English Grammatically, Writing, and Arithmetic." The earnest mechanic had his chance as well as the town lads, for Mr. Tonsey also kept an evening school.

These enterprises, while useful as far as they went, did not fill the need for an institution to teach subjects more advanced than the common branches. This need was met by the incorporation in 1787 of the Pittsburgh Academy, endowed with a list of eminent men as trustees, a modest tract of five thousand acres in the wilderness, and the block of lots bounded by Smithfield Street, Cherry Alley, and Second and Third Avenues. The academy finally got under way in March, 1789, under the principalship of George Welch. The first classes were probably held in a log house on the academy lot. The furniture was like that of the average frontier school: crude long desks hinged to the walls so that they could be dropped to enlarge the available space, split-log benches, a stove or fireplace, and a wide, painted blackboard nailed to the wall or to a standard. At some time during the seventeen-nineties a brick school building was erected, and it was partially paid for by state funds.

v

THE father of the little academy that was to grow into the University of Pittsburgh was Pittsburgh's most eminent lawyer and literary *raconteur*, Hugh Henry Brackenridge. Born in Scotland in 1745, he was brought to Pennsylvania five years later.

He was educated at Princeton; then, after periods spent as a teacher, a Revolutionary chaplain, and the editor of the unsuccessful *United States Magazine*, he came to Pittsburgh in 1781 and took up the practice of law. During the succeeding years he became known both in Europe and America as the author of a powerful political satire, *Modern Chivalry*. Elected to the state legislature in 1786, he had been chiefly responsible for the erection of Allegheny County and the incorporation of the Presbyterian Congregation and Pittsburgh Academy. But he did not play the game with the western politicians, lost his chance for reëlection, and so ruined both his influence and his law practice that for several years he was in Coventry and was forced to wage a grim fight not only for political rehabilitation but for a livelihood. Though he favored the adoption of the constitution and celebrated the ratification of that instrument by the delivery of an eloquent address to an assemblage of townsmen on Grant's Hill, yet his democratic leanings made him anathema to the Federalist party, which was already beginning to form; moreover, he had alienated the most politically potent family in Pittsburgh, the Nevilles.

General John Neville and his son, Colonel Presley Neville, both Revolutionary veterans, were men of substance and chronic officeholders; the elder Neville's brother-in-law, Abraham Kirkpatrick, held great tracts of land and was financially prosperous; Major Isaac Craig, John Neville's son-in-law, was not only a businessman but deputy quartermaster general of the United States army, and as such had at his disposal a vast amount of local patronage. The Neville lawyer, John Woods, son of Pittsburgh's town planner, was next to Brackenridge the town's most prominent attorney and no mean adversary in his own right. The outbreak of the French Revolution accentuated the political antagonisms in the West, for the democratic element enthusiastically espoused the cause of the revolutionists and even aped many of their customs; the democrats changed knee breeches for trousers, addressed each other as "citizen," and organized Democratic societies for the promotion of the ideals of the Revolution. The passage of the federal excise on distilled products

was a convenient peg on which the West could hang its grievances. These were by no means confined to the resulting high
cost of whiskey, but included opposition to the government's reputed purpose to promote aristocratic rights and privileges at
the expense of the liberties of the common people by its policies
of financial extravagance, favoritism toward industry and commerce to the exclusion of agriculture, and indifference to the
problem of opening the Mississippi for western trade.

Political controversy, though none the less bitter, had been
hampered by the lack of a newspaper in the region, or indeed
anywhere west of the mountains. In 1786 Brackenridge backed
the foundation of the *Pittsburgh Gazette* by two young easterners,
John Scull and Joseph Hall. The first issue of the *Gazette* was dated
July 29, 1786, and was printed on a hand press in a log house
on Water Street near Ferry. The venture was greeted with enthusiasm by everyone. Brackenridge was spokesman for the community, and he exemplified the current opinion that a newspaper
should print distant rather than local news when he wrote: ''Who
would not give half a guinea to know, exactly as he does his own
calf pasture, what is going on every day when he rises, at Smyrna
and Amsterdam, and count as easily as he can the stripes of his
waistcoat, the armies that are on foot in Europe ... To be able
to look up with the tail of his eye as far as Russia, and down
again with the same glance to the islands in the West Indies,
and to see all the intermediate space swarming with men and
things.'' Getting closer to home, the lawyer went on: "A principal advantage will be to know what is going on in our own state;
particularly what our representatives are doing: Heretofore, like
boys creeping into a hay stack at such a remote distance, we
could see only their heels, while their heads were hid away amongst
the cabals of Philadelphia." This was before Brackenridge had
been sent to the state legislature and had antagonized his constituents by his independence.

The *Gazette*, while its editors were Federalist in their opinions,
strove to be politically impartial, and it was not until 1800,
with the establishment of a rival paper, that all attempts to be
neutral were abandoned. Since the *Gazette* was, beside the Bible

and an almanac, the only reading matter available to many of its subscribers it published a great variety of material: a description of Pittsburgh written by Brackenridge appeared in its first issues, and was followed by essays on temperance and on women, poems in praise of this and that, witty or moral anecdotes, articles on agricultural methods, medical and culinary recipes, polemics on religion, education, politics, and the navigation of the Mississippi, and advertisements for runaway slaves, bond servants, horses, and wives. By 1787 Scull had undertaken the publication of the *Pittsburgh Almanac*, calculated for the meridian of Pittsburgh. He was spurred on to the undertaking by Brackenridge, who whimsically recited the case of a local citizen who had "almost lost his life trusting to a Baltimore almanac to draw blood" when of course "the time of the sun rising is different, having 300 miles and a high mountain to come over." Scull also kept for sale a stock of textbooks, laws, and religious books. Some of them he may have printed himself, but it is probable that the third volume of *Modern Chivalry*, which Scull published in 1793, was the first book printed west of the mountains.

Joseph Hall died shortly after the *Gazette* was started and his successor, John Boyd, hung himself on the hill that still bears his name. Scull continued to publish the paper by himself. His greatest problem during the first years, since there were no post offices in the region, was to provide for the distribution of the paper to subscribers. Even with the establishment of post offices after 1788 the problem remained only partly solved. Those who lived on the Monongahela had their *Gazettes* delivered by the boatmen who made regular trips on that stream, but isolated readers still had to submit to considerable inconvenience. The printer, besides being handicapped by the laxness with which subscriptions were paid, was often hard put to find paper when disappointed of a supply from the East. At such times the paper on which the issues were printed was much reduced in size, and on one occasion Scull borrowed a wheelbarrow and trundled to the shop some cartridge paper that he had begged from Major Craig's military stores. The establishment of a paper mill at Brownsville in 1797 finally put an end to the scarcity of paper.

THE decade following the close of the Revolution was marked by the disappearance of the Indian traders from Pittsburgh and the growing demand for more varied merchandise. Even at the beginning of the period there were nine stores in the town and by 1794 there were probably about forty; many of the proprietors doubtless manufactured in the back of their stores the goods that they sold in the front. A finer quality of goods began first to come over the mountains and then up the rivers from New Orleans, and skilled artisans began to flow into Pittsburgh and set up their little establishments, which not only manufactured goods but sold them at retail and wholesale prices. The English and Scotch-Irish had done the pioneering; it now became the turn of others to make their contributions. German immigration into the region increased perceptibly during the Revolution and a surprising number of Frenchmen, left by the French expeditionary forces or fleeing from the Reign of Terror, settled in Pittsburgh. One list of mechanics for 1792 gives "1 Clock and Watch Maker, 2 Coopers, 1 Skin Dresser and Breeches maker, 2 Tanners and Curriers, 4 Cabinet-makers, 2 Hatters, 2 Weavers, 5 Blacksmiths, 5 Shoemakers, 3 Saddlers, 1 Malster and Brewer, 2 Tinners, 3 Wheelwrights, 1 Stocking-weaver, 1 Rope-maker, 2 White-smiths. Total 36 [*sic*] Mechanics." There were in Pittsburgh at about the same time two brickyards, three or four boat yards, and near by, two or more sawmills. Whiskey-distilling was becoming an important industry, not only in Pittsburgh but in the entire region, and Monongahela rye was well known in the East.

Pittsburgh had its own rising manufacturers, such as John Ormsby, Isaac Craig, Stephen Bayard, and James O'Hara, but the real captain of Pittsburgh industry in the eighties and nineties was William Turnbull, late of Philadelphia, who lived in the only stone house in the village and entertained as befitted his station. Craig and Bayard were associated with him for some years but finally broke off relations. Bayard soon afterward left Craig and went up the Monongahela to found Elizabeth. Turnbull and his various partners engaged in a long list of activities, among them sawmilling, coal-mining, and distilling, and in 1789 and 1790 he built western Pennsylvania's first iron furnace on Jacob's Creek. The attempt in 1793 of an Alsatian named George Anshutz to run a furnace at Shadyside (now a part of Pittsburgh) proved unprofitable because of a scarcity of ore and was discontinued in 1794.

Thus Pittsburgh was scarcely a cross section of the agricultural frontier. Settled originally by hard-bitten, trigger-fingered, realistic Indian traders, it was a commercial entrepôt from the first, and as these traders prospered and loosened their belts life in Pittsburgh became easier. Master mechanics, lawyers, and medicos moved in, and a little circle of the more cultured and educated had formed even before the guns of Concord announced the beginning of the struggle for American independence. It was years, however, before travelers ceased to rail at the native's idea of cultured society or before they could pass through the town without deriding the local standards of sanitation, business practice, or morality.

Not all the people of the Monongahela approved of the encroachment of manufacturers upon their simple rural domain, and more than one hard-headed old-timer clung grimly to the products of home industry and refused to be seduced by the fancy store goods of effete Pittsburgh. There was, said these hill-billies of the eighteenth century, a well-organized attempt on foot to get them all into debt and make them slaves to the aristocracy even as were the farmers of the East. "A Countryman" even went so far as to send to the *Gazette* an article that ridiculed the ingenious contrivances of a carpenter to save labor by running his grindstone and his wife's spinning wheel by water power. Pittsburgh's enterprise and prosperity thus made it the cynosure of western eyes, and with the French Revolution's popularization of radical democratic ideas it actually became hated as the local exemplar of corrupt aristocracy and soulless materialism. The time was not far distant when this attitude was to be translated into action.

X

Tom the Tinker Comes to Town

HUGH HENRY BRACKENRIDGE rested his elbow on a bale of furs in the rear of Beaumont's store and watched the cooly indifferent clerk wait upon a woman whose homespun garments and misshapen figure, stooped with years of field labor and childbearing, proclaimed her to be from the country. Anger was evident in the tone of her voice and in the way she flung back on the counter the ribbon she had been holding. As she stalked from the store the lawyer came forward.

"What was it she said?" he asked.

"She said she'd get it for less in a few days, Mr. Brackenridge," the clerk answered.

The lawyer walked to the door and looked out into the street. The woman had been joined by a man whose red thatch gleamed in the July sun and who bore under his arm a long, murderous-looking rifle. The pair turned into another store.

"Probably intends to buy flints and powder," mused Brackenridge. He hesitated a moment, then crossed the street to the shop of Dennis McCarty, who, though he preferred to shoe horses, sometimes tried his quick Irish fingers at gunsmithing. The smith dropped the handle of his bellows as his neighbor entered.

"Ah, the tap o' the marnin' to ye, Misther Brackenridge.

What kin I do for ye?"

"Nothing, Dennis, just a spark with you," answered the law-yer. "How is business these days?"

The Irishman wiped his sweaty hands upon the grimy legs of his trousers. "Faith," he said, "I haven't seen it so good sence the Injun scare three years ago come next Christmas. Ivery Orange psalm-singer in Washington County has been in to have his gun minded."

The Scotch lawyer raised his eyebrows and smiled slightly. In spite of their differences in race and religion the two under-stood each other. "It looks bad, Dennis," he commented.

"Ye're roight, sor," returned the Irishman. He looked cau-tiously around, then spoke in lowered tones. "D'ye want to know whut it was I jist heard? That was Orris Shochan that jist left here, the red-headed, Scriptur spoutin' blaggard, an' in the coorse av the conversa-ation whut d'ye think he tould me? He said that the other Sodom was destroyed by fire from hiven, but that this Sodom"—Dennis waved a black paw in a gesture that included the whole town—"'that this Sodom *should be de-stroyed by fire from earth.*"

The lawyer left the smithy, his brows knit in thought, and walked up Front Street toward his home. Safely in his office he locked his door, pulled the curtains together, and sat down at his desk. A tiny key that he produced from his waistcoat pocket unlocked a drawer. He fished in the recesses of the drawer for a moment, then drew out a sheet of paper covered with his characteristically illegible, sprawling handwriting. The letter, as yet unfinished, was dated July 29, 1794, and was directed to Tench Coxe, supervisor of the revenue. The lawyer hurriedly scanned the lines that he had written: "——the present state of this country with respect to the Excise law. The small distillers consider themselves wronged by this tax, which in truth takes away their profit if they bear the expense of its transportation below [*to the East*] and if they keep it here they must trade it for Country produce and never see in a year enough hard cash to pay the assessment——large distillers, who sell to the Army, think to use the Law in treading down the little fellow——opposition, which, for some time showed itself in resolves of Committees——in the riddling with bullets the Stills of those who would pay the tax (from which circumstance they have become known as Tom the Tinker), advanced to Masked attacks on Insignificant Deputy Excise Officers and the pinning of threatening notes on trees near the homes of those suspect——some organizations of malcontents——Washington County the head, and this because it has the most stills——Mingo Democratic Association a power unto itself; it has taken over all the ordinary processes of the Law.

"The appearance of the federal Sheriff in this County to serve processes did so anger the people, who saw themselves ruined if they had to bear the expense of being tried in Philadelphia at 300 miles distance——on the sixteenth instant five or six hundred strong attacked Bower Hill, the country Mansion of General Neville, inspector of the excise, and burned it to the ground with the loss of two or three men killed, including Major James McFarlane, their leader——General Neville and the marshal have fled —— a meeting called for Parkinson's ferry on August fourteenth."

When he had finished his perusal, the lawyer dipped a quill in the inkstand and wrote: "July 31. The root of the trouble is far deeper than a mere quarrel over the Excise. It is, as our people see it, a stand of the democratic, poverty ridden West against the encroachments of the aristocratic Money Bags of the East; of a people who feel themselves taxed in order to fasten the yoke of Plutocrats about their necks, the whiskey excise being but one step of a series of tyrannical measures. The crisis arises from an opposition to the fiscal policies of Government which they aver are for the benefit of speculators in credits from the late war and bear hardly on the poor; to the conduct of Indian affairs; to the Eastern commercial interests that block the opening of Mississippi navigation; and to the rule of appointive officers.

"The latest news is that the Mail has been intercepted and characters in Pittsburgh become Obnoxious by letters found in which are sentiments construed to evince a bias in favour of the Excise Law. A muster has been called for tomorrow at Braddock's Field, of those who oppose the excise and who in effect, are now insurgents. The object is well known to be to invade Pittsburgh, which they say is a veritable den of Reptiles, and consign it to the torch. A town Meeting is called for tonight to decide our course on the morrow. There is no alternative but that we must put on the Masks of friendship to save our families and homes and march forth to Braddock's field. Perhaps Art may yet save us."

When Brackenridge had finished the letter he folded it carefully with the writing inside and wrote on the outside the name of the person to whom it was addressed. He sat then for a moment debating whether or not to take the letter to the post office, but he finally decided to await an opportunity to send it to the East by some trusted friend. The danger of having the letter removed from the mails by some "whiskey boy" was too great to be run. The letter was locked in the drawer once more, and the lawyer picked up his frivolously cocked hat. Perhaps, already, there was more news to be gleaned on the streets.

II

THE town meeting was in session in the upper room of Watson's tavern on Market Street when word was brought that a deputation of gentlemen from Washington desired an interview with a committee of responsible citizens. Brackenridge and two others were immediately named and quickly made their way through the gathering gloom to the tavern where the visitors were lodged. There they were informed that David Bradford, the young Washington lawyer who had assumed the leadership of those in opposition to the excise, had promised, unofficially, to spare Pittsburgh if the townsmen would exile the authors of the objectionable letters, among them Abraham Kirkpatrick, Presley Neville, and John Gibson, and would march out to Braddock's Field next day and join in the display of force against the excise. The townsmen could do nothing but comply with the demands, and a committee of twenty-one was appointed to direct affairs during the crisis. Brackenridge, because of his acknowledged ability, was in effect the leader of the committee. The exiled letter-writers, some grudgingly and some cheerfully, prepared to depart in the morning, while the members of the committee, with their tongues in their cheeks, proceeded to draw up a series of complaisant resolutions for distribution to the insurgents, and John Scull was set the all-night task of printing them.

There was little sleep in Pittsburgh that night. The houses were lit up, the women were in tears, and the men were oiling their squirrel rifles. Those who had valuables buried them in safe places and then sat up to worry lest they be found. No one thought of going to work when morning dawned. The whole population gathered in the streets to cheer the departing defenders of homes and firesides as, 250 strong, they marched away under the supervision of John Wilkins, Jr., brigadier general of militia, associate judge of the county court, and proprietor of a store that bought whiskey only from those distillers who had paid the excise. As Braddock's Field, eight miles from town, was approached, the Washingtonians were sent ahead to distribute Scull's handbills, then presently the Pittsburghers, preceded by their committee of twenty-one, advanced with fearful hearts and bold faces through the seething thousands of insurgents to the spot chosen as headquarters.

The militiamen were having the time of their lives that day, boasting themselves of the morrow as if, to quote one writer, they were so many Samsons "who each could kill his thousands with the jaw bone of an ass." The smoke of rifle fire drifted up through the trees that had witnessed the massacre of Braddock's army as the restless frontiersmen passed the time by shooting at the mark. On a splendid charger David Bradford, decked out in the plumes and gold braid of a major general, rode about giving orders and whipping up the enthusiasm of the insurgents with impromptu addresses. He seems to have seen himself as a young Lochinvar riding out of the West to save the liberties of the people; actually, poor fellow, he was nothing but a chip riding the crest of a wave that was soon to subside.

Through this Mayfield of pure democracy wandered the jittery Brackenridge, striving to keep his mask of hypocrisy adjusted as he doubled back and forth in a mass of verbiage like a fox running from the hounds. Upon one occasion young Senator James Ross, who was present as an observer, threw him into a panic by twitting him about his veil wearing thin. A young Pittsburgher, the son of the merchant John Ormsby, failed to guard his words and managed only with difficulty to escape the clutches of a party of vengeful insurgents and make his way by unfrequented back roads to the shelter of Fort Fayette. Toward evening the Pittsburgh contingent, which had not brought any food, prepared to return home. The men had scarcely started, however, before there was a clamor that they were deserting the cause, and indeed never had been sincere in it. When the committee saw the effect of the departure Brackenridge was sent posthaste to recall the men. The militia obediently turned back, each man tightening his belt to allay his hunger and willing to do anything to protect his home. This incident demonstrated the peril of the Pittsburghers' situation. Had they left the field it is possible that the town would have fallen the next day before the fury of the malcontents.

As night came on Brackenridge and others opposed to violent measures began to work upon the fears of the militia.

"Are we to take the fort?" someone would ask.

"We are," Brackenridge would reply.

"Can we take it?"

"No doubt of it."

"But at a great loss?"

"Not at all," the wily lawyer would answer. "Not above a thousand killed, and five hundred mortally wounded."

The next morning a committee representing the battalions assembled to decide upon the procedure of the day, while an eager gallery of linseyed and buckskinned militiamen looked on. Bradford was glad of the opportunity to sun himself in the popular eye and lingered importantly over this and that, and Brackenridge, cultivating any excuse for delay, became a willing stooge. As the byplay dragged on the gallery became restless and finally a tall, rough fellow leaning on a long rifle broke in:

"Gentlemen," he said, "we do not understand your counseling in mystery: do something speedily, or we will go to execution ourselves."

This rough ultimatum acted like a shock on the committee. Bradford hastened to move that the troops start for Pittsburgh. "Yes, by all means," agreed Brackenridge, "We will just march through, and, taking a turn, come out upon the plain of the Monongahela's banks; and after taking a little whiskey with the inhabitants of the town the troops will embark on the ferries and cross the river."

III

WHILE the militia was forming the Pittsburgh committee sent orders for the citizens to collect ample food and liquor on the plain east of town and to bring together all the ferry boats on the bank of the Monongahela, and at the same time Bradford, his ardor noticeably chilled, sent word to Major Thomas Butler, commandant of Fort Fayette, that no harm was intended to the fort. There were perhaps five or six thousand men in the line of march, about one-third of them mounted; by far the most of them were from Washington County or the trans-Monongahela part of Allegheny County. The men were definitely in a bad mood, patently hoping for any excuse to put into effect their threats against the Sodom of the West. It was said that numbers of countrywomen were on Coal Hill waiting to see Pittsburgh's destruction and to help their men plunder it.

Brackenridge, who had been stationed in the van as guide, led the army down Fourth Street to Market Street and then turned back to the vicinity of the site of the Baltimore and Ohio Railroad depot. Meanwhile the townsmen had been rolling their whiskey barrels to the river bank and setting out a free lunch for the visiting firemen. Brackenridge, who disclosed the extent of his own concern by admitting that he furnished four barrels of liquor, observed later: "I thought it better to be employed in extinguishing the fire of their thirst, than of my house." As a matter of fact, the artifice was successful: all but about a hundred of the troops left the town peaceably during the afternoon, to the great relief of the inhabitants.

Those who remained, it developed, had arranged with their comrades that the latter should fire the farm buildings of Abraham Kirkpatrick on Coal Hill as a signal for the firing of the houses of Kirkpatrick, Neville, and other Federalists in town. About nine o'clock a number of men in yellow hunting shirts gathered about Kirkpatrick's town house prepared to set fire to it. Fortunately several of the more moderate insurgent leaders had heard of the plot and one of them, thinking that the men were there to defend the house, called out to them:

"Boys, are your guns loaded?"

"Yes," they answered.

"Then put in a second ball; and the first man that puts fire to the house, shoot him down."

The men were taken aback and pretended to fall in with the order or else drifted away unobtrusively. Kirkpatrick's barn and haystack were fired, but the citizens of Pittsburgh who peered through the cracks of their shutters at the ruddy glare were witnessing the last flare-up of insurgency in the section, though that fact did not become apparent for many days.

IV

AT THE Parkinson's Ferry meeting held on August 14 and 15, the moderates, aided by Brackenridge's parliamentary duplicity, succeeded in pulling the teeth of the more violent, who were all for some kind of action. A committee was appointed (Brackenridge was included in it) to meet commissioners from President Washington in Pittsburgh. The commissioners were three: Jasper Yeates, of the Pennsylvania supreme court, William Bradford, attorney general of the United States, and young Senator James Ross, of Washington. There were also two representatives of Governor Mifflin of Pennsylvania: Thomas McKean, chief justice of the state supreme court, and Congressman William Irvine, once commander of the western army.

The negotiations were long and tedious, and once were recessed while the westerners held a meeting at Brownsville. Though the majority at this meeting favored peace, David Bradford and his friends were such fire eaters that the commissioners demanded a vote of the people in Westmoreland, Allegheny, Fayette, and Washington counties on the issue of submission to government. The vote taken on September 11 was so complicated by delays, misunderstandings, and outright intransigence that the result could not be taken as the ringing affirmative demanded by the commissioners. Alexander Hamilton, who had seen in the thoughtless violence of the democratic westerners an excellent opportunity to consolidate his party's control of the government by dramatizing its support of the Constitution and the laws, now eagerly set in motion the troops that he had meanwhile been gathering. By the last of October thirteen thousand men had ploughed through the mud of the Alleghenies and were swarming over the completely supine Monongahela country breathing out threatenings and slaughter against all traitors, but particularly against Brackenridge, whose opportunistic behavior had been woefully misinterpreted by the resentful Nevilles. David Bradford had fled in the van of two thousand others; he spent the rest of his life near Bayou Sara, Louisiana.

v

THE first troops to enter Pittsburgh were Philadelphia cavalry acting as escort to exiled "Horseface" Gibson; as they passed the Brackenridge house on Market Street, Gibson looked up and laughed, and the sensitive lawyer took the action to mean, "There lives a fellow that is to be hanged." Sometime later Presley Neville returned under the wing of his father-in-law, General Daniel Morgan, and several squadrons of horse, and there was joyful firing of salutes from Fort Fayette. That night a party of dragoons started for the Brackenridge house with a rope, but fortunately Morgan and Neville were warned and turned the soldiers back a few yards from their victim. Doubtless the general and his son-in-law preferred to let the law save them the trouble of hanging the traitor.

Alexander Hamilton and a corps of judicial inquisitors had accompanied the army, and they now lost no time in setting about the task of ferreting out treason. To avoid scaring away the game by isolated arrests they had General Henry Lee, the commander of the expeditionary forces, send out lists of names of men who were to be arrested simultaneously on the night of November 12-13—a night ever since known in southwestern Pennsylvania as the "dreadful night" because of the wanton cruelties that occurred then. General Irvine, in command of the Pennsylvania troops at Pittsburgh, received a list of eighteen, among them Chief Burgess George Robinson, Andrew Watson the tavern-keeper, and the merchants William Amberson and William Beaumont, but by some miracle not including Brackenridge.

Sixteen of the men were arrested at two o'clock in the morning; some were not even given sufficient time to dress completely and were obliged to start out with their shoes in their hands. They were driven at a trot before a troop of horse through the mud seven miles out of Pittsburgh, then back several miles toward town, and were finally thrust into an open pen. There they were obliged to stay in the snow and rain, subject to the jeers and insults of the guards, and driven from the fire by bayonets. The next day they were imprisoned in a "waste house" where they remained five days; they were than taken to a chilly guardhouse in Fort Fayette. Ten days after the arrest the prisoners were taken before a judge, the evidence against them was found to be insufficient, and they were released. It was not until then that General Irvine discovered that the prisoners were not all accused of being traitors. The list he had received had made no distinction between prisoners and witnesses. Robinson and Beaumont were both incapacitated for some months as a result of exposure during their imprisonment.

Meanwhile General Lee had come to Pittsburgh and had been quartered on Brackenridge—who, incidentally, had once been tutor to the general at Princeton. Alexander Hamilton followed and continued his investigations in the town that, ironically enough, had been anathematized as a Federalist "Sodom" by the jealous country people. Brackenridge's case came up for action. The most damaging bit of evidence was a letter the lawyer had written to Bradford, which had been picked up in a tavern and which asked for certain papers in order to enable "the business" to go on. Hamilton laid the letter before James Ross in the presence of General Neville and John Woods.

"What do you make of that?" he said. "You have averred that Brackenridge had no correspondence with Bradford; look at that, is it not the handwriting of Brackenridge?"

The senator looked at the letter carefully while the examiners waited. Brackenridge's crabbed handwriting was unmistakable.

"It is the handwriting," answered Ross finally, "and there is only this small matter observable in the case, that it is addressed to William Bradford, attorney general of the United States, not to David Bradford."

One could have heard a pin drop in the room; Neville and Woods stood motionless and speechless. Hamilton was the first to break the silence.

"Gentlemen," he said acidly to Neville and Woods, "you are too fast; this will not do."

From that time the tide turned. Hamilton, after a personal examination of Brackenridge, gave him a clean bill, a fact that somewhat broke the blow when General Lee made his apologies to Mrs. Brackenridge, saying that "for the sake of retirement" he was withdrawing to a less central part of the town. As a matter of fact he had been embarrassed by the refusal of certain men to enter the house of the hated Brackenridge. General Neville, when he heard of the acquittal, exploded with wrath, and Brackenridge was diverted by what he was reported to have said: "'The most artful fellow that ever was on God Almighty's earth; he has deceived Ross, he has put his finger in Bradford's eye, Yate's eye, and now he had put it in Hamilton's eye, too." The lawyer, in spite of his newly white-washed record, found himself back in the political Coventry from which he had been beginning to emerge after five years of unceasing effort.

The army did not remain in the Monongahela country even three weeks, but by November 19 began the return trek, carrying with it a string of miserable prisoners to grace its triumph— though upon trial all but two of them were acquitted, and they were pardoned. General Morgan remained behind during the winter in charge of a detachment of fifteen hundred men encamped near Elizabeth, but their chief usefulness was as foils for the tough mountain wagoners in tavern brawls.

Brackenridge's exoneration did not restore him to the good graces of society. The presence of the troops had occasioned a number of social events, which went off rather brilliantly, to the surprise of one eastern volunteer who admitted that he had "vainly anticipated a Country awkward Society." The climax of the social season was a dinner for General Lee that was to be followed by a ball. When James Brison, prothonotary of Allegheny County and manager of the ball, refused to send an invitation to Mrs. Brackenridge she protested to her husband with unconcealed indignation.

"What," he exclaimed, "you are hurt at this? You insult me, because it is on my account you suffer the indignity. Did you not read to me, the other evening, the life of Phocion,—after having rendered services to the state, and accused of treason by the arts of malignant individuals, and acquitted by the people; suppose his adversaries to have taken their revenge, by getting a master of ceremonies to exclude his wife from a ball; would you not think it more honourable to be the wife of Phocion, under these circumstances, than of a common Athenian, though you had received a card, and been called upon to lead down the first dance?" In his account of the incident Brackenridge added quaintly, "By this address to the pride of the human mind, I had a philosopheress in a moment, perfectly reconciled with the circumstance."

XI

The Gateway to the West

THE customhouse of Marseilles was a squat stone structure not unlike a prison, so that it was no wonder that the ruddy-faced American seaman was a little apprehensive as he walked across the quay toward its grim portal. A slim youngster, wearing the uniform of the "Little Corporal" who was at the moment in Tilsit dictating terms to the Czar of all the Russias, saluted courteously and opened the door of an office. Almost lost behind the vast expanse of table littered with papers and books was a man who somehow seemed to fit the grim fortress in which he sat—perhaps it was because the stiff gray spikes of his mustachios rose at a belligerent slant from the corners of his mouth.

The American laid an oilskin dispatch case before the customs officer and introduced himself in execrable French. "Captain John Brevoort, ship 'Western Trader,' out of the port of Pittsburgh, United States of America, laden with flour and pork. The ship's papers, sir."

The little man nodded curtly, pulled the papers from the case, and hastily ruffled through them while his face darkened with anger. Suddenly he threw the papers aside and exploded in English.

"What do you mean, sir, by giving me forged papers? Do you

129

take me for a child not to know that there is no such port in America as Pittsburgh?"

"But there is," protested Brevoort. "My ship was built there and is loaded with the products of the surrounding country."

"Prove it! Prove it!" shouted the Frenchman. "Prove it, or *par Dieu*, I'll have your ship seized and you and your crew thrown into irons."

"Do you have a map of the United States?" asked the sea captain, his voice betraying some agitation.

An assistant quickly produced a map from a cabinet and spread it over the littered table. The American sought the Gulf of Mexico and the mouth of the Mississippi. "Pittsburgh is not on the coast," he explained, "but two thousand miles inland, up the Mississippi from New Orleans, then east up the course of the Ohio." The captain's finger paused at the junction of the Allegheny and Monongahela rivers. "There," he exclaimed triumphantly, "is Pittsburgh, the port from which I sailed!"

The customs officer bent more closely over the map. Sure enough, the word "Pittsburgh" was printed there in small italics and it was plainly possible for a vessel to descend from that town to the ocean. The Frenchman straightened up and eyed the American with a newly found respect.

"I was over hasty, monsieur," he acknowledged. "A thousand apologies for my reception of you. I knew America could show many wonders, but a fresh-water seaport is something of which I never dreamed."

II

PITTSBURGH had, indeed, entered world trade. As early as 1792 the sloop "Western Experiment" had been launched on the Monongahela and had floated down to the Gulf. This vessel, or another built near the same place, was captured at sea the next year; the circumstance was cited as proof of the need of a treaty with Spain concerning the navigation of the Mississippi. In 1798 and 1799, during the troubles with France, two row galleys, the "President Adams" and the "Senator Ross," were built at Pittsburgh under the superintendence of the versatile Major

Craig, who had once been a ship carpenter. The first of the two was launched in May, 1798, with the picaresque General James Wilkinson presiding at a celebration the expenses of which were paid by the government.

Soon after the year 1800 Pittsburgh entered the shipbuilding industry in a serious way, and the "Dean," the "Amity," the "Pittsburgh," the "Nanina," the "General Butler," and the "Western Trader," as well as a dozen others, followed during the next decade. There were several ship contractors but the most prominent were Eliphalet Beebe and the firm of Tarasçon Brothers, James Berthoud and Company, which in 1802 set up a shipyard (probably on the Monongahela near the end of Try Street) with smithies and rigging and sail lofts, as well as a store and warehouse where they carried on merchandising business and gathered cargoes for their vessels. James O'Hara was another local merchant who invested heavily in ships and cargoes, not always successfully, for one of them was captured by the Spanish and taken into Vera Cruz as a prize. The christenings of Pittsburgh ships were gala occasions. As many of the socially elect ladies and gentlemen of the town as could crowd into the tight little craft partook of elaborate dinners and consumed great quantities of wine in toasting the enterprise of the owners and the success of the fledglings of American commerce whose pinions would soon soar over all the seven seas. Then, as cannon boomed and the crowds on shore cheered, the newly christened vessels shook out their plumage and sailed majestically up and down the placid waters about the little town, while on the well-scrubbed decks paced the charming guests of honor, leaning on the arms of their escorts and trying to capture the thrill of world travel.

The shipbuilding phase of the early history of Pittsburgh enterprise, while interesting, was not destined to last for long. The vessels were necessarily of deep draught and consequently found it difficult to traverse the bars in which the rivers abounded and they were, moreover, difficult to manage in tortuous passages and treacherous currents. Worst of all was the Falls of the Ohio, which could be passed only at high water and which, even in its best moods, tossed the unwieldy ships about like the devil playing with a rubber ball, often with disastrous results. Jefferson's embargo was blamed for putting an end to Ohio shipbuilding, but one can scarcely avoid thinking that it was merely a welcome excuse. Old Man River had proved too uncoöperative.

III

RIVER commerce, on the other hand, was not conquered but continued to increase. The flatboat, or Kentucky boat, shaped like the modern houseboat, though with an infinite variation in detail, had by the close of the Revolution become the chief means of downstream transportation in the West. The average flatboat was about fifteen by fifty feet and carried forty or fifty tons; cheaply and easily constructed, it was too cumbersome to be brought back upstream, but its timber found a ready sale in the southern cities. Soon after the turn of the century Pittsburgh was supposed to be building boats every year to the value of twelve thousand dollars, while hundreds of others were brought in with country produce and sold at reduced prices. They were eagerly snapped up by merchants who had cargoes to sell down river and by the thousands of immigrants who every year set off down the Ohio in search of new homes.

Boat-builders were not always honest and careful in constructing and calking their boats. Cramer in his *Navigator* warned immigrants and traders that they must exercise the greatest care in buying and that they should be accompanied, if possible, by persons familiar with boats, who could detect rotten planks and defective calking. Three-quarters of the accidents, he said, were the result of bad building with knotty, rotten plank, and of using tender wood just above the gunwale. The custom of calking only as high as the gunwale joint was dangerous, and Cramer advised travelers to take along a few pounds of oakum and a mallet and a calking iron. The term "Kentucky boat" came to have a secondary meaning as applied to shoddily built boats.

An amusing tale of bad workmanship survives. In the fall of 1807 a certain Mr. Winchester's boat struck a rock a few miles below Pittsburgh and sank, ruining or damaging several thousand dollars' worth of merchandise. The proprietor, blaming the boat's master, or patroon, for carelessness, brought suit before Justice Andrew Richardson of Pittsburgh, who incidentally had gained through sad experience considerable knowledge about Kentucky boats. The defendant, with two witnesses, went to the scene of the accident and, after a great deal of trouble, procured a section of the plank that had broken on the rock and let the water in the boat. On the day of the trial he presented the plank as evidence, at the same time observing, "Your Honor will see that it was my misfortune to have been placed in charge of one of these damned Kentucky boats." His Honor received the plank and found that it was thoroughly rotten and defective. After being satisfied that it was really from the part of the boat that had failed to withstand the shock of collision Justice Richardson delivered his opinion:

"This court had the misfortune once to place a valuable cargo on a Kentucky boat, not knowing it to be such; which sank and went down in seventeen feet of water, this court verily believed, by coming in contact with the head of a yellow-bellied catfish, there being no snag, rock, or other obstruction near her at the time; and this court, being satisfied of the premises in this cause, doth order that the same be dismissed at plaintiff's costs, to have included therein the expenses of the defendant in obtaining such damnable and irrefutable evidence as this bottom plank has furnished."

No picture of any river town in western Pennsylvania would be complete without notice of the omnipresent immigrants. The farmer found the helpless newcomers his readiest and most gullible market, the boatwright did most of his work for them, the warehouseman stored their goods, and the merchant disposed of his cloth and farm implements at two prices to them. The printers found a ready sale for numerous editions of hastily thrown together and sometimes disastrously inaccurate river guides. The money spent by immigrants was doubtless one of the largest sources of western cash and the towns on the headwaters of the Ohio exploited this rich mine almost alone until the completion of the Erie Canal. The flatboat was from the first the cheapest and most convenient means of transportation for the immigrant. The time of the spring floods that followed upon the breakup of the ice was the favorite season for river travel. Those immigrants who had farm wagons drove them over the frozen mountain highways to the river towns and waited there until the ice was out of the rivers. The impromptu villages that they occupied, and of which the environs of Pittsburgh had their share, were picturesque features of the westward movement. Some occupied flatboats that had been drawn over the snow to a convenient place. These were the aristocrats of the encampment, for flatboats were comparatively snug and were often equipped with brick fireplaces. Others lived in stick and mud huts or contented themselves with lean-tos or tents. Horses and cows were stabled in even more makeshift contraptions or tethered in the open, while children and dogs swarmed everywhere. A few shrewd movers who planned to sell their means of transportation at a profit were encamped on rafts of saw logs or perhaps had erected rude huts on their craft.

The passing of the ice pack was the signal for the beginning of a scene of intense activity, for the immigrants hoped to reach their new homes in time to clear a little land and plant some corn. If the rising waters did not float the rafts and flatboats the craft were pushed into the river while everyone, young and old, ran frantically about, carrying household goods from the cabins, chasing hens from an overturned coop, or alternately coaxing and prodding an obstinate horse or cow. The animals were stowed in one end of the boat, fodder was loaded on, the farm wagon was perched on the roof, and, if the day were mild, grandma with her knitting and rocking-chair was placed beside the wagon where she could enjoy the confusion. Presently the lines were cast off and the boats, one by one, were slowly sculled into the stream. As the flotilla passed the roofs of Pittsburgh, nestling low under bare poplar trees, Brother Zeke might get his fiddle and with fingers a little stiff from the cold bid a merry good-by to the village, while the children danced a jig in anticipation of the adventures that awaited them down the winding course of the broad, ice-flecked Ohio.

IV

For upstream traffic there came into use, probably in the seventeen eighties, a craft called the keel boat. It was built on a keel and was long, narrow, and pointed at both ends. Surviving illustrations show that it resembled a Venetian gondola with a sort of freight car amidships to protect the cargo. The keel boat was from fifty to eighty feet long and from six to twelve feet wide. It was furnished with runways for the pole men and on account of its shape was more easily propelled than the bateau. Sometimes a high block was placed at the stern with notches cut in the side. The steersman mounted the block by means of the notches and straddled the steering oar while he gave orders to the crew, who were meanwhile engaged in rowing or poling. The smaller keel boats penetrated far up the tributary streams, acting as carriers between them and Pittsburgh, and the larger ones traversed the river as far down as Louisville or sometimes St. Louis and New Orleans. Freight rates, of course, varied with distance, but upstream from New Orleans they were about eight dollars a hundredweight and from Louisville about three dollars. Downstream they were roughly from a quarter to a third of those upstream. About 1805 there were said to have been fifty keels of thirty tons each plying between Pittsburgh and Cincinnati, and twelve years later, according to one authority, there were 150 engaged in the upper Ohio trade. The round trip from Pittsburgh to Louisville occupied two months and each boat was supposed to make it three times a year.

But the great contribution of the keel boat to the early American scene was not so much the transportation of goods as the colorful figures of its crew. In the gallery of American genre paintings the keel-boat man deserves a place along with the pioneer, the steamboat pilot, the cowboy, and those other types that have enriched American life and lore. For a quarter of a century before the advent of the steamboat the dwellers upon the river bank knew the haunting notes of a horn presaged the appearance around the bend of a keel boat with a dozen sinewy red-shirted men straining at the poles as they walked their boat upstream. Perhaps a fiddler atop the cargo box played to make the hours pass more lightly for the panting pole men, or if the voyage were downstream and labor at the poles was unnecessary one of the crew would be jigging on the deck while the whiskey jug circulated freely.

The keel-boat man's food was of the coarsest and plainest, his labor most killing, and his wages rarely more than a dollar a day, yet he was always ready at night for a frolic, a song, or a fight. He carried off the prizes at shooting contests, rollicked and drank in every dive from Pittsburgh to New Orleans, matched boasts with the loudest "rip-tail roarers" of the West, and made them good against any man in fair fight or rough-and-tumble. A fair fight was confined to the use of fists, but the rough-and-tumble, the characteristic combat of the frontier, was a bloody affray in which the endeavor of each man was to maim and disfigure the other by gouging out his eyes, biting off his lips, nose, or ears, or kicking him in the groin.

The archetype of the western boatman was a Pittsburgher, Mike Fink, who had graduated *cum laude* from Wayne's school of Indian fighters. During the interval between Fallen Timbers and the War of 1812, when the steamboat was for the West little more than a pipe dream, Mike Fink was the king of the western waters, living a life of such colorful adventure that it was bound to become the stuff from which legends are spun. In him was exemplified the broad humor, the rough-and-ready law, the hot loves and hates, the vaunting boasts of the boatmen. He found his relaxation in raiding camp meetings and militia musters, battling with berserk rage against other mighty "gougers," shooting the tin cup from his comrades' heads, and chasing the spangled skirts of New Orleans. Boastful, blasphemous, and brutal, save for rhetorical purposes he acknowledged no deity nor code not of his own making, and recognized no spirits beyond those that dwelt in the whiskey jug. With this familiar oracle ever waiting at his elbow to be consulted, Mike toiled and rollicked and gouged his way through the world, the living proof of the profound aphorism afterward stated by Mark Twain after years of conscientious experimentation: "Westward the jug of empire takes its way." What does it matter that Mike Fink died a violent death on the far-away banks of the Yellowstone River; he lives forever as the personification of "the strength, the exuberance, the roaring laughter of America in her glorious youth."

v

WHILE Mike Fink and his keel-boat men were fulfilling the need for upstream transportation by poling their boats from New Orleans to Pittsburgh, there was taking place a corresponding development of land transportation. From the days of the early traders to about 1790 the pack horse carried most of the freight that reached the West. As the settlements expanded and roads became smoother an increasing number of freight wagons found their way over the mountains, much to the disgust of the packers, whose ponies were unsuitable for use in harness. For years hauling was best done in the winter because the amazing seas of mud that obstructed travel in other seasons were then frozen, and it was not until 1816 and 1817 that hard-surfaced turnpikes were pushed through to the Monongahela. The Conestoga wagon, however, came into general use among freighters years before the hard roads were constructed. These wagons were distinguished by the upward slope of the box at both ends and the enormous flare of the canvas cover at front and back. The wagon boxes were usually painted blue and the running gears red so that these parts formed a striking and patriotic contrast with the white covers. A special breed of immensely powerful black "Conestoga" horses was developed to pull the wagons, and when a six-horse team was hitched to one of these "ships of inland commerce" wagon and team were strung out for sixty feet. The horses were equipped with hame bells, and the jingle of these bells was to inland towns what the boatman's horn was to river ports.

Freight wagons were driven by their owners or by hired men in trains headed by the owner. The wagoners who worked at the business all the time were known as "regulars"; the part-time freighters were called "militia" or "sharpshooters." By far the majority of the wagoners were Pennsylvania Germans, which was only to be expected, since most of the wagons in the state were owned by that frugal and industrious race. Hired wagoners received eight or ten dollars a month, just about the time required for the three-hundred-mile journey from Philadelphia to Pittsburgh. Freight rates were five dollars a hundredweight, but the wagon boxes often returned empty to the East because that rate was too high for all but the lightest products of the western country. Passengers were carried by the freighters, or, as was more usual, immigrants loaded their goods upon the wagons and trudged along behind.

It was not until 1804 that regular stage service was opened from Philadelphia to Pittsburgh, and it was possible then only because of a subsidy in the form of a generous mail contract. The trips, which by the end of the year were being scheduled twice a week, occupied six or seven days and cost the traveler twenty dollars. Even at that many a bone-racked passenger wished he had walked, for the vehicles were but springless "stage wagons" and the customers were expected upon occasion to help push their conveyance up a mountain or through a particularly bad stretch of mud. In spite of the difficulties stage facilities were slowly expanded during the following years; one line was extended to Wheeling, Chillicothe, and Lexington, and a branch line from Baltimore was established to meet the Philadelphia-Pittsburgh line at Chambersburg.

VI

THE fact that land and water transportation focused at Pittsburgh strengthened the historical role of the city as the gateway to the West. In 1802 François Michaux aptly described the town's commercial importance:

"Pittsburgh is not only the staple of the Philadelphia and Baltimore trade with the western country, but of the numerous settlements that are formed upon the Monongahela and Alleghany. The territorial produce of that part of the country finds an easy and advantageous conveyance by the Ohio and Mississippi. Corn, hams and dried pork are the principal articles sent to New Orleans, whence they are re-exported into the Carribbees. They also export for the consumption of Louisiana, bar-iron, coarse linen, bottles manufactured at Pittsburgh, whiskey, and salt butter. . . . All these advantages . . . contribute to its improvements, which daily grow more and more rapid."

River trips from New Orleans to Pittsburgh were made frequently; and in June, 1814, a firm advertised the cargoes of six keel boats expected up from New Orleans that month. In 1817 a two-masted barge of 150 tons burden was carrying trade goods, and in 1814 Cramer recorded that "a great number of barges constantly ply between this and the country below." A barge was the river equivalent of a small ship and was propelled by oars, poles, and sails, or towed by a cordelle from shore. In 1810 Pittsburgh imported from down river between May 1 and November 14, hemp worth about two hundred thousand dollars, 689 tons of spun yarn, 10 tons of tobacco, and 120 tons of cotton. One thousand tons of Kentucky goods were said to have been shipped from Maysville to Pittsburgh during the boating season of 1812. These statistics can give only an incomplete picture of Pittsburgh's trade and of the city's dependence upon the West and the South. The manufacture of cotton, tobacco, rope, and bagging were directly dependent upon those sections. In addition, Missouri lead, Mexican copper, Spanish hides, Kentucky glazed powder, whiskey, country linen, saltpeter, bacon, sugar, Spanish wool, and West Indian products came up the river.

Each year scores of flatboats left the forks of the Ohio outfitted with shelves and counters, often arranged with attractiveness and ingenuity. They served as the department stores of the rivers and carried large stocks of all the varied products of their parent city. Each trading boat bore a calico flag to indicate its character and would respond to hails from dwellers on the banks or would tie up near a plantation or hamlet too small to afford a store. Its arrival was announced by a blast on a tin horn, and the natives with money to spend or goods to barter would flock to the landing.

The most serious obstacle Pittsburgh merchants encountered was low water, and in consequence most shipments were timed to leave before the summer drought set in. The average loaded keel boat drew about three feet and, since the stage of the rivers was often less than three feet, it was not unusual for a boat to wait weeks or months for a sufficient depth of water. At one time in 1818 there were thirty keel boats tied up at Pittsburgh waiting for enough water to float them to Kentucky and three million dollars' worth of goods was being delayed. It was this handicap that made merchants and immigrants prefer Wheeling in the summer, though there is evidence that the river for a hundred miles below that town was well nigh as shallow as it was above. During most of the year, however, Pittsburgh's ample warehouse facilities, its manufactories, and its larger outfitting stores gave it the advantage over Wheeling.

In October, 1793, Jacob Myers inaugurated a fortnightly packet service between Pittsburgh and Cincinnati. The first boat left Pittsburgh on October 14 and the second on November 5, and Myers planned to add two more boats so that there would be weekly service. He stated in his advertisement that "the Proprietor . . . being influenced by a love of philanthropy and desire of being servicable to the public, has taken great pains to render the accommodations on board the Boats as agreeable and convenient as they could possibly be made." Protection against the Indians was provided by high bulwarks thick enough to withstand rifle bullets and pierced with portholes. Each boat carried six one-pounders, probably swivel guns, and a number of muskets. The crew was supposed to be of sufficient size for defense. To obviate the necessity of landing in dangerous vicinities the boats were provided with sanitary conveniences. Passengers were boarded and liquored by the management "at the most reasonable rates possible," and a separate cabin was provided for the women passengers. Freight and letters were carried and insurance was sold at a "moderate" rate, but the amounts charged are unknown. Myers' boats were propelled by oars and sails and were intended to serve not only as conveyors of freight and passengers but also as convoys for other boats. In spite of this expenditure of liquor and rhetoric the venture seems not to have outlasted the winter, for the next May, in discussing the advisability of carrying passengers on the proposed Ohio mail-boat line, Major Craig stated it as his opinion that "the idea of Passenger Packet-Boats ought at Present to be abandoned."

The War of 1812 was a positive benefit to Pittsburgh. By cutting off the sea route, it caused more of the commerce from south to north to flow through Pittsburgh, and the resulting impetus to trade was sustained until the day of the railroad. The trade for 1813 was estimated at four million dollars and more than four thousand wagonloads of goods crossed the mountains from Pittsburgh to Philadelphia. Bosler and Company alone imported 275 tons of goods from New Orleans between April 1 and September 1, 1814.

VII

IMMENSE as this trade seemed to the citizens of early western Pennsylvania, the region was to advance even more during the following years. In 1810 the progressive author of the *Navigator* announced a new mode of navigating the western waters. Steam had been applied to a boat on the Hudson River in such a manner as to drive it against wind and tide at the rate of four miles an hour, and now there was such a boat building at Pittsburgh and another at Frankfort. "It will be a novel sight," he concluded, "and as pleasing as novel to see a huge boat working her way up the windings of the Ohio, without the appearance of sail, oar, pole, or any manual labour about her—moving within the secrets of her own wonderful mechanism, and propelled by power undiscoverable!"

The first steamboat that plied the western waters was the "New Orleans," which owed its construction to the enterprise of Robert Fulton, Robert Livingston, and Nicholas Roosevelt. The last named was in charge of the building of the "New Orleans" on the bank of the Monongahela near the mouth of Suke's Run, now Try Street, just under the brow of Boyd's Hill. Mechanics were brought from New York and they may have used imported parts in building the engine or have cast them in Beelen's foundry near by. The lumber was sawed in local saw pits from trees obtained in surrounding forests. Several times the Monongahela flooded the shipyard and on one occasion almost launched the boat before it was ready. The craft was a side-wheeler topped by a long cabin and with a broad, deep keel perfectly designed to ground on sandbars. It took nearly a year to construct the "New Orleans," but at last in March, 1811, it was launched amid the huzzas of the townsmen. Low water prevented the boat's departure for months, but on Sunday, October 20, an enthusiastic crowd of Pittsburghers gathered on the bank and watched the "New Orleans" chug a short distance up the Monongahela to prove she could breast the current, then swing into midstream and steam swiftly by the town and disappear around the bend of the Ohio. The voyage to the lower Mississippi had begun. As the "New Orleans" steamed down the river and the keel-boat men dropped their poles to watch her pass at the terrific speed of eight miles an hour, she was acting as the harbinger of a new era in western transportation.

The supremacy of the steamboat, however, was not to be won without difficulty. For almost a decade the keel boats and barges flourished. Business increased so consistently that merchants found it profitable to build their barges larger and larger, until river craft actually rivaled the smaller ocean-trading vessels in size. The keel-boat men, moreover, anchored by self interest to the old ways, were frankly contemptuous of the steamboat. In their eyes it was "a scheme to destroy their business and expose people's lives. They would like to see that new fangled machine try 'Horsetail Ripple' or 'Letart's Falls,' to get up them without the aid of good setting poles, or 'cordelles.' It could not be done 'nohow.' "

Truth to tell, the keel-boat men were not far wrong. The first steamboats were clumsy, unwieldy affairs, hard to manage on a curve and too deep set in the water to battle successfully the swift western currents even had their engines been more perfect. It was supposed that only sea captains could manage them, so the West had the ludicrous spectacle of bluff old salts with trumpets clapped to their mouths shouting nautical phrases at deck hands who had never seen the ocean. Then when they were misunderstood the captains went into spasms of sea-going blasphemy that must have aroused the admiration of western connoisseurs of billingsgate. For some time it was not at all certain that steamboats would win. They were distrusted because of the delays caused by low water, because they could not breast rapids, and, most of all, because of the frequency of explosions. Engines were improved, of course, but the most significant improvement was in the hulls which finally were built so that they scooted over the surface of the water instead of plowing the depths.

VIII

With the victory of the steamboat the keel-boat men gradually retired with their craft to the tributaries, where their rival could not follow them, or perhaps went over to the enemy and became steamboat men, pilots, or captains. Not a few, like Mike Fink, expressed the disgusted opinion that the country was getting too civilized and dropped their poles to go out to the unspoiled hunting grounds on the eastern edge of the Rockies. With the keel-boat men passed the last reminders of the western Pennsylvania frontier. Modern Pittsburgh has even forgotten that one of its sons was the mighty hero of an entire cycle of early American legend. It is high time that he be honored in the city of his birth.

Dare we imagine the scene as Mike Fink's soul rises from his body to the American Pantheon on some cloud-enshrined peak of the Tetons? Davy Crockett, the bear-hunting politician, John Henry, the Black River roustabout, Paul Bunyan, the titanic lumberjack of the north woods, and old Dan'l Boone are sitting around the campfire passing the whiskey jug and swapping yarns. Presently, striding over the boulder-strewn mountain meadows, seven leagues at a step, comes Mike Fink, swinging in his hand the familiar brown jug. Old Dan'l looks down and sees him coming. "Davy," he says to the great b'ar hunter, "go on down and see who thet brash young feller is a-hornin' in on our convention." So Crockett leaps down the mountain side and confronts the keel-boat man. Mike, unabashed, faces the champion. "Mannee," he says, "who are you?" "Why, don't you know me?" replies Davy. "I'm little Davy Crockett, I am, the greatest b'ar killer in Tennessee. I've killed so many b'ars their skins would carpet the continent of Europe and their claws would make a necklace to encircle the moon. Whoop! I pick my teeth with a pitchfork, comb my hair with a rake, fan myself with a harricane, wear a cast-iron shirt, an' drink nothin' but creosote an' aqua fortis."

The Mississippi keeler contemptuously flourishes his jug, prances a few steps like a gamecock before a fight, and launches forth on the old boast: "Well, maybe you was the high muck-a-muck in these hyar parts, but you ain't no longer. I'm Mike Fink, the greatest keeler thet ever pushed a pole on the ol' Massassip, an' I've come ter claim my rightful place by your campfire. Whoop! I'm a Salt River roarer! I'm a ring-tailed screamer! I loves the wimming an' I'm chockful o' fight! I'm half horse and half cock-eyed alligator an' the rest o' me is crooked snags an' red-hot snappin' turkle. Whoop! I kin hit like fourth-proof lightnin' an' every lick I make in the woods lets in a acre o' sunshine. I kin out-run, out-jump, out-shoot, out-brag, out-drink, out-fight, rough-an'-tumble, no holts barred, ary man on both sides the river from Pittsburgh to N'Awlins an' back ag'in to St. Louiee. Come on, you b'ar hunters, you lumberjacks, an' you cotton rollers an' see how tough I am ter chaw! I ain't had a fight fer a hundred years an' I'm spilein' fer exercise. Cock-a-doodle-doo!"

A glad light gleams in Davy Crockett's eyes as he holds out his massive paw. "I hope to be shot ef you ain't a reg'lar ol' time screamer from the muddy Massassip," he cries. "Come on right in, mannee, an' don't fergit the jug." With which Crockettesquerie he jovially gives Mike a mighty thwack on the back, and the two go up to the gate of the American Pantheon.

XII

Genesis of an Industrial Empire

THE impetus given to Pittsburgh's growth by its strategic location in the early days as the gateway to the West has never been lost, though it is no longer the only important gateway. River transportation had aided in setting the mold for the development of the region. The fact that goods could be floated to the markets in the West and South not only made Pittsburgh an entrepôt for eastern wares, but led to the early utilization of western Pennsylvania's ore and wood in the production of iron. This start, together with vast coal deposits, enabled the region to hold its lead in the iron industry, even when the ore had to be brought from Michigan and Minnesota. The same factors to a greater or less degree influenced the development of lumbering, woodworking, boat building, glassmaking, the ceramic industries, and a dozen others.

The success of the national government in quelling the Whiskey Insurrection not only stimulated immigration but encouraged the investment of new capital in Pittsburgh by those who were keen enough to see that transportation rates would enable its manufacturers to undersell those of the East. This fact, together with the progress of invention and the stimulus to manufactures afforded by the War of 1812, made the Pittsburgh of

1814 appear a metropolis in comparison to the village of 1792, with its sixteen industries and thirty-six mechanics. In 1814 Pittsburgh boasted a population of six or eight thousand and about 130 separate manufactories of all sizes. By 1817, in spite of the slump that followed the War of 1812, there were 259 factories employing 1637 men and producing annually goods to the value of two and a quarter million dollars.

II

THE development of Pittsburgh from an Indian trading post to a manufacturing city is best epitomized in the career of James O'Hara, Pittsburgh's first captain of industry, who lived from 1754 to 1819. Though he was the scion of a line of Irish soldiers of fortune, James O'Hara showed a predilection for trade, and he was trained in business methods in Liverpool. Before he was twenty years of age he appeared in Pittsburgh as a clerk for Simon and Campbell; shortly afterward, with the capital from a small inheritance, he joined the Indian trading firm of Devereux Smith and Ephraim Douglass. During the succeeding years he showed ability, tact, and courage in meeting the crises incident to the trade. Though he raised and equipped a company of forty men during the Revolution, most of his energies were devoted to the supply of the army, and his men, save for seasons of garrison duty, were engaged in the service of supply. In those days it was common for officers to engage in speculations, and O'Hara improved his opportunities with such acumen that the end of the war found him able to enter a merchandising partnership in Philadelphia.

In 1784, however, he moved back to Pittsburgh armed with lucrative contracts for provisioning the western army and for supplying food and goods to the commissioners who were about to hold a series of treaties with the Indians. He met with such success that the following year he felt justified in bringing his bride, the beautiful and accomplished Mary Carson, to Pittsburgh; he established her in the King's Artillery Gardens in what was probably the most luxuriously appointed home in the town. The following ten years were devoted by O'Hara principally to the arduous and complicated task of provisioning and equipping the armies engaged in the Indian wars. During the latter part of the period O'Hara bore the title of quartermaster general and spent most of his time with the army in Ohio. Pittsburgh was the chief entrepôt for army stores. There Major Isaac Craig, as O'Hara's deputy, collected provisions, received clothing, arms, and other supplies from the East, and sent them down the river in flatboats as they were needed.

In 1800 O'Hara retired from the business of army contracting to devote more time to his private interests, which had been developing rapidly during the past few years. The number of enterprises in which he engaged is truly amazing. Before 1790 he kept a retail store in Pittsburgh but withdrew his investment from it to engage in more grandiose schemes, though he seems never to have given up some activity in his earliest love, the fur trade. About 1795 he began reserving the provision barrels sent to the army posts in New York and had them returned to Pittsburgh filled with salt from the Onondaga salt works. The operation was not as simple as it sounds, for vessels had to be provided for use on Lakes Erie and Ontario and on French Creek and the Allegheny; wagons had to be provided for the portages and roads had to be improved. In spite of these difficulties, however, O'Hara succeeded in landing Onondaga salt in Pittsburgh at half the cost of that brought over the mountains. In 1800 Erie received 723 barrels, which were distributed all along the lake; in 1809 it received 14,346 destined for Pittsburgh and vicinity. But before long brisk competition began from the salt works on the Kanawha River and elsewhere.

In 1803 James O'Hara built the Pittsburgh Point Brewery, which flourished under the management of George Shiras, and whose brand of porter became famous in the South. A sawmill, a tanyard, and a gristmill, were among O'Hara's Pittsburgh enterprises. A flier in the iron business, entered upon when he took over the Hermitage Furnace near Ligonier in payment of a debt owed him by General St. Clair, did not prove successful, perhaps because of the panic that followed the War of 1812. In addition to all these activities O'Hara built at Pittsburgh an unknown number of ships and sent them to sea laden with western products. He was a principal organizer of a company that was formed at Pittsburgh in 1802 with a capital of a hundred thousand dollars to encourage exports from the region, and he was also active in the branch that the Bank of Pennsylvania established in Pittsburgh. He engaged with Ebenezer Denny in building a row of houses on Market Street with bricks taken from Fort Pitt, and at the time of his death was one of the largest real-estate holders in Pittsburgh, not to mention his ownership of great tracts of land held as far away as Illinois.

The enterprise for which Pittsburgh owes O'Hara the greatest debt of gratitude, however, was his establishment, with Major Craig as partner, of the first glass factory in the vicinity. The technical expert who directed the undertaking was William Eichbaum, a Westphalian glass cutter who had been employed in France before the outbreak of the French Revolution, and who in 1792 had gone to Philadelphia as superintendent of a glassworks on the Schuylkill. In 1797 he went to Pittsburgh and devoted himself to planning and erecting a frame factory building on the south side of the Monongahela opposite the Point, and to locating suitable sand, clay, and coal. The use of coal in the making of glass seems to have been introduced by O'Hara and Craig. Though the first glass was blown in 1798, the technical difficulties involved were not conquered for some years. Suitable clay for crucibles could not be found in the region and had to be brought from New Jersey at great expense; inexpert workmen were continually breaking the pots and ruining the contents. Pittsburgh sand proved to contain too many impurities to be used in high-grade work and sand had to be brought in from some distance up the Monongahela. Window glass, in sizes less than two feet square, was produced, and after tireless experimentation the first bottle was turned out at a cost of thirty thousand dollars. In 1804 Craig sold his three-eighths interest to O'Hara, and the latter carried on alone.

O'Hara's products were of green glass and, though he made many experiments in search of a better product, it remained for an Englishman, Benjamin Bakewell, to establish Pittsburgh's first successful flint-glass factory. By 1812 there were half a dozen glasshouses in town, and their products were being distributed widely over the West and were finding their way down the rivers and around by sea to the Atlantic ports, and even to some extent to Europe. Pittsburgh flint glass was acknowledged to be superior to that made in the East and was in demand all over the country. William Eichbaum, who had left O'Hara and Craig in 1800, set up a glass-cutting business. A six-light, cut-glass chandelier that he had made for Kerr's tavern was a show piece of the town, and it is probable also that he executed the brilliant chandelier, the gift of General O'Hara, that hung in the First Presbyterian Church and furnished such a contrast to the severely plain interior of the edifice.

III

O'HARA's chief fame is connected with the glass industry, but Pittsburgh's future was to depend more on iron than on glass. Pittsburgh has never produced its own iron but has imported it either as ore or pig iron, first from the ore-bearing sections of western Pennsylvania, later from Michigan and Minnesota. Blacksmiths, of course, were active in Pittsburgh from the first, and wire, nails, tools, bells, and guns were being made soon after 1800. Anshutz had failed in his blast furnace and foundry business in the seventeen-nineties, but in 1806 Joseph McClurg, whose training for the role of ironmaster consisted of the manufacture of "plug and pig tail tobacco, segars and rappee snuff," associated himself with two or three others and opened the Pittsburgh Foundry, located at Smithfield Street and Fifth Avenue on the northwest corner. The venture was successful. Though other foundries and metal-working factories sprang up on every side, no blast furnaces for the conversion of ore into pigs were erected until 1859. Pittsburgh's role was that of ironworker and ironmonger.

The rapid growth of heavy industry was attributable both to the strategic location of Pittsburgh with respect to the commerce of the West and to the plentifulness of coal, which afforded a cheap fuel for the production of steam power. In 1809 a flour mill powered by one of Oliver Evans' engines was operating in Pittsburgh under the management of George Evans, the inventor's son. The mill was built of stone and was located on the Monongahela River front west of Redoubt Alley. In 1812 the inventor built, just behind the mill, a steam-engine works, which he placed under the management of Mark Stackhouse. By 1815 Boulton and Watts low-pressure engines were also being manufactured in Pittsburgh by Thomas Copeland, and the Mississippi Steam-Boat Company was making Fulton engines. There were at least six steam mills in operation: one erected in 1812 by Christopher Cowan for slitting iron, and others for spinning cotton and wool, and for making nails, wire, flour, and paper ——"does your child want a catechism, spelling book, bible, &c. Rags will purchase them . . . at the Franklin Head Bookstore, Market Street, where the highest price is given for clean linen and cotton rags, either in books or money." Six steamboats had been built, there were two white and three green glasshouses, three iron foundries and two brass foundries, three white or red lead factories, three ropewalks, three buttonmakers, a pottery, a woollen-weaving establishment and several for the weaving of cotton——"for the encouragement of our useful *manufactories* the members of the [Pittsburgh] Tammany Society agreed to attend their next meeting dressed entirely in HOMESPUN." There were in addition the usual tanners, tinners, hatters, smiths, jewelers, cabinet-makers, and, inevitable concomitant of commercial empire, banks—three of them. There were, according to one report, 1960 workmen employed and the annual value of their products was $2,617,000.

Common laborers were paid wages that averaged less than a dollar a day; prices of manufactured goods were rather high but they were balanced by the low price of food, so the workingman, inasmuch as he had not become bogged down in trying to provide the complex array of "necessities" that torment the modern man, got along very well. His living quarters, of course, were crowded, conveniences were few, sanitary arrangements were primitive, and cleanliness was impossible, since a pall of soot covered everything and was even killing off the vegetation.

Already travelers had begun to revile Pittsburgh as the smoky city and to set down jokes anent the atmosphere.

With the multiplication of industries there inevitably came labor trouble. The first of the strikes, or "turn outs" as they were called, was probably that by the journeymen cordwainers, or shoemakers, in December, 1804. Two years later the journeymen tailors struck, and evidently won their demands.

The *cause célèbre* of Pittsburgh labor, however, was the trial of the cordwainers in 1815. About 1809 the journeymen of that trade had organized a "society" and appointed a "tramping committee" to inspect shops and wages. The rise in the cost of living brought on by the War of 1812 led to friction between journeymen and masters, and a series of strikes followed. Eventually the patience of the masters was exhausted and they induced the commonwealth's attorney general, Jared Ingersoll, to prosecute the members of the union for conspiracy. Henry Baldwin laid down for the prosecution the broad rule that an act was indictable when it was "against good morals, injures society, or is destructive to the trade of a place." The presiding judge, the choleric Samuel Roberts, left the jury no alternative, but in his charge informed it that the organization of a union was an action in restraint of trade. The defendants were accordingly found guilty and fined one dollar each.

Pittsburgh's first bank was organized in 1802 as a branch of the Bank of Pennsylvania. The institution occupied a two-story stone house on Second Street (now the Boulevard of the Allies) between Market and Ferry Streets and was opened for business January 9, 1804, with John Wilkins, Jr., as president and Thomas Wilson as cashier. In September John Thaw, of Philadelphia, came west as chief clerk of the bank; thus was introduced to Pittsburgh a name that was to become famous in its annals. John Wilkins served as president until his death in 1816; most of the time acting also as quartermaster general of the United States army. James O'Hara succeeded to the presidency of the bank in 1816 and served until the parent bank failed in 1818.

Pittsburgh's second bank was the Bank of Pittsburgh, founded in 1810 under the loose banking law of the state with William

Wilkins, younger brother of John Wilkins, as president; but an act passed subsequently so restricted the lawful activities of private banks that the bank reorganized as the Pittsburg Manufacturing Company and carried on an insurance and partial banking business until another act, passed in 1814, provided for the incorporation of the Bank of Pittsburgh. Thus began the career of a financial institution that was to continue in existence until 1931. The law of 1814 also incorporated in Pittsburgh the Farmers' and Mechanics' Bank, and the institution did fairly well until in 1818 the safe was robbed of a large part of the assets of the bank by Joseph Pluymart and Herman Emmons. The robbery so shook public confidence in the institution that it gradually retired its notes and about 1825 discontinued business. Both robbers were caught; Emmons turned state's evidence and Pluymart, though he was sentenced to prison, managed to escape. Amazingly enough, the latter was pardoned by Governor Shulze while he was a fugitive from justice, an action that was to be recalled in later years as one of the reasons why the Antimasonic movement became so powerful in western Pennsylvania. The Second Bank of the United States established a branch in Pittsburgh in 1817, and it took over the business of the defunct branch of the Bank of Pennsylvania and made John Thaw cashier.

IV

The War of 1812, as has been seen, was no small factor in promoting the prosperity of Pittsburgh manufacturers. An abnormally high tariff as well as the British blockade of American ports not only stimulated the demand for domestic manufactures but reversed to a large extent the direction of western commerce. Southern cotton and sugar, Missouri lead and peltry, and Kentucky saltpeter, hemp, and hides came up the rivers to Pittsburgh, where they were transshipped to the East. The movement was not temporary, for the development of the use of the steamboat enabled western goods to be carried rapidly and cheaply up the river.

Local units of soldiers, save for the swank Pittsburgh Blues, some volunteers with Perry, and a body of mutinous militiamen who disgraced themselves on the Niagara front, took little part in the military events of the War of 1812. Pittsburgh factories, however, were the chief sources of equipment for the western armies, with the exception of certain classes of military supplies such as cannon and gunpowder. Perry drew upon Pittsburgh for much of the ironwork, cordage, and cannon balls used in building and equipping his fleet, and the transportation of supplies to Erie was aided by the unusual height of French Creek and the Allegheny during the summer of 1813. In 1814 the establishment by the United States government of Allegheny Arsenal on the site of Arsenal Park added an important industry to Pittsburgh's list of enterprises. The arsenal was planned by Benjamin H. Latrobe, who also had built the new United States Capitol, and was erected at a cost of three hundred thousand dollars under the direction of Colonel Abraham R. Wooley. It was divided into two parts by Butler Street. The lower part, next to the Allegheny River, contained the officers' quarters, barracks, various shops, and the magazine of arms, all arranged in the form of a hollow square. The upper part, also a hollow square, held the stables and the powder magazine. Military equipment was manufactured and reconditioned there until after the close of the Civil War.

The end of the War of 1812 brought not only a cessation of large purchases by the government but also an attempt by British manufacturers to regain lost markets by dumping their immense surplus of goods into the United States with intent to drive native manufacturers out of business. The effect was to bring on the depression of 1817-21, which very nearly proved the ruin of Pittsburgh industry. Local manufacturers, who in 1815 had employed 1960 hands and produced goods to the value of $2,617,000, in 1819 employed only 672 hands and produced goods to the value of only $832,000. Pittsburgh manufacturers, particularly those in the glass industry, became prominent in the movement to lay a protective tariff on imports; this activity was to continue even after the phenomenal growth of the West had once more set the wheels of industry to turning.

XIII

Life Under the Poplars

DURING the two decades that followed the Whiskey Insurrection of 1794 Pittsburgh spread out over the flood plain between the rivers with all the gangling awkwardness of a rapidly growing youngster. The town that at the beginning of the period had perhaps twelve hundred inhabitants boasted eight thousand at the end, but it was still small enough for everyone to hear the courthouse bell, which was rung for courts, public meetings, church gatherings, and fires. Then, as now, the citizens liked to change residences frequently, and April 1 was recognized as the official moving day. The log houses that had furnished shelter at first were soon outnumbered by frame and brick houses—it was said that altogether there were thirteen hundred houses in 1815. Those built of bricks from Fort Pitt were easily distinguishable by their dirty white color. There was little rhyme or reason in the placing of the houses; sides, gable ends, or even corners faced the streets if the fancy of the owner so dictated, and of course there was no attempt to attain architectural beauty. The only thing that saved the hodgepodge of log, frame, brick, and stone houses from being positively ugly was the profusion of Lombardy poplars, locusts, and weeping willows that had taken the place of the primeval forest.

There had been no effort to number the houses; strangers found their ways by ardent inquiry, and the score or more of taverns were known by signs that bore flamboyant paintings of the person or device by whose name the place was known. One famous tavern was first the "Whale and the Monkey" and later the "Green Tree"; others were the "General Butler," the "White Horse," the "Harp and Crown," and the "Negro." Wood and Market Streets were paved and several others were graveled, but most of the streets alternated with the seasons between mud and dust. Pedestrians had for their use "footways of brick, stone or gravel, bounded by curb stones, or by squared pieces of timber"—if the property owners had seen fit to obey the ordinance requiring them to be laid. Even then Pittsburgh had parking troubles, and with the passage of years ordinances became stricter against allowing vehicles to stand in the streets.

Domestic garbage was all too frequently thrown into the streets and there was periodic complaint that the authorities did not trouble to enforce the ordinance against allowing hogs to run at large or even the one requiring the removal of dead dogs. Stables, backhouses, hencoops, pigsties, stagnant ponds, and slaughterhouses vied with each other and with the streets for olfactory attention, and the medical fraternity insisted that these conditions made Pittsburgh's disease rate high in proportion to the population. Those townsmen who opposed sanitary measures on the ground that they would entail higher taxes were sarcastically drubbed in the *Gazette* of June 3, 1803: "A little clean dirt, more or less, is neither here nor there—it is believed to be wholesome, and some folks have no objection to the smell of warm tripe and garbage, to wading through puddles of green, stagnant water, or to skating over dabs of ordure. What if a few of the citizens should be carried off by fluxes or fevers? It would be of no great consequence, as our population is rapidly increasing." What a paradise for bluebottles! It was to be eleven years before the fastidious citizen could take refuge in the "BATH HOUSE, next door to the Pittsburgh Steam mill, on the bank of the Monongahela" and soak himself "from 5 o'clock in the morning till 10 in the evening."

The ferries across the two rivers were reached by perilous descents from the plateau on which the town was built and by circuitous paths across the mud flats. On the Monongahela side there was usually a row of keel boats and flatboats nudging the bank like water bugs about a lily pad; there was less traffic on the Allegheny side, where the river washed the bank away so rapidly that finally in 1798, by special act of the state legislature, a lottery was set up to raise money to build "piers" along the Allegheny. The Monongahela bank was claimed by certain citizens as private property, and for years the municipality was forced to defend in the courts its right to reserve the area as a landing place for boats. It was not until 1832 that the issue was settled in favor of the city.

The natives of Pittsburgh, at least before about 1800, were quite content to use river water for all household purposes and even developed such a prejudice in its favor that strangers twitted them with the accusation that they stirred up the mud in the bottom of the water bucket before they took a drink. Spring water was said to taste of sulphur and wells were too hard to dig. After 1800, however, wells increased in number, and in 1802 the borough provided for four public wells. These wells were necessitated not simply for sanitary reasons but because of the constantly increasing danger of fire. The town had possessed a fire engine as early as 1792 or 1793 and by about 1815 there were no less than three volunteer fire companies, the "Eagle," the "Vigilant," and the "Neptune," all busily occupied in the "exercising" of their engines. Rivalry between the companies was intense and often led to fistic encounters. It was told that when an unauthorized man laid a hand on the dark green surface of the engine of the Eagle Fire Engine and Hose Company the Quaker captain of the company warned him: "Friend, thee had better remove thy hand." When he met with insult instead of compliance the Quaker so far forgot himself as to swear "By ——, I shall smite thee then" and actually carried out his threat, to the great scandal of the Friends Society. Though time after time destructive fires visited the aggregation of tinder boxes that constituted the town of Pittsburgh, the

optimism and indolence of human nature prevented the con-
script fathers and the volunteer companies from providing adequate fire buckets and taking proper care of their engines.

One feature of Pittsburgh life had attracted the attention of
visitors long before 1800. That was coal smoke. The fat little
cannon stoves and the open grates of the period were not very
efficient and cast off a great amount of smoke, which was sometimes merely piped out at the side of the house, much to the
annoyance of passers-by. Each household had one or more fires
burning the year round and steam mills were increasing in numbers so it was no wonder that strangers from the wood-burning
East complained of the "sulphureous vapour." A strolling actor
who viewed the town in 1815 noted the somber appearance of
the buildings and complained that the poor street lighting served
only to show the "horrors of the place." The citizens were already writing letters to the newspapers advocating the "general
and spontaneous" adoption "of some plan for smoke abatement."
In March, 1815, when smog (smoke plus fog) must have been
at its worst, the "Yankees," a social organization of New Eng-
landers exiled in Pittsburgh, drank a toast to "The Pittsburgh
Lasses—a Contrast to the Stygian Gloom of their Native Place."

II

WHATEVER fault might have been found with the physical aspects of Pittsburgh, the town was certainly improving morally,
socially, and intellectually. The Presbyterian church of logs was
replaced in 1804 by a brick edifice on the same site, but a schism
in the congregation soon followed and the Second Presbyterian
Church was organized. The members of the latter congregation
worshipped at first in the courthouse, but in 1814 they built a
church on Diamond Street on the site of the Warner Theater.
In 1805 the Episcopalians finally organized a congregation and
began to erect a quaint octagonal structure, the "Old Round
Church," on the lot now bounded by Liberty and Sixth Avenues
and Wood Street. In this building the popular Reverend John
Taylor conducted weekly services and married and baptized as
set down in his quaint "Commonplace Book"; when not engaged

in performing these offices he was teaching school or making mathematical calculations for the local almanacs. The Reverend Mr. Taylor's almanacs made an attempt to prognosticate the weather throughout the year, and since he usually allowed several days' margin he often hit the mark. On one occasion, when by some error he had prophesied a snowstorm in June, the date was signalized by a cold drizzle and a frost, and the next day the Philadelphia stage rolled in from the mountains covered with snow and sleet. The circumstance undoubtedly contributed greatly to Mr. Taylor's fame as a weather prognosticator.

The Methodist Episcopal Church in Pittsburgh probably owed its origin to John Wrenshall, an Englishman who started a store in the town in 1796 and simultaneously gathered about him a group of the pious. Mr. Wrenshall, who had been a local preacher in England, worshipped with his congregation in the deserted log church of the Presbyterians until the building was padlocked. They then moved to one of the barrack buildings in dismantled Fort Pitt. Eventually in 1810 a brick church was built on the north side of Front Street (First Avenue) a little below Smithfield Street, and in 1818 another was erected on the southeast corner of Smithfield Street and Seventh Avenue, still known to the less serious minded as Brimstone Corner. Baptists and Covenanters were also increasing in number, as well as Catholics. By 1808 there were enough Irishmen in Pittsburgh to organize a Roman Catholic congregation and erect a chapel near the site of the Pennsylvania Railroad depot. The church, appropriately enough, was dedicated to St. Patrick. It is interesting to note that several of Pittsburgh's early churches were built in part with money raised by lotteries.

Pittsburgh charity did not remain at home, for the town's first recorded venture in the field was a gift in 1798 of four hundred dollars to the yellow fever victims of Philadelphia—a generous return, it must be admitted, for the eastern city's contemptuous vilification of the West during the Whiskey Insurrection only four years before. The Pittsburgh Humane Society was organized in 1813 and laudably undertook to relieve "the sons and daughters of adversity." Committees in each of the wards solicited donations and distributed aid to those in need. The current interpretation of charity was a combination of the Lord and Lady Bountiful concept with the inculcation of moral precepts. A Sunday School was instituted in 1809 to teach reading and writing to the poor children of the town. In 1802 the Western Missionary Society organized for the "purpose of diffusing the knowledge of the gospel among the inhabitants of the new settlements, the Indian tribes, and if need be, among some of the interior inhabitants." A similar organization, the Pittsburgh Bible Society, founded in 1815, was dedicated to the dissemination of the "word of God among the poor and destitute." The most vigorous uplifters, however, were the members of a succession of "Moral" societies that devoted themselves to the "suppression of vice" with the efficient aid of the state's blue laws. Not only were the proprietors of tippling and gambling houses arraigned, but profane cursers were fined, rioters quelled, and wagoners prevented from working on the Sabbath. They did, however, allow sleighing on Sunday, much to the disgust of a visitor who was used to seeing such indulgences rigorously punished in the enlightened country east of the mountains.

Slavery was never a flourishing institution in western Pennsylvania, more because of economic reasons than moral scruples. Slaves were brought to Pittsburgh, probably as early as 1759, by British or colonial soldiers and advertisements for their sale or recapture were common during the next half century or more. Hugh Henry Brackenridge observed that many men in the district who would not "for a fine cow have shaved their beards on Sunday" held and abused slaves. The historian Boucher is authority for the statement that at least half a dozen of the ministers near Pittsburgh and most of the elders and officials of the churches owned slaves— probably chiefly household servants. In 1790, ten years after the state legislature had decreed the gradual abolition of slavery, there were 159 slaves in Allegheny County; in 1800 there were 79, in 1810 there were 27, in 1820 there was only 1, but in 1830 there were 27. This wide variation arose chiefly from the changes of residence among the older negroes; slave children born after 1780 became free at the age of twenty-eight.

III

WHEN in 1786 John Scull and his partner had established the *Pittsburgh Gazette* they set for themselves the highest ideals as censors of public morals and educators in literature, religion, science, and politics. The course of western Pennsylvania politics, however, made the newspapers of Pittsburgh organs of propaganda rather than institutions of liberal education, but fortunately the cause of letters was not left to perish. A succession of small circulating libraries limped through the years (they could scarcely have been said to have flourished), some of them in connection with more or less ephemeral bookstores.

The Pittsburgher whose writings first obtained national recognition was Hugh Henry Brackenridge, and however his efforts may be judged by modern standards, it must be acknowledged that he was head and shoulders above his closest contemporary Pittsburgh rivals. His *Modern Chivalry*, published piecemeal in four volumes from 1792 to 1813, has already been noticed. It was an imitation of *Don Quixote*, occasionally inspired and witty, but more often long winded and tiresome, chiefly devoted to political satire but occasionally branching out into other fields. The chief character was Captain Farrago, a substantial citizen of western Pennsylvania whose common-sense analyses of the state of the nation were brought out by his stooges, a comical Irishman named Teague O'Regan and a dour Scotsman called Duncan Ferguson. Captain Farrago, of course, was none other than Brackenridge himself, attempting to demonstrate the folly of government by ignorant men, whether commoners or aristocrats, and preaching the advisability of placing in office the men of sense, learning, and intelligence—a combination admittedly hard to find, but still existent, as Brackenridge broadly hinted by running for office several times and finally accepting an appointment to the supreme bench of the state.

Brackenridge's poetry, while it often tripped over tangled feet, yet possessed a sarcastic lash that stung those at whom he aimed. There was in it also a bitter note of disappointed ambition. As a matter of fact, the lawyer was too faithful to his principles and too outspoken in his castigation of the ignorant and time-serving to scale the heights of political success. His career remains as the perfect paradox—an example of how genius can rise in a democracy and of how a democracy can refuse to utilize the gifts of genius and so stifle their development.

Brackenridge's closest literary rival was Robert Patterson, a Presbyterian clergyman who had been educated at Canonsburg Academy and the University of Pennsylvania. He had preached near Erie for several years before he began a three-year term in 1807 as principal of Pittsburgh Academy. In 1810 he opened a bookstore in Pittsburgh, and during the quarter century that followed he dabbled in the publishing and paper manufacturing businesses. Under the name of "The Recluse" he produced reams of poetry that brought him some little attention at the time.

The man who undoubtedly did the most to spread literary culture in Pittsburgh in the period immediately following 1800 was Zadok Cramer, a New Jersey Quaker, born in 1773, who settled in Pittsburgh in 1800. He began as a bookbinder, soon acquired a bookstore and circulating library, and distinguished his place on Market Street to the seekers after intellectual fodder by putting up a painting of his "patron saint" and dubbing his store the "Sign of the Franklin Head." He had enterprisingly labeled himself a publisher and now lost no time in justifying the assumption. By the end of the year he had issued the first of a long line of variously named almanacs. The next year he published in pamphlet form the first edition of the *Navigator*, a guidebook for river travelers that was to make him probably the best known publisher in the United States, for it was eagerly bought by the thousands of merchants and immigrants who sought to thread the mazes of the Ohio and Mississippi. The first book published in Pittsburgh was probably Scull's 1793 edition of the third volume of *Modern Chivalry*, but Cramer took the lead in the number of books published, chiefly sermons, textbooks, and journals of travel. His was the most flourishing book business in the town—probably the only flourishing one. He sold books in French, German, Spanish, Latin, and Greek; he carried music instruction books, dictionaries, and law books; he sold all sorts of stationery supplies and was the first to offer wallpaper for sale in Pittsburgh; he carried playing cards and patent medicines, and was not too dignified to advertise that he would give cash or books for rags. In 1808 he took John Spear into partnership, and in 1810 added to the concern young William Eichbaum, son of the glass cutter, who had served an apprenticeship of seven years in the bookstore.

It was almost inevitable that a man with the enterprise of Cramer would eventually ruin his health, and this was just what he did within a decade after he entered business. He departed for the South in search of health and died there in August, 1813, a victim of tuberculosis. The firm was continued by his widow and his partners, who made a brave attempt to carry out his most cherished plan, the publication of a magazine. The first number of the *Western Gleaner or Repository for Arts, Sciences, and Literature* was published in December, 1813, and the publication lived precariously until June of the next year, when financial reasons forced its discontinuance.

IV

Two racial elements contributed no small influence to the broadening of Pittsburgh culture—the German and the French. Though it was probably true that the majority of the Germans were handicapped in their relations with the community by their ignorance of the English language, they largely filled the ranks of the mechanics, the more prosperous farmers, and even the merchants. Jacob Bausman, the most prominent of the Germans, had come to Pittsburgh as early as 1771, had served in the Virginia militia as an ensign, and had been a ferryman and tavernkeeper for years. He was one of the original trustees of Allegheny County, and with Jacob Haymaker, a German boat-builder, was trustee of the land deeded by the Penns to the German church. Michael Huffnagle was one of the county's first lawyers. Melchoir Beltzhoover, Alexander Negley, Conrad Winebiddle, and Jonas Roup were German landholders near Pittsburgh who left their marks upon the progress as well as upon the map of the city. The mechanical talents of the Germans had been cultivated in the factories of the East and found ready utilization in Pittsburgh's rising industries, where the names of Eichbaum, Lorenz, and Anshutz became prominent.

The French element of Pittsburgh, while negligible in numbers, furnished a surprising number of prominent citizens. Albert Gallatin, a French Switzer, though a resident of Fayette County, entered Congress as a representative of the district comprised of Allegheny and Washington counties; Peter Audrain, the Chevalier Dubac, Barthelemi Tardiveau, the Tarasçon brothers, and James Berthoud were Pittsburgh merchants; Felix Brunot, who began the practice of medicine in Pittsburgh in 1797, had been a surgeon in the Revolutionary War and became the founder of a prominent local family; John B. C. Lucas served in the state legislature, in Congress, and on the county bench, and finally left the region to accept an appointment as district judge for the Territory of Louisiana; John Marie was the proprietor of a tavern on Grant's Hill, and made it the center of such a tasteful display of flowers, shrubbery, arbors, and graveled walks that it became the show place of the town and the favorite resort for lovers and picnickers. Anthony Beelen, for many years a prominent merchant and industrialist, was the son of a Belgian diplomat.

v

THE Pittsburgh of the period between 1795 and 1815 furnished improved opportunities for the young person who sought an education. The children of merchants and gentlemen began their studies in one of the many ephemeral schools that were as like as half-educated and wholly uninspired teachers could make them. Occasionally there were schools that specialized in the instruction of young ladies—crude precursors of the modern finishing school. The French Revolution, among its other terrors, loosed upon the defenseless world an avalanche of aristocratic instructors in the French language, fencing, dancing, and deportment; Pittsburgh drew its share of these refugees, and local society took on a perceptible gloss as a result.

The Pittsburgh Academy (now the University of Pittsburgh),

which had opened its doors in 1789, continued to top the local educational field with the mouth-filling curriculum announced in 1795 by its principal, the Reverend Mr. Arthur: "English Grammar; Writing, Arithmetic, and Book-keeping; the Latin, Greek, and French Languages; Rhetoric, and the Belles Lettres; Geography, and the most useful parts of the Mathematics; to which will be added an Introduction to Natural, Civil, and Ecclesiastical History, Astronomy, Natural Philosophy, Logic, Moral Philosophy, and Chronology."

There were, of course, evening schools for instruction in the rudiments of learning, but more interesting were the singing schools held in the grand jury room of the courthouse and the instruction in architecture and mechanical drawing offered by a traveling Scot. Even more fascinating was the amazing variety of practical arts, from the making of furniture, jewelry, and musical instruments to the concoction of paints, medicines, confections, and cordials, "expeditiously taught without much loss of time" by Doctor J. T. B. B. Prentiss.

VI

In spite of the elaborate educational apparatus set up by the elders to torture the younger generation, the boys, as always, did what they could to initiate themselves into the mysteries of life. Young Henry Marie Brackenridge learned to write "like copper-plate," dutifully absorbed Latin and Greek from James Mountain and mathematics from John Taylor, and spouted orations at the public performances of the Academy students in the courthouse; yet he found most pleasure in stealing from bed and lying before the fireplace half the night reading the "singular sufferings and persecutions" of Baron Trenck. When his father sent him to the attic to study he discovered and devoured "four folio volumes of *State Trials*, twenty-four of the *European* and twelve of the *Literary Magazine*, beside an enormous pile of the *Hibernian*" before he was discovered and dragged back to the office where his father occupied himself with the much more congenial task of writing *Modern Chivalry*, the book that was to do so much to place the thriving little frontier town at the Forks of the Ohio on the literary map.

Those were the happy days for Pittsburgh lads who were not burdened with the necessity of cramming the classical curriculum into their skulls. They could play about the fascinating mounded ruins of Fort Pitt and Fort Duquesne and crawl into the abandoned powder magazines or through the dank drains, though some of the boys had their freedom of movement constricted by the necessity for watching small brothers and sisters to see that they did not approach the crumbling sand pits, where two children had been buried alive. If the water were low they could wade across the rivers, or they could go swimming in the cool muddy current, to the loud envy of the adults, who by borough ordinance were forbidden to disport themselves in the rivers during the daylight. Those with pocket money could purchase delicious gobs of ice cream at the confectioner's, though jolly Peter L'Horton must have lost many a sale because the lads were saving their pence to make up the twenty-five-cent tax levied on their dogs. The tax had been necessitated, so the unromantic elders said, because dogs were so numerous and so vicious that unprotected women did not dare to go out at night. In truth, travelers reported, it did seem that the dogs of Pittsburgh felt that their baying was an essential part of the mechanism that hoisted the moon up over Quarry Hill and across the sky.

Young Brackenridge, who stole enough time from the classics to be a real boy, roamed the hills with his comrade Joe, the son of a village cobbler, and was introduced to a "midnight club of youthful outlaws"; he engaged in the battles between the gangs of the upper and lower towns, and lost his marbles to General Neville's Black Andy. When a slack-wire walker named Passamonte came to town young Henry was so fired with the ambition to emulate him that he stretched up a wire in the stable and practiced at every opportunity. Six months later Passamonte returned to town and was in the midst of a performance in the courthouse when he was forced to descend to repel an invasion by a crowd of juvenile hoodlums. What was his fury upon returning to find Henry on the wire prancing before the delighted spectators! The young usurper was fain to hop from the wire and make his escape behind the benches.

One morning when young Brackenridge climbed into the barn loft to throw down hay for the horse a negro popped his head out of the mow, greatly to the lad's alarm. "Don't be scared, young massa," he implored, "I'se a po' nigga run away last night from de boat, come down from Figginy on de Monigehale, and gwine to Kentuck; pray, massa, only let me stay."

Henry smuggled food to the negro and kept the secret of his presence until danger was past; the man then came out and procured a job as an hostler. A few days later he begged his young benefactor to get him an old pair of pants, and when they were abstracted from the attic he gave the boy a dollar. The latter, fearful of being caught with such an enormous sum, gave it to his friend Christopher Magee. Unfortunately Christopher's father learned of his son's wealth, and, certain that he had stolen it, thrashed him repeatedly in a vain effort to learn whence it had come. Christopher refused to betray his friend and finally his father tired of the exercise; the boy grew up to be a prominent businessman of Pittsburgh and the founder of a famous family.

Something interesting was always happening aside from the routine life in a river town. Perhaps in the earlier years Johnny Appleseed, dressed in cast-off clothing and with his mush pan on his head, was to be seen at a cider mill where he washed out apple seeds for his nursery a short distance from the town. Once a sudden May flood of the Monongahela brought a mill floating by the town, and men in boats surrounded it and carried out the grain; another flood, in the fall of 1815, covered the banks and low-lying town lots with ripe, golden pumpkins; an elephant actually appeared in Pittsburgh in 1808, perhaps the first pachyderm to cross the Alleghenies since prehistoric times. The year 1811 brought an African leopard, the peripheral tremors of the New Madrid earthquake, and the launching of the "New Orleans," each eminently satisfactory to small boys. Soon afterwards the War of 1812 began. The crack Pittsburgh Blues at once volunteered for service, and thousands of other uniformed heroes were at one time or another congregated about Fort Fayette. The taverns were full of rollickers, endless lines of Conestoga wagons wound down to the Allegheny ferry on the way to Erie, Fort Fayette was crammed with prisoners taken at Perry's victory, and occasionally there was the thunder of a 24-pounder from the military encampment on Grant's Hill to announce that another poltroon had deserted his country's service. The red-letter year, however, was 1814, for then there were not only soldiers and a war, but the aurora borealis, a menagerie, and, best of all, a circus headed by Messrs. Pepin, Brischard, and Cayetano.

VII

PITTSBURGH life was not all work for adults. The young men and women found means to pass the time gaily, whatever the circumstances. In 1826 Samuel Jones, the respected register and recorder of Allegheny County, looked back with a twinge of nostalgia upon the simple days at the turn of the century. "The long winter evenings," he wrote, "were passed by the humble villagers at each other's homes, with merry tale and song, or in simple games; and the hours of night sped lightly onward with the unskilled, untiring youth, as they threaded the mazes of the dance, guided by the music of the violin, from which some good-humored rustic drew his Orphean sounds. In the jovial time of harvest and hay-making, the sprightly and active of the village participated in the rural labors and the hearty pastimes, which distinguished that happy season. The balls and merrymakings that were so frequent in the village were attended by all without any particular deference to rank or riches. No other etiquette than that which natural politeness prescribed was exacted or expected . . . Young fellows might pay their *devoirs* to their female acquaintances; ride, walk, or talk with them, and pass hours in their society without being looked upon with suspicion by parents, or slandered by trolloping gossips."

A favorite resort of the townsmen was the parklike expanse of Grant's Hill near Marie's Tavern. Here Fourth of July celebrations were held, complete with oratory, and while the *hoi polloi* ate picnic dinners on the greensward the political bigwigs ate Marie's roasts and toasted this and that in his excellent wine. The fraternally inclined in the town found a place in the Freemasons, the Society of the Cincinnati, the Mechanical Society, the Hibernians, or the Society of Friendship and Union, or perhaps in turtle soup parties at James Tustin's "Sign of the Ark" on Front Street. There were occasional concerts given by the Apollonian Society under the direction of one S. H. Dearborn, a New Englander, who had come to Pittsburgh to paint portraits. There were also scientific lectures for those who found them entertaining or instructive and cared to lay down the price. Waxwork exhibits found their way to the Forks of the Ohio, and for twenty-five cents the interested citizens could gaze upon the authentic features of General Bonaparte and of the Sleeping Beauty. In 1806 Francis Scachi appeared in Pittsburgh and ladies and gentlemen of fashion flocked to him to have their "profiles taken with the Physiognotrace." Doubtless in many cases succeeding generations have the artistic Scachi to thank for the only likeness ever made of the revered founder of the family.

The fashionable balls of Pittsburgh were occasionally honored by the presence of famous personages. The picaresque General James Wilkinson often appeared at the Pittsburgh wharf in his magnificent barge rowed by twenty-five or thirty men, with his musicians playing and the wives of the officers, like angels in filmy lace, seeming to float a little above the deck that ordinary men trod. Napoleon's exiled general, Jean Victor Moreau, who was later to give his old commander a drubbing at Leipzig, visited Pittsburgh and astounded the citizens by warmly embracing a French sausage-maker whose claims that he had been an aide of Moreau had been considered as mere gasconade by the skeptical villagers. The Duke of Orleans, later King Louis Philippe, with his two brothers visited Pittsburgh and was entertained by General Neville. Hugh Henry Brackenridge seems to have made quite an impression upon the future monarch, who in later years was to recall the author of *Modern Chivalry* with pleasure.

VIII

THE temple of justice was not dedicated solely to musty legal arguments or town meetings. It was the favorite resort of Thespians and upon occasion was taken over by slack-rope walkers and Punch and Judy shows. The taprooms of the taverns were sometimes utilized for stage shows; in 1801 the Academy students presented *Cato* and *The Anatomist* in an attempt to raise money "to be appropriated for the pailing in of the Grave Yard." Two years later a theatrical company rented the courthouse for a short season and offered in their repertoire the comedy *Trick upon Trick, or, the Vintner in the Suds*. In 1804 the town fathers suddenly clapped a ten-dollar license fee upon each dramatic performance given in the borough. The fine Italian hand of the Pittsburgh Moral Society may be detected in that levy, or perhaps merely the prejudice of the prosaic Scotch-Irishman, who balked at the townsmen's wasting in riotous living the time and money that might have been applied to business.

At any rate the fee must have been removed within a few years, for in 1808 two amateur dramatic societies were flourishing, one of them composed of students of law and the other "of respectable mechanicks." The aforementioned S. H. Dearborn designed and painted scenery for the stage in the courthouse, and shifted scenes or acted with equal enthusiasm. William Wilkins, a rising young lawyer who was to become a prominent officeholder, excelled in "genteel comedy." Others among the actors were Morgan Neville, George Wallace, and Tarleton Bates. The chief weakness of the Thespians was their inability to portray feminine roles with appropriate grace, but they persisted in their efforts and offered a play once a month during the winter. Young Brackenridge, because he acted in two minor parts, fell under his father's displeasure and was exiled to Jefferson College in Canonsburg.

By 1813 Pittsburgh possessed an auditorium known as the Pittsburgh Theatre. This was probably the building located on the north side of Third Street near the northwest corner of Third and Smithfield. "It contained a pit and one tier of boxes, as they were called. The form was after the old style,—two

parallel elongations, with an elliptical curve at the entrance."
The first extensive theatrical season was probably the three-
month stay in the summer and fall of 1815 of the troupe of
Samuel Drake, which had descended the Allegheny from New
York in a flatboat. The offerings of the first evening were the
comedy *Honeymoon* and the comic opera *No Song, No Supper*.
A few days later Sheridan's *Pizarro* was given. A lavish temple
of the sun was provided with the aid of paint and gold foil but
the half-grown lads who took the parts of Spanish soldiers were
lost in their equipment, and a wit suggested that the armor
looked as though it had been hung on stakes to be aired. The
house was filled to capacity, about four hundred persons at a
dollar a head, with foundrymen and keel-boat men predom-
inating, but they accepted the ludicrous Spanish army and even
the one-violin orchestra quietly. It was too much for them, however, when the sun virgins filed upon the stage and the white
veils failed to conceal the bay window of the portly property
man and the bent figure of the old Irish charwoman. Even the
tragic mien of the actors was dissolved in the wave of laughter
that swept the house.

Lectures, balls, and theatricals were all very well for the
"gentlemen of respectability" or mechanics and boatmen with
money to burn, but those without the means or the taste for
such things gathered in the beer cellars, gambling houses, and
the less reputable taverns. There was one sport, however, at
which everyone rubbed elbows—racing. Races were held each
spring and fall in connection with the county fair. The fairground and race track were located just northeast of Pittsburgh
until 1801, but with the advance of the town they were moved
to McKeesport. In the days when the fair was held at Pittsburgh almost the whole town dropped its business and attended.
There were the booths of petty merchants and tents of tumblers
and slack-rope walkers and occasionally there rose above the
roar of the crowd the "bragg" of a famous gouger spoiling for
a fight. Undisturbed by the tumult paced the blind rhymester,
Dennis Loughy, who never lost an opportunity to match a
great event with an appropriate epic. Now he was "casting his

pearls before swine, chanting his masterpiece, in a tone part nasal and part gutteral,—

> Come, gentlemen, gentlemen all,
> Ginral Sincleer shall remem-ber-ed be,
> For he lost thirteen hundred men all,
> In the Western Tari-to-ree!

But the real interest of the people was in the races and at the cry "To horse! To horse!" blind Dennis, acrobats, and sweating gougers were alike left to their own devices while the crowd rushed to surround the track. The races were run according to the rules of the Pittsburgh Jockey Club, and all jockeys were required to wear the distinctive garb of their calling. The prizes were sixty dollars on the first day, forty dollars on the second, and sweepstakes on the third. Race days were exciting times in Pittsburgh, but there were those who found fault and who rejoiced when the fair was moved to McKeesport. One writer in the *Gazette* complained that the races attracted the worst characters from all quarters and taught the youth of Pittsburgh idleness and debauchery.

XIV

Clapboard Democracy

PITTSBURGH politics before the Whiskey Insurrection had been dominated by the "gentlemen of respectability," chief among them the members of the Neville connection. Though the Nevilles were openly Federalist and aristocratic in their sympathies they managed to keep their offices and influence even in a predominantly democratic region because their enemies had not learned to unite. As a matter of fact that was the situation all over the country. In consequence, Jefferson, presumably in innocuous retirement upon his Virginia hilltop, was actually devoting himself untiringly to the work of building up a democratic opposition party. The growth of the Democratic party in Pittsburgh, however, owed little to Jefferson; it was the work of that old stormy petrel of the perilous days of 1794, Hugh Henry Brackenridge.

It will be remembered that Brackenridge had become an enemy of the Nevilles even before the insurrection, and that the events of that abortive political revolt merely furnished additional pegs on which each side could hang its grievances. The end of the insurrection found Brackenridge an outcast from Pittsburgh's polite society and with his battle for political rehabilitation to fight all over again. This time, however, he did

172

not attempt a comeback by quiet industry as he had before. Old John Neville, who had lamented the lawyer's uncanny ability to stick his finger in the eyes of Ross and Hamilton, soon found the same long finger extended in a much more vigorous and menacing fashion toward his own eye. Brackenridge had been a candidate for Congress in 1794 but had been defeated, as he felt, by the machinations of the Nevilles, who were supporting their protege, the lawyer John Woods. As a matter of fact it had not been the Neville influence that had bested him.

The Reverend John McMillan, referred to by his contemporaries as the "Presbyterian Cardinal" of the West, distrusted Brackenridge because he had "given up his license to preach and learned to swear" and had resolved to defeat him. At the last moment McMillan had dragged into the race Albert Gallatin, a scholarly genius, late of the city of Geneva and not a resident of the congressional district, and had actually succeeded in swinging the election for his candidate. In Congress Gallatin proceeded to prove the adage that genius is ninety-nine per cent perspiration, and made himself so indispensable that it was plain to see that he was destined for great things. He was reelected handily over Woods again in 1796, but the election in 1798 proved to be a more difficult matter. The Federalists took advantage of the current fury against France (it was the time of the X Y Z affair) to accuse Gallatin of being a Francophile, and at the same time they sought to revive old issues and tar him with the blame for the Whiskey Insurrection. As a matter of fact, he was peculiarly vulnerable to assault because he had sympathized with the aims of the insurgents although he had deplored their methods.

Perhaps up to 1798 it would not have been too late for the Federalists to have saved themselves by winning over Brackenridge to their side, for it must be acknowledged that he was insatiably ambitious, and, moreover, he cared little for party labels but believed that personal fitness was the true criterion for the selection of officeholders. At any rate the Nevilles made no gestures toward him but, smugly certain of victory, assured themselves that the Whiskey Insurrection had clipped his claws.

Their dismay, then, was almost comic when they discovered that Brackenridge, taking advantage of the rivalry between Pittsburgh and Washington Federalists, had actually entered their camp and had induced the heir to the family dignities, Presley Neville, to announce his candidacy against the regular choice, John Woods. In vain the party leaders strove to convince young Neville that the wily lawyer was merely using him to split the opposition and assure the election of Gallatin; his vanity had been so subtly flattered that he proved obdurate. Brackenridge had correctly judged his man.

The Federalist guns swung from Gallatin and hastily concentrated upon the imperturbable Brackenridge. His *Incidents of the Western Insurrection* was thumbed assiduously, and not in vain, for remarks derogatory to the Nevilles, and these were spread upon the pages of the *Gazette* cheek by jowl with tremulous Federalist prayers that Presley Neville would leave off eating husks with the swine and return to his father's house. A fortnight or so before the election young Neville finally withdrew from the race, but it was too late to repair the damage he had done. Gallatin sailed through handsomely while the grinning old Scot strolled by the Federalist wailing wall and ostentatiously wiped the canary feathers from his chin. From then on the Federalists made no mistake: Hugh Henry Brackenridge was their Public Enemy Number One.

II

THE congressional campaign of 1798 clearly demonstrated that Brackenridge was the logical leader for the scattered democrats of Pittsburgh and they did not wait long to gather about him. The new Democratic-Republican party did not lack for leadership in the counties of western Pennsylvania, but its membership in the borough of Pittsburgh, while zealous, enterprising, and loyal, had yet to develop men of high caliber politically; as a consequence the work of organizing party activities and planning strategy fell upon Brackenridge. It so happened that several of the more prominent men of the new party lived on the east side of Market Street between Third and Fourth Streets in a row of clapboard houses, so the Democratic-Republican hierarchy in Pittsburgh came to be known as the Clapboard Row Junto, or the Clapboard Democracy. Here in Molly Murphy's General Butler Tavern the Democrats held their dinners and rallies, and here were developed some of the political methods that have become traditional in Pittsburgh.

The caucus had already come into use as a means of nomination, but the men who pulled the strings had tried to make its decisions appear as those of the whole community; the Democratic-Republicans now frankly made it a party instrument. A committee was appointed to urge foreigners to become naturalized and to vote the party ticket—not a very difficult matter, as most immigrants were violently democratic in their sympathies. The craze for French republican titles and customs that had begun in 1793 with the advent of Citizen Genêt was intensified. Men discarded their knee-breeches and began wearing trousers; cocked hats gave way to low crowns and straight brims; powdered wigs and clubbed hair survived only among the old fashioned. "Jacobin" became an epithet proudly borne by the more radical, and every Democratic-Republican on occasion was addressed by his fellow partizans as "citizen."

The best-known Democratic-Republicans before 1800 were a newly arrived Irishman named William Gazzam; Adamson Tannehill, former proprietor of the Green Tree Tavern; Samuel Ewalt, Allegheny County's first sheriff; Nathaniel Irish, a county commissioner and storekeeper; Tarleton Bates, a debonair young Virginian of good family; Alexander Fowler, who had resigned a British commission to serve as auditor of the western military department (much to the grief of General Brodhead) and who loved to flourish his title of brigadier general of county militia; and Dr. Andrew Richardson, Fowler's son-in-law.

The Federalists of Pittsburgh possessed, in addition to the Nevilles, several prominent leaders. Foremost among them was Senator James Ross, a young man of grave and distinguished appearance, who had married a sister of John Woods and moved to Pittsburgh soon after the Whiskey Insurrection. Ross, who had been born in York County in 1762, was among the youngest men to enter the United States Senate. He served there for two terms, until 1803, then returned to Pittsburgh to practice law; and in a day when the local scene boasted some of the country's most distinguished legal talent he became by far the most prominent and respected member of the bar, and he was not too proud to serve for seventeen years in the city council. His personal popularity in the western part of the state made him the logical choice as Federalist candidate for governor in 1799 and 1808 in the hope that he might carry that democratic section for the party.

Alexander Addison, the president judge of the western circuit and a resident of Pittsburgh, had been educated for the ministry in Scotland but had emigrated to the United States in 1785 and had taken up the law. His capacity was proved by the fact that only six years after he entered the country he had been appointed to the bench. He was a man of such humorless and uncompromising devotion to his duty as he saw it that he made many enemies. In addition to Ross and Addison the Federalists also boasted the allegiance of John Gibson, industrialist; James O'Hara, quartermaster and banker; General John Wilkins, Jr.; John Scull of the *Gazette;* and a promising bevy of youngsters, among them William Wilkins, a brother of John Wilkins, and Morgan Neville, eldest son of Presley Neville.

The gubernatorial campaign of 1799 was bitterly fought between James Ross and Thomas McKean, the chief justice of the Pennsylvania supreme court, who had but lately been converted to Democratic-Republicanism. McKean garnered the Presbyterian vote by accusing Ross of having sung songs over a card table and of having committed the even more heinous offense of mimicking the Reverend John McMillan (after all, who could have resisted doing it?). McKean lost Allegheny County but carried the state by a comfortable majority. The day after he resumed office he rewarded Brackenridge for his share in bringing about the victory by making him a justice of the supreme court. Soon afterward the Pittsburgher paid off an old score by having the governor dismiss Prothonotary Brison and appoint a Brackenridge relative in his place. Thus was Mrs. Brackenridge finally avenged for Brison's insult in not inviting her to the ball in honor of General Lee. The Pittsburgh Democratic-Republicans celebrated McKean's victory by a dinner at Smur's Tavern, where Brackenridge presided. After the dinner some of the celebrants went around to Ross's house to gloat and took along a band to play the rogue's march. Unfortunately for them the Federalists still controlled the borough and the next day they found themselves arrested and fined as rioters.

III

BRACKENRIDGE did not propose to rest with this victory, but like a good general, prepared to win others. Scull, who had sincerely prided himself upon the political impartiality of his *Gazette*, had developed a curious blind spot; he refused to publish articles directed against the Federalist regime because that would be forwarding the work of rascals, traitors, atheists, and Jacobin sans culottes, but he gladly printed Federalist propaganda because that party was led by the heroes of the Revolution and was the palladium of liberty and the Constitution; but still, praise be to Washington and Hamilton, he was not, like other men, afflicted with the virus of political prejudice. As a matter of fact it was not long before the editor, who at first had only grudgingly consented to let break a lance in defense of the government, was riding through printer's ink to the crupper of his horse while he manfully swung his compositor's stick in defense of God and the federal constitution. Witness this salutation in a mock petition to his erstwhile patron craving pardon for having dared to vote for James Ross: "To H. H. B——e, Esq., President of the Jacobin Society, Professor of Chivalry, Privy Councillor to the Governor of Bantam, Poet Laureat to the Herald of Sedition, Biographer to the Insurgents, Auctioneer of Divinity, and Haberdasher of Pronouns, &c. &c."

It is scarcely a matter of surprise that any "Haberdasher of Pronouns" with the spirit of Brackenridge should retaliate by backing a rival newspaper. A tool was ready at hand. For some time a young Hebrew named John Israel had been publishing in Washington a sheet that specialized in language as venomous as that of Scull and his friends, and he readily consented to set up a press in Pittsburgh. Accordingly on August 16, 1800, there was published the first issue of the *Tree of Liberty*. The banner head bore a nobly proportioned tree beneath which there lay on the ground a number of spherical objects that may have been the detruncated heads of aristocrats, while Brackenridge had drawn upon his studies for the ministry to furnish the motto that was flaunted in a scroll beneath the gruesome Golgotha, "And the leaves of the tree were for the healing of the nations." With whoops of joy the surrounding Democratic-Republicans dashed for their poison pots to set down the pent-up virulence that seethed within them. It was the beginning of a merry journalistic war that has never wholly let up, even to the present.

The next year Brackenridge's new judicial duties prompted him to move to Carlisle, where he lived until his death in 1816, but he by no means neglected the West, for his duties occasionally took him back. His place as the inspiration for the *Tree of Liberty* was soon taken by a handsome and brilliant young Yale graduate, Henry Baldwin, who was destined to become a justice of the United States Supreme Court. Baldwin was ably assisted by Tarleton Bates, by now prothonotary, and by a long-faced young law student, Walter Forward, a penniless Western Reserve Yankee who had paid his way into Pittsburgh by giving the ferryman a horseshoe he had picked up for luck. By 1801 party animosity had become so strong and social divisions so pronounced that there were not enough socialites well disposed toward Jefferson to hold a ball in honor of his inauguration. Even the militia divided on politics; part of the regiments insisted upon wearing the black and white cockade of the American Revolution, while the greater part adopted the red, white, and blue cockade of the French Revolution. Brackenridge, never at a loss for a quip, suggested that an attempt be made to cement the political breach by arranging "inter-marriages of young persons" from the camp of each political faith.

Perhaps it was in pursuance of Brackenridge's advice that Baldwin fell in love with a certain young lady who was also favored by young Isaac Meason, the son of the iron manufacturer of that name. The rivalry ended in a duel, which was usually explained as the result of political antagonisms, an explanation that may have been true in part. The duel was held at what is now Tenth Street and Penn Avenue. At the first fire Baldwin fell to the ground spitting blood, but examination showed that Meason's bullet had hit a Spanish silver dollar in his opponent's waistcoat pocket and raised a lump over the heart. A second exchange of shots was prevented by the opportune arrival of a posse under Judge Riddle. The affair must have been hushed up, for neither of the principals was punished by fine and the deprivation of citizenship for seven years as the law against duelling provided.

The Democratic-Republicans were undoubtedly beginning to make progress locally. The Federalists, in a clumsy attempt to gain the good will of the voters, began to call themselves Federal-Republicans; the action opened a chink in their armor big enough to drive through a Conestoga wagonload of ridicule, and their opponents did not hang back through any mistaken sense of chivalry. John B. C. Lucas, a Frenchman who had served as associate judge of the county court, was criticized because he allowed his wife to plow *on Sunday* but was nevertheless elected to Congress. The unsuccessful attempt of a quondam friend to beat him with a cudgel while he was dining in John Marie's tavern was interpreted as the long prophesied last resort of Federalists to hold their political domination by assassination. Judge Addison then so far forgot his judicial dignity as to deny Lucas, his associate on the bench, certain rights as a judge and to read him a lecture upon his political sins. It was the long-awaited opportunity. Under the able generalship of Brackenridge the state assembly tumbled Addison from his bench and forbade him ever again to hold judicial office. It was the handwriting on the wall for Pittsburgh and Pennsylvania Federalism. In 1803 the Democratic-Republicans worked as they never had before and their industry was magnificently rewarded.

They won the borough elections for the first time and, when noses were counted in the state assembly, lo, there were only a half dozen Federalists to be found.

IV

BUT it is a long worm that has no turning. McKean had been gradually returning to his first political love and was continually embroiled with his radical legislature. When he ran again for gubernatorial stakes McKean found himself confronted by Simon Snyder, a man more to the liking of the radicals. The Democratic-Republican party was split wide open. The *Tree of Liberty*, in the opinion of the extremists, under the aegis of Henry Baldwin was no longer a sturdy Democratic oak but a quaking aspen. The result was that on July 24, 1805, the *Commonwealth* was begun under the editorship of Ephraim Pentland, a short and stocky youth of twenty who had served his apprenticeship on the Philadelphia *Aurora*, and whose love of jokes did not hamper his style as a master of invective. Israel and his triad of angels had at last met their match, and the despondent Federalists who had not even smiled for two years held their sides with merriment, then in good time marched to the polls and threw their strength to McKean. Pentland could not forgive this defeat; it was obvious to him that he had proved himself so much the superior in the art of vilification that his side should have won, and he refused to let up in his attacks.

Finally Tarleton Bates took umbrage at Pentland's tactics and on January 2, 1806, sought out his tormenter and gave him a cowhiding. Pentland sent Bates a challenge to a duel by Thomas Stewart, a young Irish merchant; Bates refused to fight and Pentland gleefully posted him as a coward. Bates published his reasons in the *Tree of Liberty*, and Stewart took offense at a reflection upon himself contained in them and challenged the author. Bates accepted. The encounter took place on January 8 on the bank of the Monongahela near the foot of Bates Street in Oakland. Morgan Neville acted as second for Stewart and William Wilkins acted for Bates. The Virginian fell at the second fire and died within the hour.

Tarleton Bates had been liked by all who had not been blinded by prejudice, and the whole town mourned his death. The seconds were unjustly accused of not having tried to stop the duel, and so strong was the feeling against them that William Wilkins considered it prudent to visit his brother in Kentucky for a year. In October Israel died in Washington of blood poisoning, and the *Tree of Liberty* quietly withered and died.

Meanwhile Pittsburgh society had been titillated by two visits from that fascinating international pettifogger, Colonel Aaron Burr; one visit was in April, 1805, and the other in August, 1806. These visits occasioned considerable speculation as to their purpose, and this speculation was made all the more piquant by the colonel's mysterious hints on his second visit of great things to come. George Morgan, the Revolutionary Indian agent who was then living at Morganza near Canonsburg, wrote to President Jefferson of his suspicions, and this missive may or may not have had some effect in making the government Burr conscious. The story is still told in Pittsburgh that Queenie Millesmere, daughter of a prominent citizen, became "fashionated" by him, and that after his departure Burr sent her a small statue of a satyr. Thirty years later when Burr died poor Queenie went mad and worshipped the statuette until her father had it buried secretly.

Pittsburgh furnished a few recruits for Burr when he was ready to undertake the fulfillment of his schemes of empire. In December, 1806, a group of fourteen young men from Pittsburgh Academy, including Morgan Neville and William Robinson, started down the river to join Harmon Blennerhassett at his island paradise and accompany him to the rendezvous of Burr's troops at the mouth of the Cumberland. When they arrived at the island they found it in the possession of a band of riotous Virginia militia who proceeded to put them under arrest. They obtained their release only with difficulty and continued the voyage down the river with Mrs. Blennerhassett in their company. There the account of the Pittsburgh boys stops, and even this much was told only in a gallant but unsuccessful attempt to aid Mrs. Blennerhassett in her endeavors to get recompense from the government for the destruction wrought by the militia on Blennerhassett Island.

The gubernatorial campaign of 1808 was an especially bitter one. The Federalists, who had been joined by some of the more conservative Democratic-Republicans, nominated James Ross; their opponents again ran Simon Snyder. Ephraim Pentland led the radical cohorts, now organized as the Tammany Society, and developed a messy and unscrupulous but effective bit of strategy. It seems that John Marie, proprietor of the well-known tavern on Grant's Hill, had become estranged from his wife, and in 1803 he decided to abandon her and return to France. Without informing anyone of his intention, he disposed of his Grant's Hill property to James Ross in 1803 and departed. Mrs. Marie claimed that, according to an agreement made with her some years before, her husband could not sell the property without her consent, and she refused to vacate it. A forcible ejection carried out with unnecessary brutality followed, but though it was at the instance of her husband's lawyers she blamed it upon Ross, and the latter's political enemies found that it made excellent political capital. They even cooked up an addendum to the effect that Ross had wantonly given her a horsewhipping one evening a few months later as she was passing by her former residence. The lies had their intended effect; the kindly Ross was transmogrified into a monster of cruelty and in the eyes of his opponents became the personification of tyrannical oppression. In vain Scull and the Federalists trumpeted the warning that "your constitution is at stake"; the Republicans cautioned the people that a sadistic Federalist was waiting behind every bush to pounce upon the liberties and the persons of the people, and Snyder, their paladin, was swept triumphantly into office.

v

But enough of stale political campaigns. Suffice it to say that it was a dull year when the Constitution was not saved or destroyed (depending on the point of view) in a bitter election contest. With the opening of the War of 1812 the Federalists metamorphosed themselves into a "Peace Party," but nothing they could do prevented the recruiting of men at Fort Fayette or delayed the tramp of feet carrying their owners to the shores of Lake Erie to die an inglorious death by dysentery and small-pox. Eventually in 1814 the popular recoil from military incompetence and extravagance gave John Woods his long-sought ticket of admission to Congress, but the demand for a tariff, which arose from Pittsburgh's rising industrialists when England dumped her surplus goods into the country upon the close of the war, resulted in the election of Henry Baldwin to lay before Congress the demands of western Pennsylvania. The platform upon which he stood for election was, save for familiar catch phrases, everything that the old-time Federalist might have sought. The cycle had been completed. The lean young radicals who had "fought the good fight" in 1800 had grown prosperous and fat, and now without realizing the change they accepted the guardianship of the national heritage of conservatism. A few bewigged and knee-buckled oldsters took a melancholy pleasure in mumbling into their stocks that the eternal verities must always win, but there were few to regard them; the supplanters believed in all sincerity that they themselves had created the brave new world, and faced about to defend it against the starry-eyed young idealists in the conflict that begins anew with every generation.

XV

From Turnpike to Railroad

THE decade that followed the War of 1812 was one of hardship and humiliation for the proud "Gateway to the West." The slump that came as the result of the cessation of the wartime demand for manufactured products and the dumping of British goods could be counteracted by time and the tariff, but the looming threats to Pittsburgh's supremacy as an entrepôt were more serious.

The first blow to Pittsburgh's commercial prestige was the decision of Congress to make Wheeling rather than Pittsburgh the point at which the National Road should cross the Ohio— thus, it was argued, affording access to the river at a point below which the water was never too shallow to be navigable. The Pittsburghers, the while they in turn berated and supplicated the legislators at Harrisburg and the merchants of Philadelphia for succor, whistled nonchalantly before their rivals of Wheeling. "The worthy citizens of that little borough," wrote the editor of the *Gazette*, "are actually doing nothing but walking about on stilts and stroking their chins with the utmost self complacency. . . . 'Poor Pittsburgh,' they exclaim, 'Your day is over, the sceptre of influence and wealth is to travel to us.'" Editor Scull's stiff upper lip was in danger of collapse even as he wrote, and Pittsburgh's businessmen, with the threat of the road added to the hardships of the current depression, were closer to a blue funk than they had ever been before or have been since.

For a decade after the completion of the road in 1820 it actually looked as though Wheeling's boast might come true. As many as five thousand Conestoga wagons were unloaded annually at Wheeling's warehouse doors, and factories were springing up on every side. It is true that Wheeling did act as the way station for most of the trade between Baltimore and the West, but in an age of expanding commerce there was plenty left for the wide-awake commission merchants of Pittsburgh. The Pittsburghers also were saved from commercial ruin by the facts that Wheeling's citizens lacked enterprise and capital, Virginia was cautious and unprogressive, and the National Road itself was so expensive to maintain and congressional appropriations for repairs were so hampered by constitutional quibbles and sectional jealousy that it was finally turned over to the states through which it ran. The net result, however, was a commercial victory for Wheeling, a victory that she enjoyed for thirty years before expanding railroad systems thrust trunk lines past her on both sides and left her to struggle on as best she could.

The gain of Wheeling was in a very real sense Pittsburgh's loss, for western commerce that had been passing through Pittsburgh was visibly transferred to the rival city. The business that went to the Erie Canal, on the other hand, was only in part taken from Pittsburgh. The Great Lakes region owed its development mostly to the Erie Canal—a development for which it would have waited many more years had it depended on Pittsburgh and Philadelphia to provide the transportation facilities. Pittsburgh thus lost little save what she had dreamed of having. On the other hand, so rich were her manufacturing potentialities and so rapid were their development that the transportation of her products alone soon more than made up for her commercial losses to Wheeling. Before many years an increasing share of the intersectional commerce began to find its way back through Pittsburgh in order to utilize its improving transportation facilities.

II

PENNSYLVANIA'S answer to the challenge of the National Road was an act to provide for the incorporation of turnpike companies that with funds provided by private subscription and by the state legislature would undertake to pave the Pennsylvania Road from Harrisburg to Pittsburgh; thus a turnpike all the way from Philadelphia to the Ohio was afforded. The work was completed in 1818 and the road immediately became one of the great national commercial highways, despite the fact that it had to compete with the toll-free Cumberland Road. The Conestoga wagons that had formerly required six to ten weeks for the round trip between Philadelphia and Pittsburgh could now accomplish it in a month, unless snow and ice obstructed the way. A second road, the Huntingdon Turnpike, was constructed between Harrisburg and Pittsburgh by way of the Juniata and Conemaugh valleys. A third important highway was laid out by way of Butler, Mercer, and Meadville to Erie and was completed in 1821. About the same time feeder roads were constructed from the main pikes to Washington, Steubenville, and Beaver.

The freight carried by the two great trans-state highways was said to have been about fifteen thousand tons annually in the early 1820's. About two-thirds of it was bound westward. A wagon carried an average load of between three and four thousand pounds and paid a toll for the round trip between Philadelphia and Pittsburgh of about twenty-four dollars. The Huntingdon Turnpike had scarcely been completed before it justified its existence by affording a cheap means of transportation for Juniata iron, which otherwise would have been forced off the market by a sudden drop in the price of European iron. The long trains of Conestoga wagons that had thundered into Pittsburgh each winter during the thirty years after the disappearance of the pack horse were now able to keep to the road in all seasons. The "wagon stands" of Pittsburgh, where wagoners and their teams could put up at the end of their journey, increased in number; and the trees in their courtyards sheltered growing fleets of red, white, and blue Conestoga schooners, while the thick dialect of the Pennsylvania Dutch wagoners became more familiar than ever to Pittsburgh's Scotch-Irishmen.

At the same time stage travel was developing regularity, speed, and convenience. The bone-shaking old "stage-wagons" were replaced by Concord stages that were, comparatively speaking, models of lightness and comfort—some of them were almost egg-shaped, so desirous were the old-time builders to give the impression of grace and speed to their vehicles. The panels were decorated with scenes from Watteau or allegorical representations of American ideals, and the harness of the horses was handsomely mounted with burnished silver ornaments. What a brave sight a stagecoach must have made as, with bugle blowing and whip cracking, it dashed into town—a stagedriver would as soon have committed hara-kiri as have *walked* his team into town—and pulled up with screeching brakes before Mc-Master's Spread Eagle Hotel! Chickens, pigs, and children scattered to right and left and loafers and apprentice boys came rushing up to view the event of the day and perhaps to catch a glimpse of a pretty ankle as some fair damsel bedecked in Philadelphia finery alighted from the coach.

The natural course of evolution led inevitably to a consolidation of staging interests. By 1831 a single company had monopolized passenger traffic on the Pennsylvania Road and was operating three lines that traveled at different speeds. The names of the Despatch, Good Intent, and Telegraph lines were as familiar to the Pittsburghers of that day as are the bizarrely named motor-coach lines of the present; the drivers were by way of being public characters, respected by adults for their skill and reliability and admired by small boys and older sisters for their nonchalance and dashing courage. The fare to Philadelphia was from twelve to twenty dollars, depending upon the line selected, and the trip took from two and a half to four days. Passengers stopped overnight in the company hotels along the way or slept in the coaches as best they could. Stops were made for meals at convenient places. The stages sometimes left Pittsburgh at unreasonably early hours, and citizens came to anticipate the three o'clock round of the stage calling at the hotels and residences for passengers. The stage agent, with the list of passengers and the order in which they had reserved places, accompanied the driver and knocked thunderously upon the doors of those who were tardy in appearing.

While the stages that traveled the Pennsylvania Road were probably the chief centers of Pittsburgh interest, yet scarcely less important were those that went to Harrisburg by the Huntingdon Turnpike, or that journeyed to points west by way of Wheeling, Steubenville, Beaver, and Erie. It was considered a remarkable feat when in 1824 a gentleman covered the 360 miles from Detroit to Pittsburgh through Erie by means of steamboat and stage in just three days.

The building of the Pennsylvania Canal did not ruin the wagoning business entirely. The sluggish waters of the canal were usually frozen during the winter months, and during that time the Conestogas were still called into service. Stages continued to run and were preferred by those who were in haste or who were bound for points distant from the canal. It was not until the Pennsylvania Railroad had spanned most of the distance between the Susquehanna and the Ohio that the great trans-Allegheny stage lines went out of business.

There was a curious sequel to the history of toll roads in the craze for plank roads in the decade that followed 1845. Plank roads were just that—heavy planks laid across parallel lines of stringers. Most plank roads were short and were laid on the beds of dirt or macadam. Their advantages were said to be their cheapness, smoothness, and usableness in all kinds of weather, and a few misguided enthusiasts even touted them as rivals of the railroads.

Pittsburgh must have had a dozen or more of these short-lived answers to the farmer's prayer radiating like drunken spokes from a hub, and some of them bequeathed names that are still borne by modern motor roads. From Allegheny alone there were four leading to—or rather aimed at—Butler, Perrysville, the Beaver Road, and New Brighton. The Perrysville Plank Road was made long and winding by its shrewd builders, so it was claimed, in order to enable them to collect more tolls. The famous criminal lawyer, Thomas M. Marshall ("Glorious

Old Tom"), who habitually drove in to Pittsburgh over this road, became tired of jouncing over broken planks and wash-outs. One day he refused to pay toll, and when the gate-keeper refused to let him pass took an ax from his buggy, cut down the gate, and went on. The lawyer got away with his high-handed action because the road company feared to sue him lest he hale it into court for not living up to the terms of its charter, which provided that it must keep the road in repair.

As a matter of fact, the proponents of plank roads were overly optimistic. The stress of heavy traffic and most of all, decay, made repairs continually necessary, and if they were not made the users and their horses were seriously endangered. In the end it was found that a complete rebuilding was necessary at least once in five years, and, since reasonable tolls from the aver-age road's traffic could not meet this strain, the planks rapidly vanished and the roads were consigned to their primeval mud or were macadamized.

III

THE enterprise of Robert Fulton and Henry Shreve had settled for three-quarters of a century one aspect of Pittsburgh's busi-ness activity. The steamboat as a means of transportation was to outlast the Conestoga wagon and the canal, to rival the rail-road for a generation, and even to stage a revival in the age of the airplane.

The Monongahela wharf was the favorite landing place of steamboat captains almost to the time of the Civil War, and the commission merchants and their warehouses were largely grouped there. During the weeks following a rise in the river the cobblestoned wharf became a scene of intense activity. Boxes, bales, barrels, and other freight were piled six feet high on the bank and in front of the stores on Water Street, some-times for the greater part of the mile from Try Street to the Point. The low two-wheeled, one-horse drays then in use clat-tered over the cobblestones, and long cues of negro "mudsills" droned their minor refrains while they carried boxes and barrels to or from the waiting steamboats. At one such time as this in

1857 a visitor counted 124 steamboats lined up along the Monongahela wharf. It was nothing unusual for thirty steamboats to arrive in a day, and in the decade before the Civil War arrivals were averaging close to three thousand a year.

Packet lines were operating at one time or another to Brownsville and to all the Ohio River cities, and an unsuccessful attempt was even made to open a steamboat service up the shallow Allegheny to Olean, New York. The steamboats of that day were not like the present-day grimy tramps and the antiquated excursion boats. The favored packets were up-to-date luxury liners of the inland waters, scrupulously overhauled and repainted every season, and furnished with pier glasses, rosewood and mahogany furniture, and carpets with piles so deep that passengers might well have thought that they were walking on bearskins. Their menus and wine lists would have delighted an epicurean and the service was consciously modeled upon that of the best metropolitan hotels.

In only one particular did the steamboats fall short—one could never depend upon them to depart at the times advertised —at least not in the early years. Captains universally strove to entice passengers and freight by announcing an early departure, then delayed for days while they and their agents attempted to drum up more business. It was not until the 1840's that the lines were sufficiently well organized to justify a boat's departing at a specified time and leaving some business to the next boat. By then the lines maintained a common wharf boat and agent, though the various steamboats did not necessarily charge the same rates. Sometimes boats agreed to "load in turn," that is, a boat loaded goods for only one port, such as Louisville, and left the Cincinnati freight for another boat.

From 1811 steamboat building was one of Pittsburgh's most important industries, and it is probable that about half the western boats built were constructed in Pittsburgh yards. The firm of Robinson and Minis had the distinction of building at their Washington works the first large iron steamboat. It was launched in September, 1839, and christened the "Valley Forge." To the astonishment of the uninitiated it did not sink but rode the water as well as a wooden boat; moreover, it was lighter in draft, and was impervious to the thrusts of hidden rocks and snags. The venture was the beginning of a great industry. Pittsburgh yards in 1840 alone constructed about one hundred iron boats, most of them for use on canals. Ocean vessels of iron were soon being constructed; an account of the United States iron bark "Allegheny," launched at Pittsburgh in February, 1847, states that it was an object of intense interest to the naval officers of all nations stationed at Rio de Janeiro.

Theoretically the rivers were open to navigation during a long spring season and a short fall season, and they were closed by low water in the summer and by low water or ice in the winter. Actually the seasons were not always as regular as shippers and steamboat men could have wished. Navigation was so dependent upon the depth of the rivers that an unusual drought or a severe winter sometimes worked hardships upon the dwellers along the shores. At one time in 1857 the cotton mills of Allegheny were forced to close because they could not obtain cotton from the South, and the poor of Cincinnati and Louisville suffered during the winters because the closing of the river by ice forced the price of coal beyond their means. In September, 1854, the mayors of Pittsburgh and Allegheny appointed a day of fasting and prayer to obtain the "withdrawal of the divine displeasure" that had brought on a severe drought. It was in such times as this that the keel boats crept out of their refuges on the smaller streams and reaped a harvest by transporting goods at high rates on the Ohio.

It was inevitable that such conditions should lead to river improvements. As early as 1824 state commissioners were appointed to clear obstacles from the Ohio and the unusual freedom from accident of the keel boats that summer was credited to their work. The legislature's authorization in 1817 of a company to improve the navigation of the Monongahela River came to nothing, though the state did undertake to remove some obstructions. In 1836, however, the Monongahela Navigation Company was formed, and state aid was granted in a proposed program of building dams and locks. The work progressed slowly because of financial stringency, and it was not until after the management was taken over in 1843 by a group of Pittsburghers headed by James K. Moorhead that the project was completed to Brownsville. The value of the slackwater system can be gauged by the increase within ten years from three million to fifteen million bushels of coal shipped from the Monongahela, and in the considerable reduction in the price of that commodity downstream.

River traffic, however, was not confined to the steamboats and keel boats. It was calculated in 1838 that one hundred million feet of lumber annually, exclusive of logs, joists, shingles, and lath, was finding its way down the Allegheny to be used in Pittsburgh or sent on down the Ohio. Hundreds of flatboats left the vicinity of Pittsburgh every year laden with agricultural products, manufactured goods, or coal. Shipping coal in flatboats was expensive, because it required the services of a crew of several men for each pair of boats, but in the 1840's steam towboats that could push several flats were constructed and put into use. As time went on the skill of the towboat men increased until they were able to handle in one trip as many as sixty of their unwieldy parasites. The stern-wheel steamboat was best for towing purposes, and the pilots of such craft developed great facility in maneuvering in narrow waters. Trips were made regularly to Cincinnati, Louisville, and New Orleans after 1854. Large wooden or iron barges came into use, and by 1858 they were carrying down the Ohio almost twenty-five million bushels of coal annually.

IV

IT WAS not until 1834, when the Pennsylvania Canal system was completed at the state's expense, that Pittsburgh found a fairly satisfactory answer to Wheeling's challenge. The canal system was built at a time when the success of the railroad was already foreshadowed, and the new route was actually a combination of canal and railroad. The Columbia Railroad was utilized from Philadelphia to the Susquehanna, where it joined the eastern division of the canal which extended to Hollidaysburg. From that point the Portage Railroad crossed the Allegheny Mountains to Johnstown by means of ten inclined planes up which stationary engines with cables hauled little passenger cars or freight cars bearing sections of canal boats. The western division of the canal extended from Johnstown to Pittsburgh. The new transport system was not a complete success. The first cost, because of the graft involved, had been enormous, and the canal often suffered from breaks caused by floods or faulty construction. It did, however, do a vast volume of business. During its first year of operation the Portage Railroad carried twenty thousand passengers and fifty thousand tons of freight, and traffic increased until private railroads were developed to the point where they could compete favorably.

The construction of the canal cheered western Pennsylvanians and renewed their faith in the great destiny of their region. In 1831 Neville B. Craig, the editor of the *Gazette*, exhibited a map showing Pittsburgh with a great system of already built or proposed roads, canals, and railways radiating from it, and this project was known far and wide as "Craig's Spider." As time went on Craig's dream, or something very much like it, was realized. A canal was constructed from Beaver to Erie, and with its completion in 1844 half a dozen steamers daily plied the river between Pittsburgh and Beaver as contrasted to the one boat only a few years before. The Cross Cut Canal connected the Beaver and Lake Erie Canal with the canal system of Ohio and drew more commerce to Pittsburgh. The railroad era continued the movement of diverting trade to Pittsburgh until today the city, while it can no longer boast of being *the* "Gateway to the West," can claim to be on one of the great intersectional trade arteries of the nation.

The Pennsylvania Canal entered Allegheny City on the line now occupied by the Fort Wayne Railroad and continued west to Cremo Street, where there was a basin surrounded by commission houses and from which a branch extended down to the Allegheny River. The main line of the canal crossed the Allegheny River over a leaky wooden aqueduct and followed what is now Eleventh Street to Liberty Avenue (there were bridges over it at Penn and Liberty Avenues). Thence it followed Grant Street to Seventh Avenue (where there was another bridge over it); thence it turned and passed beneath Grant's Hill almost on the line of Tunnel Street, emerging a little north of the present Fifth Avenue, then known as Watson's Road. From there the canal followed the old course of Suke's Run and Try Street, now occupied by the Panhandle Division of the Pennsylvania Railroad, to the Monongahela River. The tunnel had been dug and lined with masonry at great expense with the object of effecting a union with the Chesapeake and Ohio Canal, but in the end the expenditure proved to have been useless, for the latter never even crossed the mountains. The tunnel fell into disuse and was seldom visited save by rats and adventurous boys, until the mouths were finally closed and the cavern left to the stalagmites and stalactites. About the only good ever accomplished by the tunnel was that the dirt taken from it enabled the city to fill up that old eyesore at the foot of Grant's Hill, Hogg's Pond.

The chief center of canal activity in Pittsburgh was at the basins between Penn and Liberty Avenues, just below the present Pennsylvania Union Station. About the docks of these odoriferous havens of bilge water gathered the offices and warehouses of those whose business was the handling of goods that traveled by the "raging canawl," and nearby there sprang up a multitude of hotels, rooming houses, and laboring men's homes. The volume of business transacted there may be judged by the fact that in six weeks during the spring of 1839 there were over fourteen hundred canal boats arriving and departing that carried a total freight of twenty-five thousand tons. There were at the time 121 boats plying between Pittsburgh and Johnstown, and their crews numbered between eight and nine hundred persons. There were at the time thirteen lines of boats, each with daily departures for Johnstown. The three leading men in the business of canal transportation were Samuel M. Kier, Benjamin F. Jones, and William Thaw; they all became prominent later—in oil refining, in steel manufacturing, and in railroads, respectively.

In 1842 the canal transport lines formed a combination to

raise freight rates, but the public clamor was so great that they were prosecuted and fined; their officers received prison sentences. The resentment against the high-handed tactics of the lines was probably owing to the fact that labor unions were being suppressed in western Pennsylvania and to the failure of the canal to wean away much of the business of the Erie Canal. As a matter of fact, the Pennsylvania Canal was not paying its way, and it probably never could have repaid the immense sum of close to twenty-five million dollars that had disappeared into the pockets of contractors and politicians. The United States Bank of Pennsylvania had been forced by the terms of its charter to handle the financing of the public works, and had crashed in 1841, as a result of the strain on its resources and the pressure of the panic of 1837. A strong sentiment grew up in favor of selling the canal and the Portage Railroad, but obviously there could be no takers for such a lemon. The system limped along under state management until finally in 1857 the officers of the Pennsylvania Railroad purchased it for seven and a half million dollars in order to remove the weak competition it offered.

v

It was evident to the observant that canals did not solve the transportation problem any more than did turnpikes or steamboats, but that the world still awaited a means of transportation that combined cheapness and speed and that was practical in all kinds of weather. Public interest in railroads was evident from the first and in 1825 the *Gazette* published a quarter-page picture and diagram of a "Locomotive Steam Engine." Five years later a railroad car was exhibited in Pittsburgh. Even the ladies flocked to see "this neat and ingenious structure"—perhaps because half the proceeds were to be given to the Female Benevolent Society. In 1839 Editor Craig of the *Gazette* discussed the feasibility of a railroad from Pittsburgh to New Orleans, though he prefaced his article with an apology for arousing horse-laughs by his suggestion.

In 1828, before the completion of the Pennsylvania canal system, the Baltimore and Ohio Railroad had obtained from the

Pennsylvania legislature a charter giving it fifteen years to extend its line to Pittsburgh. By 1842 the railroad had reached Cumberland, and it appeared to be only a matter of a few years before it would advance into western Pennsylvania and drain the business of the section away from Philadelphia to Baltimore. In 1837 a group of Pittsburghers headed by William Larimer and William Robinson had been granted a charter for a railroad from Pittsburgh to Connellsville. The Baltimore and Ohio's Pennsylvania charter lapsed in 1843, but it was discovered that, concealed in an act for the "Relief of the Overseers of the Poor" in Erie County, the legislature had granted the Pittsburgh and Connellsville Railroad the right to extend its tracks southward. To the jaundiced eyes of patriotic eastern Pennsylvanians, and especially those from Philadelphia, this looked like a clever move on the part of the Maryland railroad. The Pittsburgh and Connellsville officials, however, demanded such an exorbitant sum from the Baltimore and Ohio that the latter decided to try to get another charter from the Pennsylvania legislature.

The session of the Pennsylvania General Assembly held in 1846 was confronted with the necessity of choosing between renewing the charter of the Baltimore and Ohio Railroad and authorizing a new home-owned corporation, the Pennsylvania Railroad. Pittsburgh and the western end of the state were almost violently in favor of the Baltimore and Ohio and asserted that the proposed alternative was merely a shadow created to please them but with no likelihood of solid realization. Western feeling ran high and there were even threats heard of a secession from Pennsylvania if the favored bill were defeated. In the end both railroads were authorized, but it was stipulated that if the Pennsylvania met certain conditions, among them the subscription of three million dollars in stock, by July 30, 1847, then the rival Maryland company should lose its charter.

To the surprise of the public the Pennsylvania Railroad met the conditions promptly, thanks to some earnest dabbling in Philadelphia politics and a consequent subscription by the city councils of four million dollars in stock. The next year Allegheny County hopped on the band wagon to the tune of a million dollars. Western Pennsylvania was enthusiastic in its support of the home company, and the Pittsburgh and Connellsville Railroad continued to refuse to allow the Baltimore and Ohio to use its charter save on unreasonable terms. The result was that the latter chose Wheeling as its terminus and swerved around the southwestern corner of Pennsylvania to attain its objective. Already the Baltimore and Ohio had its eyes fixed on Cincinnati and St. Louis, however, and it was not long before its main line was changed to reach the Ohio at Parkersburg.

The Pennsylvania Railroad was opened to through traffic between Philadelphia and Pittsburgh on November 29, 1852, though the Columbia and Portage railroads had to be used part of the distance. Two years later, with the completion of the mountain division, the Pennsylvania's own trains covered the entire three hundred miles thrice daily each way, requiring from thirteen to seventeen hours for the journey.

The completion of the Pennsylvania Railroad between Philadelphia and Pittsburgh was the climax of a dramatic struggle, but there were other victories as other railroads were pushed farther and farther to the west and north. The Fort Wayne Railroad, then known as the Ohio and Pennsylvania, was the first railroad to run locomotives out of Pittsburgh. On July 30, 1851, it was opened as far as New Brighton with a celebration and an excursion of political and industrial bigwigs. A few months later connection was made with the Cleveland and Cincinnati Railroad and rail transportation between Pittsburgh and Cleveland was instituted. The Allegheny Valley Railroad was opened in 1856 and the Panhandle in 1865. In 1871 the Pittsburgh and Connellsville connected with the Baltimore and Ohio at Cumberland; in 1879 the Pittsburgh and Lake Erie was opened; and, last of all, in 1904 the Wabash, that child of adversity, found its way into the city.

Telegraphic communication was established with the East six years before the Pennsylvania Railroad ran its first train through from Philadelphia to Pittsburgh. The first telegraph line was strung into the city by the Atlantic and Ohio Telegraph Company, sometimes known in Pittsburgh as the O'Reilly Line from

Henry O'Reilly, the promoter. The first message was sent from Pittsburgh, December 29, 1846, by Adjutant General Bowman of the Pennsylvania Militia and was a report to President Polk that the Second Pennsylvania Regiment was nearly ready to leave for Mexico.

The lines were extended west and north within the following two or three years. There were as many jokes told about the telegraph in those days as there were later told about the flivver. One newspaper twitted the editor of another paper for having climbed one of the neat white telegraph poles "each surmounted by a gilded ball" and having put his ear to the wire in an effort to solve the mystery of the "magnetic telegraph." The *Post* was the first Pittsburgh newspaper to utilize the telegraph, when in 1847 it began publishing each morning a column of dispatches captioned, "Received by Lightning, Printed by Steam."

VI

THE extension of railroads met with opposition not only from the farmers, who thought that they would do away with horses and feed crops, but from many substantial citizens of Pittsburgh who resented the manner in which the public thoroughfares were appropriated by the new masters of transportation. The first depot of the Pennsylvania Railroad was in an old white-lead factory at the northwest corner of Liberty Avenue and Twelfth Street. After the canal was abandoned and filled up with the earth from basements and railroad cuts the line was extended another block, and a new station was erected near the site of the present Union Station—a shanty town of saloons and tenements was razed to make room for it.

It is an interesting commentary upon railroad rivalry that the locomotives of the Allegheny Valley Railroad were not allowed any farther west than Seventeenth Street and the company was forced to use horses to drag its cars to the station at Pike and Eleventh. When in 1854 the Pennsylvania Railroad planned to run a spur down Liberty Avenue to a freight depot at the Point in order to be able to transship to steamboats, however, draymen and public-spirited citizens alike objected, and some of the latter went so far as to dig up the rails in protest. The railroad, just the same, had its way and soon the unwary citizen who had been used to crossing Liberty Avenue in peace learned to listen for the dinner bell, which in the vigorous fist of a brakeman always warned that a train was coming.

It was seen from the first that a connection between the Pennsylvania and the Fort Wayne railroads would provide a convenient through route and would obviate the necessity of transferring passengers and freight from one station to the other. The roads came to an agreement and the Pennsylvania furnished the capital to build a bridge across the Allegheny. The bridge was completed in 1856, but the connection was delayed for two years by the objections of draymen and certain other citizens to allowing the track to be laid across Penn Avenue. The dispute was finally settled in 1858 and unbroken steel bands bound Pittsburgh with the East and West.

The popular hysteria for railroad building in the 1850's had resulted in the exchange of six per cent bonds by Pittsburgh and Allegheny County for railroad eight per cent bonds to the sum of five and a half million dollars. It was expected, of course, that interest payments made by the railroads would enable the city and county to meet their obligations and to have a sizable profit left over, as well as be enabled to enjoy the benefits of the railroads. The panic of 1857, however, interfered with the regularity of the railroad's payments, and the chicanery of certain railroad officials in exchanging the city and county bonds for equipment at a low rate did much to alienate public confidence. When in 1857 the Allegheny County commissioners levied a four-mill tax to enable them to meet the county's indebtedness there was great public indignation. An anti-tax mass meeting was held in Lafayette Hall and a committee, headed by Thomas Williams, a lawyer, was appointed to find a way out of the difficulty. The result was that a policy of repudiation was recommended and new county commissioners pledged to such a course were elected by the people that fall.

The commissioners who took office in January, 1858, were faithful to their pledges and before long were served with a mandamus requiring them to provide for payment. The case was carried through to the state supreme court, which decided for the bondholders, though one justice held that had the constitutionality of the original subscriptions to the railroads been open to decision the court would have been obliged to declare them void. On the strength of this opinion and by the advice of Thomas Williams, the commissioners flouted the mandamus and were thereupon fined and committed to jail. There two of them remained for more than a year with nothing to do but watch the new prison sundial until in May, 1861, the county paid their fines. Two years later the bonds were refunded at lower interest. The last of the old railroad debt was paid off in 1913.

XVI
Civic Pittsburgh, 1816-1860

BY 1816 Pittsburgh had so far outgrown the provisions of the
borough charter that, just as a parent fits his growing son with a
larger suit of clothes, the state legislature formulated and passed
a bill incorporating as a city "The Mayor, Aldermen and Citizens of Pittsburgh." This measure, signed by Governor Simon
Snyder on March 18, set up a city government that consisted
of a mayor, select and common councils, a recorder, and twelve
aldermen. The select council consisted of nine members, and the
common council of fifteen; both were elected by popular vote,
and were to enact ordinances for the government of the city and
to elect the mayor and the other executive officers. The governor
appointed the recorder and the twelve aldermen, and the mayor
was to be elected annually from among the latter.

It is probable that the burden that devolved upon the county
court as the result of the growth of Pittsburgh was one of the
reasons for passing the city charter. At any rate the mayor's
court was created, consisting of the recorder and the aldermen,
and they were authorized to try any cases formerly handled by
the Court of Quarter Sessions of the Peace as well as any viola-
tions of the city ordinances. The mayor and the aldermen were
separately to have the powers of justices of the peace, and it was

also the duty of the mayor to draw warrants for expenditures and to issue licenses to draymen and tavern-keepers and permits for theatrical entertainments. Ebenezer Denny, a prominent merchant and a veteran of the Revolution and the Indian wars, was the first mayor of Pittsburgh.

In 1833 the charter was changed so that the mayor was elected by the people, and each ward chose three select and five common councilmen. In 1839, as a part of the general reorganization of courts, the mayor's court was abolished (except probably for certain minor functions) and in 1848 it was provided that each ward should elect only two selectmen and a proportion, based on its taxables, of a common council limited to thirty members. Beginning with 1858 the mayor, treasurer, and controller were elected by popular vote for two-year terms.

In 1816 the city had been divided into two wards, but these were further divided in 1829 into four: West, or Point Ward; South, or Monongahela Ward; East, or Grant Ward; and North, or Allegheny Ward. In 1837 the names were changed respectively to First, Second, Third, and Fourth, and Bayardstown was added as the Fifth Ward. Thereafter there was a steady stream of new wards created as portions were taken into the city from Pitt Township on the east, until in 1868 Lawrenceville and Pitt, Peebles, Oakland, Collins, and Liberty townships were annexed, and the city moved the eastern boundary of the metropolis to about the position it now occupies.

II

"PITTSBURGH is without exception, the blackest place which I ever saw," wrote Anthony Trollope. "Nothing can be more picturesque than the site.... Even the filth and wondrous blackness of the place are picturesque when looked down upon from above. The tops of the churches are visible and some of the larger buildings may be partially traced through the thick brown settled smoke. But the city itself is buried in a dense cloud. I was never more in love with smoke and dirt than when I stood here and watched the darkness of night close in upon the floating soot which hovered over the house-tops of the city."

Visitors like Trollope were able to appreciate the unrivaled grandeur of Pittsburgh's situation, which offset for them the palpable civic backwardness of the place, but the more forward-looking citizens who had to live there were not so easily consoled by the view from Coal Hill. They complained that, in what should have been broad daylight, the judges sometimes had to read their charges by candlelight, so thick was the atmosphere; they criticized the helter-skelter architecture of the place, with "demure looking" cottages nestling beside imposing structures whose cornices were so cumbrous that they looked like "an individual with a brick in his hat"; many streets were seas of polluted mud where hogs and dogs ran wild, and one newspaper editor said that he would advocate proposals for the construction of a suspension bridge across a certain street were it not that the mud was too deep to find firm foundations for the piers; even the pigs were said to resent the unreasonable quantities of mud in those areas "humorously termed streets by the wag of a Street Commissioner," and when they stuck fast they squealed, like other irate citizens, "Where's the Street Commissioner?"; building constructors, auctioneers, livestock salesmen, merchants, and draymen used the streets and sidewalks as parking places, to the great inconvenience of passers-by; sewers were left open and cellarways were built without covers, so that the unwary were subject to hazard of life and limb, especially in the years before the streets were lighted.

The animal life of Pittsburgh's streets was a never ending source of wonder. Hogs, dogs, and rats found them a paradise until at least 1860. The attacks of savage porkers upon children in 1850 and 1851 finally stirred the authorities to take some measures to enforce the long-standing law against hogs running free. A pound was set up and a reward of one dollar was paid for each hog brought in, much to the delight of the street urchins, who found it an entrancing mode of earning pocket money. These drives were put on at intervals throughout the decade whenever the owners became careless, and as late as 1860 thirty-nine hogs were impounded in one day.

It is probable that some of the unpleasant features of Pittsburgh life owed their persistence to the parsimony of the tax-payers, but improvements were being made continually. Grant's Hill was cut down, and the Point section raised perhaps as much as twelve feet. Virgin Alley was widened in spite of the protests of a coterie of old-timers who felt that it was a desecration to move even a part of the old burying ground next to the First Presbyterian Church. Diamond Alley was widened and its name was changed to Diamond Street. Another fault of the Woods plan of Pittsburgh was remedied in 1836 and 1837 when Duquesne Way was laid out next to the Allegheny River. It was along this new street that Mayor McClintock proposed that the city set out trees and plant shrubs and grass, but in spite of several years of agitation the project failed to materialize. Pittsburgh had to wait about half a century for its first park. The city did undertake one improvement, however, when about 1837 it began numbering the houses.

Street paving with cobblestones was the answer of the city fathers to the complaints of the citizens about mud. This did make it possible to scrape the streets more efficiently or to flush them with water but it did nothing to prevent noise. In 1837 a pavement of wooden blocks was laid on St. Clair Street (now Sixth Street), but the first flood caused the blocks to swell and burst from their anchorages. The chastened city engineers then went back to the old reliable cobblestones.

III

PITTSBURGH's progress in the way of erecting bridges and commodious public buildings and in providing public utilities was striking. In 1842 a new county courthouse was completed on Grant's Hill. It was a huge rectangular building of gray sandstone with a massive central dome and with an impressive double row of Doric columns on the side facing the city. The designer was John Chislett, who was also the designer and landscape architect for the new Allegheny Cemetery that was begun in Lawrenceville in 1844. The old courthouse was converted into a market house and continued in use until it was torn down in 1852 to make way for a new city hall and market. The next year a new federal building, containing the post office and custom-house, was completed on the northwest corner of Fifth Avenue and Smithfield Street.

The facilities in Pittsburgh for public gatherings were very poor until 1840. Philo Hall, located over the post office on Third Avenue, was the first hall considered worthy of a name, and for years it had to serve in lieu of a better. During the next two decades additional concert and lecture rooms were built or adapted from lofts over saloons or stores. In 1851 Masonic Hall was erected on the north side of Fifth Avenue above Wood Street, and one of the first functions held in it was a recital by Jenny Lind; it remained in use until it burned in 1887. Lafayette Hall, chiefly noted because the first Republican national convention was held there, was an L-shaped building that opened on both Wood Street and Fourth Avenue a few feet from the southwest corner. In later years the hall was used for minor receptions and public dances and it finally gathered a reputation as a low resort. It was torn down in 1895.

Pittsburgh's hills and rivers have made it a city of bridges. The first bridge was a covered wooden structure across the Monongahela River at Smithfield Street completed in 1818 and opened to the accompaniment of cannon salutes and the drums and fifes of the swank military companies. The bridge gave good service until 1832, when a sinking pier caused two arches on the Pittsburgh side to fall. It was completely destroyed in the great fire of 1845 and was replaced by a wire suspension bridge built by John A. Roebling.

The first bridge across the Allegheny River was completed in 1819 between St. Clair and Federal Streets and opened with a banquet served at a table that reached almost from shore to shore. It was replaced in 1860 by a suspension bridge. The bridge built at Hand Street (now Ninth) was completed in 1839. The roof of the bridge was surmounted by a promenade which was for a time a fashionable resort, but finally had to be closed because of its popularity with questionable characters. This bridge was connected with one of Pittsburgh's best known practical jokes. In the summer of 1846 it was advertised that M. Anser would at a certain day and hour fly from the top of the bridge. At the appointed time the shores of the river were crowded with people who had come to see the exploit. Finally a man in a long black cloak appeared on the promenade and sauntered toward the center. There he paused for a moment, then threw back his cloak, produced a big gray goose, and tossed it into the air. Those who knew a little Latin saw at once how they had been sold and explained to their fellows that M. Anser had indeed flown.

Other bridges were erected from time to time. The Mechanic's Bridge at Sixteenth Street was opened in 1838, burned in 1851, rebuilt, torn out by the flood of 1865, and built again. The canal aqueduct at Eleventh Street was completed in 1834 and was replaced by a suspension aqueduct in 1845, said to have been the first of its kind in the world. Another bridge spanned the Allegheny at Sharpsburg in 1856. Pittsburgh's bridges were paid for and maintained by tolls, but during the eighteen-fifties there was a growing sentiment in favor of free bridges, and the proponents of the latter delighted to quote a bit of doggerel in derision of the owners:

So long as our globe continues to roll,
So long will our bridges expect to take toll.

IV

BY 1820 the water problem in Pittsburgh had become acute. Lines of people formed in the morning before public and private wells and every morning and evening women and children could be seen wending their ways to the rivers. Many householders kept tanks in their back yards and had them filled by the old men with barrels, on carts or runners, who made a livelihood by selling river water for three cents a tubful or six cents a barrel.

These old men were, of course, the most vigorous opponents of the movement for putting in a city water system, but they lost out when in 1824 an ordinance was passed for the construction of waterworks. The system was completed in 1828 but for some time operated poorly, and householders were strictly limited in the use of their hydrants. The pumping station was at the foot of Cecil's Alley on the Allegheny River, and the reservoir was located at the southwest corner of Fifth and Grant. Both proved far too small to fill the need, and the cutting away of Grant's Hill left the latter so high in the air that new water-works were projected. The new reservoirs were located on Quarry Hill and the pumping station on the bank of the Allegheny at Twelfth Street. The new system was in partial operation by 1842. The first water system in Allegheny was not finished until 1849.

No attempt was made to purify the water before it was piped into the homes of Pittsburgh, and doubtless many continued to use well water for drinking and cooking; even that, in a city where there were as yet no sanitary sewers, was bound to be impure. But city water was at least cheap. Householders paid from three to ten dollars a year, hotels twenty to forty, and factories from fifteen to one hundred and fifty.

Pittsburgh's first street lights seem to have been a few whale-oil lamps put up about 1816, but they were taken down because mischievous boys kept breaking them. The streets then remained dark until about 1830, when oil lamps were once more installed. Already in 1829, however, the curious could see gaslights in Lambdin's Museum, to which the gas was piped from a retort heated over the kitchen stove of a Mr. Bain. There were several false starts made toward supplying the city with gas but they failed because of the public outcry against financial chicanery, so it was not until April, 1837, that hotels, stores, and street lamps were able to use the illuminant. Allegheny's gas system was put into use in 1853 and Birmingham's in 1856 or 1857.

v

THE police protection of Pittsburgh was, until well past the time of the Civil War, tragically inadequate and amusingly antiquated in its organization and methods. The day constables and the night watchmen were kept religiously separate until 1868 and even as late as that there were only about 122 men in both.

When the city was organized in 1816 a high constable and four constables were provided for, in addition to a captain of the watch and twelve watchmen. A watch-house and twelve watch boxes were authorized, though the watchmen were not to occupy them save in "very inclement weather." The watchmen were to call the time and the state of the weather hourly until four o'clock in the morning during spring and summer and until six in other seasons, and a fine of five dollars was laid upon anyone caught mimicking them. The organization had hardly gotten under way, however, before on April 1, 1817, it was abolished as an economy measure.

The night watch was not revived until 1836, when the councils authorized the hiring of a captain, two lieutenants, and sixteen watchmen. They were not uniformed, and the ordinary watchmen received only twenty dollars a month salary. They were armed with clubs with which they not only persuaded wrongdoers to see the right but with which they also signaled to each other by rapping on the pavement. The watchmen were entitled to certain fees when they made arrests and were charged with the care of the street lamps. The watch boxes were intended chiefly as safe lockups for offenders until the officers were ready to take them to "Mount Airy," as the jail on Grant's Hill was called.

The custom of calling the hours was abolished in 1845 but was revived later on the plea that it kept the watchmen awake and enabled the citizens to find them when they were needed. It seems not to have occurred to anyone that thieves also would know better how to avoid them. The usual form of watchmen's cry, depending upon the state of the weather, was "One o'clock and a starlight morning!" or "One o'clock and a cloudy morning!" It was said that a German watchman afforded considerable amusement to the people on his beat by his cry of "Pasht twelve o'glock, and the moon peeps out a coupla times."

There was plenty for constables and watchmen to do. There were the usual crimes incident to a city: burglary, prostitution, and murder; and counterfeiters, pickpockets, and gamblers were occasionally arrested. There was even a crime wave of thievery and incendiarism in 1851. Boys were prone to juvenile delinquency then as now, and gang wars, the robbing of missionary boxes, and attendance upon "free concert saloons" of questionable reputations were among their activities. There was an influx of Europeans after the unsuccessful revolutions of 1848; many of those who found their way to Pittsburgh attempted to impose upon the sympathy of the citizens. Italian beggars became so numerous that in 1857 they were banished from the city. Two years later they were back in full force, however, and assembled to the number of a hundred about a sort of "beggar's court" on Enoch Street kept by one Antonio Baltel. He kept monkeys and "grind organs" that he rented to his followers, always taking in return a goodly share of the money they collected.

VI

PITTSBURGH'S fire protection continued on a volunteer basis until the organization of paid companies in 1870. Legally every citizen was subject to call, and before the installation of a city water system every householder was required to keep a leather fire bucket ready for use. In those days the fire engines were kept supplied with water by a line of bucket men that extended to the nearest well or to the brink of the river. There was a legend among the firemen of later years that at least one woman was always to be found in the bucket line. She was a tall, dark, rawboned individual named Marina Betts who hesitated not to say what she thought of men who failed to do their duty, and if malingerers came within her reach they could expect the contents of a leather bucket in their faces. The older men of the city were organized as fire wardens; they carried long poles and it was their business to form a barricade around rescued goods. Even small boys had their uses as torch bearers to light the firemen's way through the dangerous streets as they pulled their engines along at breakneck speed.

By 1870 Pittsburgh boasted at least a dozen volunteer engine companies and there were probably as many more in Allegheny and on the South Side. Each company had its distinctive color or color combination, and most of them had a series of canine mascots. Jack, the bull terrier of the Niagara Company, not only ran with the engine, but when the Civil War began went with some of the fire laddies to battle, was wounded, captured, and exchanged. Each company kept its engine in a shed located conveniently close to the homes of the members, and it was the pride of the enginemen to keep their machines spotless and in the best of condition. They even carried rags and bits of chamois skin in their pockets to use in wiping away any flecks of sacrilegious dust that might light upon the objects of their affections. Every man and boy kept his oilskin coat and his peaked tin hat in his bedroom ready to don at the first stroke of the alarm bell.

Fire companies always went to fires on the run and always returned to their headquarters on the run, until a number of needless accidents put a stop to the latter practice. The rivalries between companies were so intense that very little excuse was ever needed to start a fight, and there were even times when the fires were forgotten while the engine companies directed their hoses at each other or fought out their differences with fists and stones. Such battles usually stopped suddenly, however, when a constable appeared and began writing down the names of the combatants. On one occasion, when the Allegheny and Eagle companies were returning from a fire and spoiling for a fight, a strapping laddie from the former slipped and fell. A little Eagle man, not five feet in height, leaned over him and shook his fist:

"There," he cried, "you might have known I'd have knocked you down if you looked at me that way."

"You? You knock me down?" cried the big fellow, leaping to his feet. "Why, you little runt, I could eat you for quail on toast and swallow your engine for dessert." The laugh that followed ended the prospect of a fight for that trip.

Houses built of materials as inflammable as were those of Pittsburgh were bound to furnish plenty of work and excitement, but there were many occasions when trifling blazes or false alarms failed to keep the firemen busy. At such times the companies would dash to a low resort near the foot of Virgin Alley (now Oliver Avenue) called the "Crow's Nest" and proceed to deluge it with water, on the principle that even if there were no fire that place at least needed cleaning out. One of the false alarms, long a joke among the townsmen, was sent out when someone saw the aurora borealis and took it for the glare of a fire.

There was one historic occasion in July, 1849, when the firemen of Allegheny refused to aid in extinguishing a blaze in a carpenter shop because the city council had not increased their annual appropriation. They not only refused to allow their own engines to be wheeled from their sheds, but prevented the fire companies of Manchester and Pittsburgh from giving aid. As a result the fire spread to at least thirty-five buildings, including the Presbyterian church, and burned them to the ground. The ringleaders of the mutineers were afterward prosecuted and entirely new fire fighting organizations were formed in Allegheny.

The great annual event in Pittsburgh was the parade of the fire companies. The parade was formed on Liberty Avenue west of Sixth Street and was given a preliminary inspection by the chief engineer—who for twenty years was the popular William Eichbaum, on prosaic days a publisher and postmaster. The firemen appeared in full regalia, marching behind their engines, which were pulled by as many as a dozen profusely decorated horses, each ridden by a boy dressed in company colors. The engines and hose carriages were decked out with flowers or bunting. Sometimes one of the members dressed as an Indian warrior rode upon the engine, while on top of the gallery perched a small girl dressed in Greek robes.

The old hand engines used about 1840 threw streams of water a little over two hundred feet. Shortly after 1850 interest in steam fire engines began to develop and one of them was tested as early as 1856. In 1859 Pittsburgh's oldest company, the Eagle, undertook to design and build a steam engine. The first test was made at night to avoid the ridicule of other companies in case of failure. The engine did indeed prove to be a failure, and spies from other companies who were looking on from darkened doorways and behind fences jeeringly cried, "Take your old steamboat home; she can't squirt." In the end, however, proper alterations were made and Pittsburgh's first steam fire engine was put into successful operation.

VII

DISEASE was almost inevitable in cities with no better sanitary facilities than those that existed before 1860, and Pittsburgh was no exception to the rule. The local newspapers, with an amusing disregard for accuracy, stoutly denied the existence of an epidemic or glossed over its extent, even while the paper's columns were noting deaths from the disease and were printing the calls of the clergy to oppose the full prayer strength of the churches to its spread. For example, in August, 1834, shortly after the *Gazette* had reported forty-four deaths from cholera in the vicinity during the past ten weeks, it proceeded to attribute the good health of the citizens within the city limits to "our coal smoke, pure air, and excellent hydrant water."

There were visitations of the cholera in 1832, 1833, 1834, 1849 1850, 1854, and 1855, and perhaps others as well. In August, 1849, the South Side was hardest hit and for a while Birmingham was almost depopulated as the frightened inhabitants took refuge in the country. Twenty-five were said to have died there in one day. A coal fire or a pitch pot was burning on nearly every street, and a luckless farmer lost a load of hay that he was attempting to deliver when it was set ablaze by one of the fumigating fires. The cholera panic almost banished river travel, and in other places people even refused to accept Pittsburgh scrip lest they take the disease. The cholera epidemic of 1854, however, seems to have been the worst, and the candid *Post* reported that in two weeks of September there were four hundred deaths from the scourge.

The sanitary committee of the earlier years was replaced in 1852 by a board of health and the rudimentary nursing facilities in the city were improved. The epidemic of 1854 was combated by the Howard Association, which was specially organized to meet the emergency. Mercy Hospital had been founded in 1847 by the Catholic Sisters of Mercy and had rendered excellent service during the ensuing cholera epidemics. Passavant Hospital was begun in 1849 under the name of the Pittsburgh Infirmary by the Reverend William Passavant, a native of Zelienople and a great humanitarian whose activities extended to many other regions. In 1851 the federal government opened at Woods Run a marine hospital for the care of rivermen.

The humanitarian institution projected upon the most ambitious scale during those years was the Western Pennsylvania

Hospital, founded in 1853 on a tract of land in Bloomfield donated by the Harmar Dennys and the Schenleys. Impetus to the organization was furnished by a visit in 1844 of Dorothea Dix, a well-known advocate of reform in the care of the sick and insane, as a result of which she severely castigated institutional conditions in Allegheny County. Miss Dix did not limit herself to criticism but threw herself into the legislative fight for reform and was chiefly instrumental in obtaining the funds for the foundation of the insane department of the Western Pennsylvania Hospital at Dixmont in 1859.

Pittsburgh's first home for the care of paupers was located on the south side of Virgin Alley near Wood Street. In 1822 a new home was erected in what is now the North Side, and in 1848 another move was made to Mifflin Township, on the site of Munhall. The Allegheny City poor farm was located on the site of Millvale until 1873.

Quaintly named charitable societies, some of them more or less long-lived, flourished during these years. The Female Benevolent Society, mainly concerned with poor relief, was active around 1820. Twenty years later the Ladies Society for the Encouragement of Indigent Industrious Females was engaged in promoting work for seamstresses. The Irish had their own Erin Benevolent Society around 1820, and the Germans organized for the relief of immigrants of their nationality. The giving of balls and suppers, of course, was a popular method of raising money. Institutional relief was furnished by a House of Refuge for juvenile offenders, opened in 1854, and the Pittsburgh and Allegheny Orphan Asylum, founded in 1832 in Allegheny. Both had been founded with state aid but were maintained and administered by local organizations.

In the too frequently recurring times of financial stringency thousands of indigent citizens were made dependent upon charity. The favorite means of dispensing relief was for ward committees to collect cash, food, clothing, and coal and to distribute them; but individuals and fraternal organizations, as well as churches, also engaged in the work. Soup houses were set up by ladies' organizations, and in less than two weeks in January,

1855, over nineteen thousand people were fed. At least one of the cotton factories in 1839 supplied its former employees with coal and flour. During the same depression the city undertook to furnish the needy with coal. A modern note had been struck as early as 1819, when the editor of the *Mercury* ventured the opinion that it was "better for charitable organizations and corporate bodies to give *Work* to the poor, rather than to support them in idleness."

Pittsburgh boasted a number of businessmen who gave more than the average attention to philanthropy. Perhaps those best known in this way before the Civil War belonged to the foremost glass manufacturing family, the Bakewells. Benjamin Bakewell, the founder of the family, began the tradition of service, and his sons, John Palmer and Thomas, continued it so ably that for years a benevolent enterprise was hardly complete without one of their names on the executive committee.

VIII

ALTHOUGH Pittsburgh's public schools were begun in 1834 it was many a year before the old-fashioned private schools yielded before them. In 1841 a directory named thirty-three "Select Private Schools and Seminaries" in the vicinity, and there were in addition many individuals engaged in tutoring. Many of the schools were very small. Harriet Preble's school, for example, had eight pupils—just enough so that teacher and pupils could each quaintly assume the name of one of the muses. Business training was offered as early as 1833, but the first business school that enjoyed a long life seems to have been Peter Duff's "Mercantile College," which was established in 1840. The Iron City Commercial College was incorporated in 1855.

There were in or near Pittsburgh a number of women's colleges and academies, but the best known was Edgeworth Ladies Seminary at Braddock's Field, and it was probably typical of the group. The institution occupied a large stone house with wings at either end, set in the midst of gardens and orchards; the girls' rooms, white washed and scantily furnished, were on the upper floors, and the recitation and living rooms were on the first floor. The school terms occupied all the year save April and October. The students, about a hundred in number, rose at six o'clock in the morning and, especially if the weather was cold, dashed for the dressing room at top speed. Prayers came at nine o'clock and were followed by classes, dinner at noon, and then more classes until four or five o'clock. During classes the pupils sat at large tables and responded to the random quizzing of the teachers. Wednesday and Saturday afternoons were half holidays and Saturday mornings were devoted to reading the "compositions" of the students, occasions second only to the public examinations given at the close of the terms, when all comers were free to question the classes. The evenings were devoted to study and lights were presumed to be out at ten o'clock, but it may safely be presumed that many a midnight "feed" was indulged in thereafter.

In February, 1819, the Pittsburgh Academy was rechartered as the Western University of Pennsylvania. Its first faculty consisted of four Protestant ministers and a Catholic priest, and the Reverend Robert Bruce was the principal. The buildings at the old location on Third Street were burned in the great fire of 1845 and the school moved to a new building on Duquesne Way. This building, in turn, was burned in 1849, and the university was suspended until 1855, when it was reopened in a third building at Ross and Diamond. The institution had never been very strong financially and suffered considerably when the Civil War, by drawing away its students, set back its enrollment. Through all its adversities, however, the university managed to keep the spark of higher education alive and even began to expand at the close of the war.

As early as 1809 the county commissioners were authorized by the legislature to provide schooling for those unable to afford attendance at private schools, but the social stigma attached to "county scholars" was so pronounced that many did not avail themselves of the opportunity. In 1816 the Adelphi Society was providing free school facilities for the children of the poor and continued to do so for a number of years. At last in 1834, after a merry war between the opponents and the advocates of free schooling, the public schools as the term is now understood were established. A board of education was elected for each Pittsburgh ward and the schools were opened in 1835. Two years later there were over two thousand pupils enrolled, though the attendance was much under that figure—perhaps fortunately, for there were only fourteen teachers. Temporary quarters gave way to permanent buildings during the next few years and the number of scholars increased. In 1855 there were almost six thousand scholars, fourteen male teachers and seventy-three female teachers. In that year a central board of education was established, and Central High School was opened in a building on the site of the present Mellon National Bank. J. L. G. McKown was the first principal; he was succeeded by Philotus Dean, a remarkable educator whose memory is still revered by those who sat under him.

The teaching facilities and methods of the public schools in the early days seem very odd and inadequate today. The boys and girls were taught in separate rooms, often on different floors. The effort to keep them apart even extended to having them enter the building by different doors. Some schools provided separate departments for beginners. The great number of pupils, often well over a hundred, to each teacher necessitated the use of the monitorial system, by which the older pupils taught the younger ones. Each monitor's rank was indicated by a brass badge, which he proudly wore on a massive brass chain around his neck.

William G. Johnston, who attended one of these first public schools, has left an amusing picture of the master. It was nothing unusual for him to appear in the classroom perceptibly off balance from too much liquor. He habitually tilted back in his chair on the high platform, cocked his feet up on his desk, and smoked a cigar while he listened to recitations or watched the monitors at work. On one occasion, when he ran short of cigars, he sent one of the boys out for a fresh supply, with instructions to bring one back lighted; when the lad appeared vigorously puffing the lighted cigar the school master seemed in no wise offended, but transferred the weed to his own mouth and went on with his duties. This master was a strong believer in the educative mission of the rod, and his supply of switches was occasionally renewed by the older boys, who were sent for them to the slopes of Coal Hill across the river. He sometimes administered whole-sale whippings, though the sons of the school directors were always excepted, unless the master happened to be unusually drunk. At the time locofocos, or friction matches, were just coming into use, and the boys delighted in teasing the master by lighting them noisily when his back was turned, and they ceased the prank only after he had engaged in one of his brutal but effective general whippings.

XVII

"The Birmingham of America"

"To this place is the attention directed of every one, who speaks of America and her prospects. To it the emigrant looks; and if he asks, which is the most flourishing town, or where he is the most likely to succeed, in almost any branch he may mention, 'Pittsburgh,' is the answer."

This statement, made by a British traveler in 1818 during the post-war depression when Pittsburgh was industrially at its lowest, speaks volumes for the optimism of the American and of the immigrant who came to these shores. Their confidence was more than justified. Pittsburgh began a phenomenal recovery soon after 1820, and so rapidly did her industries and shops multiply that it would be impossible in this short space to catalogue them, let alone describe their importance to the community and to the expanding West.

The most illuminating guide to Pittsburgh's growth is found in the population statistics and in the summaries of manufactories. In 1820 the city and its suburbs contained only about ten thousand people; in 1860 the metropolitan district boasted close to one hundred thirty thousand. In 1820 there were about eighteen hundred houses in the city; by 1860 they had increased to nearly ten thousand, exclusive of those in the suburbs. The number of industries (many of them handicraft) in 1817 was 54, and the number of manufactories was 259; by 1857 there were about one hundred industries and just under four hundred manufacturing establishments. In 1817 there were said to have been 109 stores; forty years later there were three hundred wholesale and retail establishments, exclusive of drugstores and retail groceries, which may well have doubled the number.

II

THIS phenomenal progress was not the result of steady growth or unbroken prosperity. Two major depressions had intervened, those of 1837 and 1857. Business had been hampered perenially by the scarcity of specie and frightened by the popular clamor for the issuance of scrip and banknotes. The city actually issued scrip in 1837 and 1838 to the value of one hundred thousand dollars, and the county issued a great deal more during the next decade. Business sentiment was expressed through desultory meetings and not through permanent organizations. A board of trade, established in the winter of 1835 and 1836, was intended to arbitrate disputes between business men, to promote coöperation by demonstrating the need for common policies, and to furnish an educational center where the members could obtain the journals and books devoted to their interests. The organization eked out a precarious existence for five or six years and then perished miserably. A newspaper commented in a discouraged tone that "our merchants have no just appreciation of the necessity of coöperation and united action to sustain their common interests and secure their trade against competition from without." An attempt made in 1854 to revive the organization seems to have failed just as completely. Sporadic attempts were made to establish merchandise marts where local manufacturers could exhibit their wares for the convenience of retailers.

The great variety of manufactures carried on has already been mentioned. Iron and metal working, of course, led the list, but there were other industries of almost equal importance. Nearly a score of glass factories in 1856 produced goods to the value of between two and three million dollars annually. As early as 1818

Bakewell and Page furnished for the table of President Monroe a complete set of flint glass, each piece engraved with the arms of the United States. The service was inspected by the editor of a local paper, who stated that he had seldom seen "any samples so perfectly pellucid and free from tint." Seven years later the Franklin Institute distinguished the company by awarding it a medal for producing the finest cut glass. In 1829 the firm became one of the pioneers in the pressed glass industry and began to use the molds first developed in New England. By that time Bakewell's was not simply the most important of the city's glassworks but was the best-known flint glass factory in America —so widely known that for half a century no tourist was thought to have seen Pittsburgh properly unless he had made a pilgrimage through it.

Most of the other glassworks of the city changed owners frequently and did not, like Bakewell's, remain in the same family. There were a few well-known names in Pittsburgh's glass industry, however, among them Frederick Lorenz, who bought out O'Hara's works, and Charles and Christian Ihmsen.

The distillery business never attained the importance in Pittsburgh that it held in the rest of the Monongahela country, and it seems to have disappeared altogether by 1860. There were four such establishments in the city in 1825; one, that of George Sutton, was well known for "the celebrated 'Tuscaloosa,' which is so highly esteemed in the Southern States for its anti-miasmatic and animalculae-destroying qualities, for the mildness with which it insurges the consumer and for the fresh and exhilarated spirits that it gives to those who may have been accidentally rendered obsolete by its power when the returning rays of translucence break upon them . . . Mr. Sutton is now engaged in making a new beverage as a competitor of the 'Tuscaloosa,' to which he has given the inspiring and beautiful name of the 'Pure Rock Water,' or, in the language of the last of the Mohicans, the 'Real Tallyvally Cord.' This is an admirable liquor, blending with the mildness of milk all the sparkling vivacity of champagne. It steals gently upon the senses like music upon the soul and animates the intellect without ever collapsing an idea." With advertising writers grinding out such gems as this it is difficult to understand why the distilling business did not flourish in Pittsburgh.

Pittsburgh's first cotton factory had been founded in 1803 by Samuel Haslam, who carded and spun both cotton and wool. The next year Peter Eltonhead, who had learned cotton textile manufacturing in England, began a more ambitious cotton business; and he was soon followed by others. By 1847 there were seven cotton factories in Allegheny; they employed fourteen hundred hands, mostly young women and boys, and produced a million dollar's worth of goods a year. Eventually, however, labor troubles and competition from other regions hampered Pittsburgh's cotton industry to such an extent that all the mills either shut down or moved elsewhere.

III

PITTSBURGH's iron industry, before 1835, was concerned largely with the manufacture of tools, utensils, and materials for the use of country blacksmiths. No structural iron and little railroad iron was fabricated. As the century wore on, however, the foundries and shops of the city began to displace the blacksmith, and there also grew up a demand for iron for specialized uses. The first complete rolling mill in Pittsburgh was set up in 1818-19. At first blooms were brought from the Juniata district, but by 1830 iron furnaces in the Allegheny and Shenango valleys were furnishing a large part of the materials used by Pittsburgh rolling mills, forges, and foundries. Pig iron also began to supplant blooms, and soon after 1840 the puddling process began to be used in iron manufacture. Coke was produced at Pittsburgh as early as 1813, and though it was slow in finding its way into general use, by 1833 a row of coke ovens at the base of Coal Hill was adding its glare to the night sky of the developing "Birmingham of America." Strangely enough, though Pittsburgh had long since become important in the iron industry, the first blast furnace (since the Anshutz failure in 1794) was only erected in 1859. The furnace was a part of the Clinton Iron Works of Graff, Bennett and Company, located on the South Side midway between the Smithfield Street and Point bridges, and the ores used were brought from the Allegheny Valley, Missouri, and the Lake Superior region. Other furnaces followed in rapid succession.

By the middle of the century Pittsburgh's importance in iron and steel was well established, though it had not yet surpassed that of the East. It possessed twenty-five rolling mills in 1857, and they consumed one hundred forty thousand tons of iron a year. There were sixteen foundries with thirty cupolas and air furnaces with a yearly capacity of forty-four thousand tons. All the iron working establishments together, well over fifty in number, employed close to eight thousand men, made nearly every sort of iron product then fabricated, and valued their output at close to fifteen million dollars a year. Steam engines alone were being produced to the value of nearly a million dollars.

It was inevitable that an industry so well advanced should attempt to control prices and wages by agreement. As early as 1830 five leading iron manufacturers published a common list of prices and terms of sale, and it seems that during the succeeding years it became the custom of the manufacturers from all over western Pennsylvania to meet annually to set prices. The reduction of wages in 1849, which led to serious labor troubles, arose from what one ironmaster frankly acknowledged was an attempt "to break up the small establishments." "The big fish," said he, "are going to swallow up the little ones." In pursuance of such a policy of combination the Western Iron Association was formed in 1862, but it does not appear that it was able to do much toward the elimination of small fry during the boom times of the war. The great age of the monopolies was still in the future.

IV

IT WOULD have been strange if Pittsburgh's industries had been built up without labor disputes, and the record indicates that the city witnessed some of the bitterest of the labor wars that enliven the history of American industry between 1840 and 1860. During that period the newspapers of the city were all but unanimous in support of the employers against the laborers; of the important papers only the intransigent *Post* dared to hold out against the popular stand. Such papers as the *Gazette* pointed out that Pittsburgh's future was in the hands of the manufacturers, that it was to the interest of the community and the worker to encourage manufacturing, and that workingmen who struck for higher wages were only injuring themselves. The *Post*, on the other hand, argued that all that had been accomplished for the workers had been brought about by strikes and urged them to " 'strike' while the iron is hot."

Pittsburgh, according to the *Gazette*, was getting a bad name because of its labor troubles. A number of glassworks that would otherwise have been founded in the city had gone elsewhere, and the cotton mill owners were considering moving. "No wise man," wrote a contributor to the *Gazette*, "will risk his capital in the uncertain and dangerous business of manufacturing in a place where his interests are exposed to increasing newspaper attacks, and himself made an object of continual abuse. . . . Here capitalists are reproached, their business interfered with, violence excited against them, their property hazarded by mobs, and every evil passion stirred up against them." There was much to be said for the attitude of the entrepreneurs. Machinery was high in cost, methods were as yet inefficient (modern concepts of the marginal productivity of labor were then almost unheard of), and cutthroat competition was the order of the day. The easiest way, and perhaps the only one, to meet such competition was to hire cheaper labor and drive it as many hours as possible. The protective tariff was not yet a settled policy but was still the football of opposing economic forces, and its benefits could not be relied upon over long periods of time.

The *Gazette* might have been correct in its statement that Pittsburgh workmen enjoyed two dollars a day and roast beef (as the Whig campaigners of 1840 had promised), but there was another side of the picture. Working hours, as portrayed upon the harplike charts in the factory offices, varied from eleven in winter to as many as fourteen in summer. Even the store clerks worked from twelve to eighteen hours daily, the longer periods on market days and Saturdays. In 1850 the clothing store clerks felt that they had gained a real concession when their employers agreed to close the stores at eight o'clock in the evening, Saturdays excepted, "in order to give their young men time for recreation and improvement." Time was allowed for meals, though one traveler asserted with pardonable exaggeration that such was Pittsburgh's intentness upon money-making that no more than ten minutes was ever given to a meal.

The institution of apprenticeship, to the advantages of which much lip service was still dedicated, had fallen out of use. It was now possible to contract for the services of an entire family during the rush seasons and to employ only the father when work fell off. Child labor had been an accepted factor in American industry ever since Samuel Slater had set up, in 1791, his first cotton mill with a staff of nine, all boys or girls from seven to twelve years of age, and Pittsburgh did not escape the blight. There was, perhaps, some justification for such conditions in the fact that life at best was hard and every available hand was need-ed at work, in the city as well as on the farm; but it is doubtful whether apologists for the system were warranted in asserting that employment in the lint-laden air of the cotton factory was healthful and beneficial because it made paupers self support-ing, kept women from vice, and gave children a necessary train-ing in habits of obedience and industry. These theories, however, were almost universally believed and even the workers, when they campaigned for shorter hours, made their pleas on the ground that they should have more time for "mental and moral cultivation."

Wages ordinarily varied between one and two dollars a day, but the girls in the cotton factories received two dollars and a half a week; and when the "boilers" in the iron mills struck for six dollars, they meant six dollars a week, not six dollars a day. It is conceivable that the girls might have managed to live by pooling their wages with the family income and that the boilers might have supported their families on one dollar for each work-ing day had it not been for the "order" system, whereby they received part or all of their wages in orders on company stores. Company stores then and since, in other parts of the country, have been accused of overcharges and of padding the employees' bills, and from the complaints of Pittsburgh working people against the system it is probable that the abuses existed there. Real estate, perhaps, was not as high as it was in some other cities, but rents were rising, as were the other costs of living. Labor naturally wanted higher wages and proceeded to win them by negotiation or force.

v

WHEN in 1823 the owners of the Phoenix Cotton Factory united with their employees in a Fourth of July dinner, the *Gazette* called attention to "the cordial feeling of sociability with which respectability and rank there united with honest industry and modest worth." Up to that time there had been little labor trouble in Pittsburgh, the celebrated case of the cordwainers in 1815 being the most important exception. It was not long, however, before the harmless educational and social organizations of workingmen gave way to more militant bodies.

The skilled trades, in which it was least possible to use the labor of women and children, were the first to organize and attempt to enforce their demands. The cordwainers' union continued to be active and found strong grounds for complaint against the competition of convict labor in the Western Penitentiary. There were moves on the part of boatmen toward united action, and in 1819 in the case of Shecker and others *vs.* the Geneva Boxer it was decided that they had the right to libel a boat for their wages. The carpenters organized and struck, denouncing "the customary usage of working from sun to sun as bearing too close an affinity to slavery." Waiters, stonecutters, stevedores, coal miners, glass blowers, boatwrights, printers, horseshoers, saddlers, tailors, ironworkers, and cotton-mill workers were at one time or other among those who turned out for higher wages or to prevent their wages from being reduced. All in all, the strikers had a surprising degree of success in attaining their demands.

There was much talk but little action upon the ideal of uniting all labor into a single organization, and in 1850 an attempt to form a workingmen's congress of representatives of all the local unions failed ignominiously after a short history of internal bickering. The foremost demand made collectively by labor was for a ten-hour law, and the vigorous campaign for its passage was met by success in 1848. It was not long, however, before the victory was seen to be as hollow as a gourd, for the law limited the working day to ten hours—except when by special contract the worker agreed to longer hours.

In 1824 the *Gazette* had boasted that the character and conduct of the women employed in the cotton mills "furnish the best evidence, that 'manufactures are not injurious to morals.' " The reaction of the cotton-mill girls of Allegheny to the ten-hour law in 1848, however, was a sad disappointment to those who looked upon factory labor as a wholesome moral influence. The girls had won a preliminary skirmish in 1843, when they had struck in protest against an attempt to lower their wages and had defied public concepts of female decorum by parading the streets with a banner inscribed with the Whig promise of 1840—"Two dollars a day and Roast Beef." Now the factory owners claimed that they could not remain in business on less than the old terms and closed down the factories until the necessary contracts could be made with workers or with the parents or guardians of minors.

The operatives refused to sign the contracts and demanded the old rate of pay for ten hours' work. In vain the owners cajoled and threatened to move their businesses out of the region. The girls stuck to their demands all through the long hot month of July. Several meetings were held in the market place of Allegheny, and were well attended by unsympathetic riffraff who shouted a derisory rhyme at the strikers:

> Cotton bumpers in a pen,
> Never get out till nine or ten;
> When they get out
> They get buttermilk and sauer kraut.

Finally it was announced that the Penn factory on River Avenue between Federal and Sandusky Streets would resume work on July 31. Those operatives who attempted to enter the factory had to run a gantlet of hisses from the waiting crowd, composed of strikers and sympathizers. Toward noon the strikers broke into open disorder, and began stoning the windows as the result, it was said, of some of the crowd being scalded by boiling water thrown upon them from the building. The factory gate and the east door of the building were cut down by axes in the hands of the militant girls and the crowd swarmed in, led by a young Kentucky girl of unusual beauty whose activity in directing the strikers won for her a fleeting notoriety as "The Unknown." The mayor and the sheriff were present but were powerless. When one of the owners attempted to address the girls there was a cry of "Take off your hat," and someone near by did it for him. The carts that had been brought up with provisions for the few who had come to work were overturned and the food appropriated by the strikers; the workers themselves had fled hastily by a back door as the infuriated crowd came in the front.

In the end the riot accomplished little. One of the factories was opened a few days later, and the bell was rung long and loud in the hope that some of the girls would return to work. When no one appeared the owners made an attempt to run the machinery themselves, but gave it up after five hours—an attempt that the *Post* promptly labeled "the five hour system." Eventually, about the end of August, the workers went back to their machines after a compromise by which they took ten to sixteen per cent reductions in return for the ten-hour day. Thirteen of the rioters of both sexes were tried (it was in aid of the prosecution that Edwin M. Stanton won his spurs), and eight of them were sentenced to terms in the penitentiary. Seven of the convicted persons jumped their bail and the eighth was pardoned after serving part of his term. There were sporadic outbreaks after the riots, and the factories were occasionally shut down, the operatives claimed, in attempts to force them to yield some of their hard-won rights.

In February, 1850, the puddlers and boilers in the iron mills struck to prevent the reduction of their wages. At first their meetings and parades were conducted with orderliness, but the importation of strike breakers from the East (who, it was said, were kept behind locked doors to prevent them from hearing the strikers' propaganda) finally led to violence. A mob composed largely of loafers and women invaded several ironworks and did considerable damage, but Mayor Joseph Barker, who was popular among the workers, finally persuaded them to disband. For the first time in Pittsburgh labor history militiamen were called out, though it does not appear that they were actually employed against the strikers. A dozen or so of the rioters were tried in April and six of them, including four women, were fined or imprisoned or both. There were at the time ugly charges that the mill owners had deliberately stirred up the riots, and the strikers registered their opposition to violent methods and asserted that most of those involved in the disturbances had had no connection with them. In the end the strikers were forced to return to work at compromise wages.

VI

THURSDAY, April 10, 1845, was clear and cloudless, with a high wind from the northwest—a perfect day for a fire. In a small yard back of an ice house at the southeast corner of Ferry Street and Second Avenue a washerwoman had kindled an open fire to heat some water, then had carelessly gone away and left it. The wind died down about noon, but the flames leaped against the ice house, and that building caught fire; then speedily several frame houses on Second Avenue were ignited. Next the fire jumped across the narrow avenue to the Globe Cotton Factory of James Woods and soon reduced it to ruins, bringing down also the brick dwelling that stood between the factory and the Third Presbyterian Church near the corner of Ferry and Third.

The volunteer firemen had before this, of course, responded to the alarm in the tower of the endangered church, but the water in the reservoir was low and the efforts of the engines brought nothing but a thin mud and, to make the situation worse, the wind sprang up again. The Eagle Company concentrated upon saving the church, and after a heroic struggle they finally succeeded by cutting away part of the wooden cornice upon the roof of the church. Meanwhile the fire had been rolling up Second and Third Avenues toward Market Street, sending before it showers of flaming embers. On the east side of Market it quickly spread from Diamond Alley (missing the immediate vicinity of the Diamond, however) to the Monongahela and then continued the march uptown, missing only by chance a building here and there. At Smithfield Street the flames began to narrow back to Third and Grant, but they spread again slightly at the factories and tenements of Pipetown. On the bare sides of Boyd's Hill the fire burned itself out.

The Bank of Pittsburgh, on Fourth Avenue between Market and Wood, was reputed to be fireproof, and the cashier confidently locked the cash and books of the bank in the vaults and departed. The fire took the bank in its course and gutted the interior, though it left the walls standing and the vaults intact. Meanwhile the Monongahela water front fell an easy prey to the flames. The warehouses were consumed and even the goods piled high upon the wharf were licked up. The Smithfield Street Bridge, a tinder-dry structure of wood, yielded readily to the flames, and the steamboats at the wharf saved themselves only by dropping down river.

At first it was supposed that the progress of the fire would be arrested and thousands of people gathered to watch it. When it became apparent, however, that little could be done to stop its course the people who lived in its path scattered to save their belongings. Draymen were scarce and much of the furniture piled in the streets was burned, and looters reaped a rich harvest. Fortunately, only two lives were lost during the entire holocaust.

By seven o'clock in the evening the destruction was almost over. Twenty squares in the most valuable part of the city, comprising about fifty-six acres and with nearly a thousand buildings, had been ravaged and twelve thousand people had been rendered homeless. About one-third of the area of the city was in ashes, and approximately two-thirds of its wealth had been destroyed. Among the buildings burned were half a dozen important hotels, including the new Monongahela House, three churches, the Western University, the customhouse, Philo Hall, and the Scotch Hill Market House. The gas works, two glasshouses, and several ironworks were also destroyed or badly damaged. Altogether the loss was conservatively estimated at no less than $2,500,000, and some estimates ran as high as $8,000,000.

For months after the fire homeless families were quartered upon the more fortunate or sheltered in the courthouse and other public buildings and in warehouses. Nearly $250,000 in money poured in from other parts of the city and from all over the country, and food and clothing were placed in generous quantities in the hands of the relief associations. No time was lost in undertaking the business of reconstruction, and though it was years before all signs of the fire were eradicated, yet in the long run the fire proved to have been a blessing because it made way for the construction of modern buildings in an old part of the city and because it drew in a great deal of eastern capital.

There was one other unexpected result of the fire. Dr. David Alter, a physician, chemist, and physicist of Freeport, took a fragment of flint glass from the ruins of Bakewell's glasshouse and ground a prism from it, and it was this prism that led to his discovery of spectrum analysis in 1853.

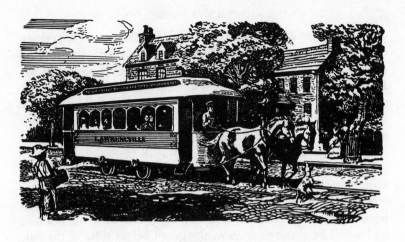

XVIII

The Emergence of a Metropolis

UNTIL about 1840 most of the business activities of Pittsburgh were confined to the triangle bounded by the rivers and Wood Street. Market Street was the hub of the town, and anyone who went beyond Wood was moving to the country. It is said that in the 1840's a storekeeper who had quarreled with his Wood Street landlord moved his business around the corner to Fifth Avenue. There he prospered in spite of the dire prophecies of his friends. Others followed and drew trade after them—one shoeman is claimed to have sold his wares to the blare of a brass band. Hogg's Pond had recently been filled by dirt from the canal and from Grant's Hill, so there was plenty of good building land available. The coming of the Pennsylvania Railroad assured the continued prosperity of the section; recognition of this fact was shown by the erection in 1853 of a new federal customhouse and post office at Fifth and Smithfield on the site of the present Park Building. Already in 1842 the county commissioners, with uncanny prescience of the trend of real estate values, or perhaps only to save expense, had erected a new courthouse on Grant's Hill, and the Roman Catholics built their St. Paul's Cathedral on the northwest corner of Fifth and Grant in 1829.

Grant's Hill, it will be remembered, had been purchased by

James Ross from the tavern-keeper, John Marie, in 1803; there until around 1830 lived the "Nestor of the bar" in the original tavern, which was located on the square bounded by Grant, Ross, Fourth, and High Streets. Below him, toward the Monongahela, developed the section called Scotch Hill, presumably because many Scotsmen lived there, and on the site of the present ramp of the Boulevard of the Allies was a market that sold that cereal dear to the heart of Scotia—real oatmeal.

The progress that had engulfed Grant's Hill was not universally admired. Henry Marie Brackenridge recalled—half seriously, half in humorous vein—the days when the vicinity had been the holiday resort of the townspeople and when he, as a lad, had rolled over and over down the green velvet sides of the hill. "The shallow pond at its base where we used to make our first attempts at skating has been wickedly and wilfully filled up, and is now concealed by brick buildings; the croaking of the town frogs having given place to men more noisy still than they. What is passing strange, as if in mockery of nature, the top of the hill is half covered by an enormous reservoir of water, thrown up there from the Allegheny River by means of steam engines, while the remainder is occupied by a noble cathedral church. What is still more lamentable, the hill itself has been perforated, and a stream [the canal] has been compelled to flow through the passage, at an expense that would have discouraged a Roman emperor. Streets have been cut in its sides, as if there was a great scarcity of ground in this New World: and in time, houses will rise up along them like those of the Cowgate in Edinburgh, thirteen stories on one side and half a story on the other."

Brackenridge's prophecy of a Pittsburgh Cowgate might well have come true had not the city fathers in their wisdom seen fit at various times to cut off layers from the top of the hill just as a housewife peels the layers from an onion. The first cut on "the hump" was probably made before 1837; it left the Roman Catholic cathedral and the water reservoir perched far above the street. Additional cuts were made in 1844 and 1847, and the final one was begun in 1911. Altogether the hill was cut down in some places as much as sixty feet.

II

UNTIL 1830 the valley between Grant's and Boyd's hills marked the southeastern limit of settlement, though there were a few small factories and a boat yard in the valley. During the next decade, however, laborers' cottages and tenements began to spring up along the course of Suke's Run and the Monongahela extension of the canal. The rapid foundation of several manufactories there was responsible for this change. One of the most important of the new entrepreneurs on Suke's Run was an eccentric but popular Englishman familiarly known to everyone as Billy Price, who erected a pipe foundry near Colwell and Stevenson Streets on the eastern border of the settlement. Billy Price himself lived near his foundry in a round house with a chimney in the center. The house was round, explained the irreverent Billy, to keep Old Nick from hiding in the corners. Near the house was an orchard that proved to be a great attraction to the neighborhood boys, so the foundryman trained a parrot to keep watch. When the marauders appeared the parrot would call "Boys in the orchard," and Billy would sally forth with shotgun and rock salt. The official name of the valley was Kensington, but it was better known as Hardscrabble or Pipetown. It was here, in 1817, that the second hanging for murder in Allegheny County was performed, while the curious crowds looked on from the boundary hills.

Suke's Run above Pipetown was not a very savory neighborhood for there resorted some of the butchers whose slaughterhouses had been outlawed in the city. The region as far as the present Dinwiddie Street was known as Riceville, and in the sections where the atmosphere was comparatively pure were located "Hatfield Garden," famous for its beer, and "Social Garden," where the initiated might occasionally witness a bear-baiting.

A little farther out, at Fifth Avenue and Moultrie Street, was the machinery and tool factory of James Tustin, who was said to have built part of the machinery for the steamboat "New Orleans." Tustin was a native of the Soho district of London, hence the name of that section of Pittsburgh. Tustin lived on the hill near Fifth and Brady in a fine stone mansion with elegant grounds overlooking the Monongahela River.

The Tustin grounds are inseparably connected, in the minds of old Pittsburghers, with an eccentric French silk merchant named Claire de Rouaud whose store and home was on Market Street but whose favorite resort on Sundays was the Tustin property. The unreasonable fluctuations in the prices of De Rouaud's merchandise led to whispers that he was connected with smugglers or robbers, but the Frenchman paid no attention to slander, for he numbered the wealthiest women of the city among his oldest and steadiest customers. No matter what the season, De Rouaud invariably wore the same old green straw hat. One time someone bought him a new one and stuffed the old one into the stove; the sudden blaze started a fire in the chimney so that the fire engines had to be called out, no doubt to the great damage of the bolts of silk. After that the old man cooked his meals on the sidewalk.

De Rouaud's inseparable companions were his two spaniels, a black one called Cricket, and a tan one called Busy Bee. When De Rouaud died he was buried on the Tustin grounds and when the spaniels died they were buried near their master, one at his head and one at his feet. Years later, when vandal progress had erased all trace of the graves, George Fleming, a Pittsburgh newspaper man, wrote a fitting epitaph for the old man's faithful companions:

> Patrician dogs who live at ease,
> With troubles naught save active fleas,
> Their "bark" is on some other shore,
> On Soho's heights they sleep no more;
> Long hushed their once lugubrious howl,
> Gone are their master's bones, we see,—
> Farewell then Crick and Busy Bee.

III

THE East Liberty Passenger Railway, opened in 1860, followed Braddock Road, known successively as Watson's Road, the Fourth Street Road, the Farmers' and Mechanics' Turnpike, Pennsylvania Avenue, and Fifth Avenue. With the convenient transportation offered by this line came the suburban developments of Oakland and East Liberty. Oakland takes its name

234

from that of the estate of William Eichbaum, whose surname is the German for "oak tree." It was on the site of the present Montefiore Hospital. Before the Civil War Oakland was the home of a group of wealthy Pittsburghers, so many of whom were members of the Third Presbyterian Church that the section was often called the "Third Church Colony." The Eichbaum house was later enlarged and occupied by John Moorhead, one of the first Pittsburghers to invest in paintings that were not family portraits. The Bidwell (later Porter) home, Oak Manor, afterward the Faculty Club of the university, was on the site of the present new Presbyterian Hospital.

In the eastern part of Oakland were the cow pastures, later known as Schenley Farms, that were to become Pittsburgh's civic center. Beyond these was Bellefield, once the property of Neville Craig of the *Gazette* and named for his wife. Modern Shadyside, Squirrel Hill, and Point Breeze were still pastoral in character, though wealthy townsmen were seeking retreats there in increasing numbers. Swissvale, Hazelwood, and Glenwood were as yet inhabited mainly by country people, though a few coal mines, salt wells, and rural manufactories were being opened. McKeesport, farther up the Monongahela, had been laid out in 1795 but did not prosper outstandingly until the meeting of coal, iron, and railroads set it on the path to becoming the "Tube City."

Wilkinsburg was a thriving village laid out about 1790 by Colonel Dunning McNair and known as McNairstown before it was renamed for Judge William Wilkins. McNair's home was "Dumplin Hall," built about 1790 at the corner of Hay and Kelly Streets and so named because it was built of cobblestones. About 1825 James Kelly became a large landholder in the community and for half a century was the patriarch of the village. He is said to have worn his uncut hair in a queue to the day of his death as the result of losing an election bet. Though he failed financially in his old age, he is gratefully remembered by Wilkinsburg as a benevolent and public-spirited citizen.

East Liberty was a village with a rural charm all its own. It possessed a couple of taverns popular with sleighing and equestrian parties, and a bleak Presbyterian meetinghouse where met:

The Negleys, Aikens, Burchfields, Spahrs,
McClintocks, Baileys, Berrys, Barrs.

The valley in which East Liberty stood was owned largely by
the members of the Negley family, who divided their energies
between farming and running a steam gristmill. Near by lived
a rising lawyer and banker named Thomas Mellon, who had
married one of the Negley girls. His sons were to inherit their
father's business acumen and during the next half century were
to build up one of the greatest family fortunes the world has
ever known.

IV

BEFORE Grant's Hill was cut down it was separated by a narrow
ravine at Seventh Street from what was then called Quarry Hill,
but is now known as Herron Hill or simply the Hill. It is about
two miles long, runs parallel to the Allegheny River, and is back
about a third of a mile from the river. Though it is now quite
thickly populated, before the Civil War Herron Hill boasted only
a few settlements, most of which were crowded upon the western
end, close to the city.

Up to 1812 the neighborhood of the present junction of Wylie
Avenue with Fifth had been occupied by pleasant country homes
surrounded by orchards and gardens. With the eastward advance
of the city, however, bucolic retreats gave way to city progress.
At first the section was the home of many noted residents, but
by 1850 they had yielded to a horde of Irish carters and laborers.
The place became a Democratic stronghold with Duffey's Hotel,
at Webster and Grant, as political and social headquarters. It
is said that no Republican parade dared to go by there, for if it
did battle and inevitable defeat would follow. The place was
popularly known as "The Battery," from one of the fortifications hastily thrown up there in 1863. The uninhabited part of
the Hill, particularly at the points that overlooked Fourteenth
and Seventeenth Streets, was a favorite resort for bear-baiting,
a sport that was indulged in chiefly at Christmas. Here also,
before the Civil War, when the law still called for a general muster of all able-bodied men, were held the military parades that

were the joy of every small boy and that, because of the opportunities for conviviality, were enjoyed even more by the men.

As early as 1850 the region of lower Wylie Avenue was known as Hayti from the great numbers of negroes congregated there. It was realized that their presence caused property to depreciate in value and efforts were made by the owners to force them out. Though the Fugitive Slave Law of 1850 did cause many to go to Canada, the negroes have remained there to the present day.

The property in the vicinity of Webster Avenue and Roberts Street had, during the early years of the century, belonged to Judge Samuel Roberts, the successor of Alexander Addison as president judge of the western circuit. About 1840 a certain Dr. Lacy conducted a young ladies' seminary, and from him the vicinity took the name of Lacyville. Like the region closer to the city, Lacyville fell before the advancing slums, and at the time of the Civil War the name became a byword for wickedness. It was sometimes known as Fort Maloney, probably from another of the Civil War forts.

Farther out, at the end of Wylie Avenue, was the village of Minersville, whose name describes the chief industry of its inhabitants. Wagoners bought close to two hundred loads of coal at the mine heads there daily and sold it to householders and factories in the city. Hard pressed for anything to say about the community, the author of an 1837 directory noted that "here, on the hours of the sacred Sabbath, is to be seen an industrious and moral people, after the labors, toils, and cares of the week, dressed in clean, genteel apparel, attending church, their children the Sabbath school and at night the prayer meeting."

The principal citizen of Minersville was Jacob Ewart and next to him ranked Alexander Brackenridge, the son of the organizer of Allegheny County's democracy. Ewart lived in the columned mansion at the corner of Herron Avenue which was later to be the home of the Montefiore Hospital for many years.

V

THE region bounded by the Allegheny River, Herron Hill, and Eleventh and Twenty-sixth Streets was long known as the Northern Liberties but was named Bayardstown upon its erection into a borough in 1829, and it was called by this name long after it had been admitted to the city in 1837. The town was laid out in 1816 by George Bayard and James Adams, and the first settlers were a number of butchers whose abbatoirs had been recently ousted from the city.

Bayardstown was strategically located to profit by the business first of the canal and then of the Pennsylvania Railroad, and capital was not lacking to seize the opportunity. Three tanneries converted the hides from the slaughterhouses into leather. Breweries were started to quench the thirst of the German immigrants who were flocking into the town, and the big, genial Irish residenters, with Galway slugger whiskers under their jaws from ear to ear, speedily acquired a taste for the Teutonic beverage. Several glassworks, a paper mill, and tobacco and soap factories were erected. Before the Civil War there were at one time or another over a dozen ironworking plants.

Schoenberger's Juniata Iron Works, one of the most important in the city, made a specialty of wire and nails, and bar, boiler, and sheet iron. The founder, John Schoenberger, a German, built a beautiful home in what later became Allegheny Cemetery, after which he moved to lower Penn Avenue. The Sable Iron Works was owned principally by another German, Christopher Zug, a large and stolid man who always dressed like a Quaker and drove the fastest horses in town. At one time his ironworks was blown up in a boiler explosion, and Zug, evidently feeling chastened for his pride, sold all his fast steppers and drove a mule that had worked near the puddling furnaces and had had patches of hair burned from his body.

The Fort Pitt Foundry, successor to the original McClurg Foundry, later Mackintosh-Hemphill Company, engaged in boiler-making and in casting heavy machinery and cannon. The dull boom of the cannon at the proving ground across the Allegheny, where they were pointed at the barren side of Coal Hill, was a familiar sound to Pittsburgh ears. These tests were attended by government ordnance experts, and the company officials always served plenty of whiskey with the lunch. Upon one occasion, when the regular company representatives had to be away, they sent a temperance man to the proving ground and he served buttermilk with the lunch. Several cannon were rejected that day, it is said.

Bayardstown was a twin for toughness with the Hill and the battles of its boys with those of the Hill and Allegheny scandalized upright citizens. The "Bayardstown Rats" did not hesitate to besiege the Hill enemies in their schoolhouse and bombard the windows with stones. The German lads of Allegheny scarcely dared venture on the ice of the river in the winter for the "Rats" outnumbered them and would sometimes shoot at them if they came within range. Nude bathing in the rivers was prohibited by ordinance, but the boys and young men of Bayardstown openly flouted such sumptuary legislation and bathed when and how they pleased. The newspaper editors were particularly outraged by such actions, and one of them wrote ambiguously that "crowds of ladies are constantly passing near them, and though such conduct might be tolerated in Otaheite, it should not be in Pittsburgh."

However, the lads had their uses. When swimming in the river they would bring up cobblestones and sell them to the contractors to use in paving the streets. These streets, in a time when no attempt was made to collect garbage and rubbish, became inordinately filthy. Finally the custom arose of having the aged or otherwise superannuated men of the town hitch themselves to scrapers and clean the streets. From the fact that they worked eight or a dozen abreast they were commonly known as the "Twelve Apostles."

Beyond Bayardstown was the straggling village of Croghansville; above it was Lawrenceville, named for James Lawrence of "Don't give up the ship!" fame. Lawrenceville owed its foundation to the enterprise of a Virginian, William B. Foster, who induced the government to locate its Allegheny Arsenal there and then laid out a village around the arsenal. During the following years a number of factories and a steamboat yard were started there. Its main industry, until after the Civil War, however, was the manufacture and reconditioning of army equipment. The existence of an army post in the village made it one of the most attractive social centers near the city, what with weekly balls, dashing young officers, and a military band.

As early as the summer of 1818 "an elegant hackney coach" was running between Pittsburgh and John Means's tavern in Lawrenceville, but there is no indication that the service outlasted that season. In the 1840's a Mr. Naser was running a hack line over the same route. Each hack, drawn by two horses, seated twelve passengers. The driver collected the fares and blew his bugle lustily at every cross street to apprise prospective passengers of his approach. In 1853 Naser was bought out by the Excelsior Line, which put twelve new omnibuses into commission, running them every five minutes. Each omnibus bore a distinguishing name, and one of them, the "Lady Jane" ungallantly upset at Third and Wood and spilled out several women who were riding. The Excelsior Line also enterprisingly started a new run out Herron Hill to Minersville, but it was not long before the company officials were haled into court and fined for operating on Sunday in contravention of the Sunday observance law of 1794. When the case was carried to the state supreme court that body weightily drew a line between riding on Sunday for necessity and for pleasure and confirmed the prior decision. This setback, however, was not serious enough to prevent a competing line from beginning business, and presently citizens were complaining that the busses of the two lines had a strange tendency to collide whenever they met.

The Pittsburgh-Lawrenceville route was the first in the region to boast a street railway (unless one counts the Pennsylvania Railroad's invasion of Liberty Avenue); in 1859 the Citizens Passenger Railway Company laid rails along Penn Avenue from Sixth Street to Twenty-sixth. Later on the line was extended to Lawrenceville. Business was begun with four cars of a bright straw color, each with its own insignia, a white or black bear, a golden eagle, or a white swan. It was considered a mark of distinction to be a conductor and, according to one chronicler, Alexander Hays, a West Point man who later became a general and was killed in the Civil War, was one of the first.

VI

THE site of Allegheny had been reserved by the state legislature in order that the seat of Allegheny County might be established there; but, as has been seen, Pittsburgh was eventually made the county seat. Early in 1788 David Redick, of Washington, surveyed the reserved tract and laid out a town with a generous allowance for public buildings, cemeteries, and pasture, ground that has since been known as the Commons. Redick was certainly no prophet, for he put on record his opinion that the site was so rough that it would never be good for anything except "to afford a variety of beautiful lunar spots not unworthy the eye of a Philosopher. I cannot think that ten-acre lots on such pits and hills will possably meet with purchasers, unless like a pig in a poke it be kept out of view." Indeed, the present symmetry of the terrain of the lower North Side is a tribute to the industry of the Irish Paddy.

The first white settler on the site of Allegheny seems to have been James Boggs, who built his cabin there in 1760. Boggs was killed by a falling tree and his widow married James Robinson. The Robinsons probably moved from Pittsburgh about 1785, for on December 17 of that year their son William was born —probably the first white child born north of the Allegheny River. Once during James Robinson's absence from home the cabin was attacked by Indians but was ably defended by Mrs. Robinson until help arrived from Pittsburgh. The settler prospered. His cabin was located beside the Franklin Road (now Federal Street), and he kept an inn and ferry for the convenience of travelers to such good purpose that in 1803 he was able to build a brick house on what is now the west side of Federal Street, between General Robinson Street and River Avenue. This house was later enlarged by his son, who occupied it until his death in 1868. William Robinson was for years the leading citizen of Allegheny and in 1840 served as its first mayor. He studied law under James Ross and was active, not simply in the law, but in banking, industry, and politics, and was one of the builders of the Fort Wayne Railroad.

Allegheny did not boom during the early years, although in

1800 the Scott, Denny, and Beelen glassworks was founded, and in 1813 the Irwin ropewalk was transferred from Pittsburgh. In 1822 the Butler Pike was completed, and five years later the Juniata Rolling Mill was started. A cotton mill was built in 1828, and the town, which had about twenty-five hundred inhabitants, was incorporated. A market house was built, two fire engines were purchased, and a paper mill and several more cotton factories were erected. In 1829 the western division of the Pennsylvania Canal reached Allegheny and with its completion in 1834 the town really began to grow. The streets were graded and graveled, the unsightly and inconvenient ravines filled, and the borough was extended east to Sawmill Run (of the Allegheny River), north to Island Lane, and west to Fulton Street. In 1840, with a population of 10,089, it triumphantly became a city. During the next years the streets were cobbled, gas street lights and waterworks were installed, and finally in 1859, the Pittsburgh, Allegheny, and Manchester Railway was built from Pittsburgh across the Allegheny River, through Allegheny, and on into the little borough of Manchester, which had been growing up along the Ohio next to Allegheny City since 1832.

The existence of the Commons, about 102 acres in extent, proved to be both a blessing and a problem. Until 1833 the streets were not demarcated, and the fields were crossed by paths and wheel ruts in every direction. Meanwhile portions of this unsightly stretch, originally intended for pasturage, had been appropriated for various purposes. In 1818 the legislature took ten acres for the Western Penitentiary and by 1826 this castellated structure, built of gray sandstone, was frowning across the Commons. There it remained until the Riverside buildings were put up in 1886. In 1819 the Western University was granted forty acres, and in 1825 a further grant was made to the Presbyterian Church as a site for the Western Theological Seminary. The seminary building was completed on Hogback Hill (now Monument Hill), but it was burned in 1854, and a new building was erected on Ridge Avenue.

Meanwhile individuals had appropriated parts of the Commons and built homes there, and the Presbyterian Church, which had followed suit, managed to have its right to the soil recognized by the predominantly Presbyterian borough council. In 1831, however, when the congregation started to erect a new building on the site of the old, the religious complexion of the council had changed and the work was stopped. The private interlopers were gradually dispossessed, and Allegheny Academy, another "squatting" institution, was taken over by the borough and became the town's first high school.

Allegheny possessed a large German population (at one time it had a German language newspaper), which was congregated largely in the eastern part, known at the time as "Dutch Town." The region bounded by the canal, East Lane, the river, and Chestnut Street was inhabited by Switzers and was popularly referred to as "Schweizer Loch."

Next to Allegheny on the east was Duquesne Borough, which had been formed in 1849 and part of which was merged into Allegheny in 1868. Herr's Island, which occupied the river front near Duquesne, was an idyllic spot that was rapidly giving way to industry. It was said that old Mr. Herr, the owner of the island, had leased it for ninety-nine years at a very cheap rate, and that, when upon reflection he came to regret the act, he asserted roundly that "when that lease expired they shouldn't have it as cheap next time."

The site of Millvale was from 1844 to 1867 partially occupied by the Allegheny City poor farm, though in 1858 two brothers, Andrew and Anthony Kloman, began there a forge that specialized in high-grade axles for use on railway cars and locomotives. It was from this humble beginning that the great Carnegie Steel Company developed. Etna, or Stewartstown, was a flourishing settlement that owed its prosperity to the Etna Rolling Mill and the wrought-iron pipe works of H. S. Spang and Son—now Spang, Chalfant and Company. Sharpsburg, named for its founder, James Sharp, owed its rise first to the fact that it was located near the locks of the canal and then to the Guyasuta Iron Works. It was made a borough in 1841.

The plain now occupied by Aspinwall was before the Civil War the property of James Ross and his heirs, and the town took its name from Ross's granddaughter, Mrs. Aspinwall, the wife of the owner of a transatlantic steamship line. The Ross home, "The Meadows," was a red brick mansion with massive pillars near the present Ross pumping station. Before it burned a few years ago the old mansion was used as a road house.

The bottoms along the Allegheny River were occupied by flourishing farmsteads and villages. Tarentum, on the site of Chartier's Old Town, had as its reigning family the Brackenridges, the descendants of "Auld Hughie" of Whiskey Insurrection fame. Just above Tarentum were the salt-wells of Natrona. Here in 1840 petroleum began to seep into the salt well of Samuel M. Kier, and between his activities as a canal transportation agent and as a salt-refiner Kier began to experiment with the substance. Presently the stuff was put on sale in bottles as medicine and a florid circular advertised "Kier's Petroleum or Rock Oil, Celebrated for Its Wonderful Curative Powers. A Natural Remedy! Procured from a Well in Allegheny Co., Pa. Four Hundred Feet below the Earth's Surface. . . . The Petroleum has been fully tested! It was placed before the public as A Remedy of Wonderful Efficacy. Everyone not acquainted with its virtues doubted its healing qualities. The cry of humbug was raised against it. It had some friends—those who were cured through its wonderful agency. They spoke in its favor. The lame through its instrumentality were made to walk—the blind to see. Those who had suffered for years under the torturing pains of *rheumatism, gout and neuralgia* were restored to health and usefullness."

Kier was not satisfied to remain a vendor of nostrums and presently he had found a way of refining the wonderful substance that "flows from the bosom of the earth" and was selling it as an illuminant to be used in a lamp of his own invention. Kier's lamps and "burning fluid" were practical and cheap, and they were soon finding considerable favor in the region. The market was thrown off balance, however, when a Natrona salt well suddenly began to produce oil instead of salt water, and Kier had to wait for the demand to catch up with the supply. By the time E. L. Drake drilled the first oil well at Titusville, Kier's pioneering had borne fruit, and the world was ready for petroleum.

THE narrow plain on the south side of the Monongahela and Ohio rivers from Sawmill Run to Beck's Run was developed industrially as soon as any section near Pittsburgh but outside of the original borough. Temperanceville (now West End), at the mouth of Sawmill Run, was laid out by Isaac Warden and it got its peculiar name from the fact that the deeds to property sold there stipulated that liquor should never be sold on the premises. There is no record that the agreements were kept, and in fact Temperanceville eventually bore the reputation of having more saloons in proportion to its size than any other place in the county. Its industrial establishments included salt, glass, and plow works, and a rolling mill. It did not, however, become a borough until 1859 and lost this status in 1872, when a blanket act of the legislature swept all the South Side boroughs into the city.

West Pittsburgh, a borough erected in 1853, extended from Temperanceville to a line about one third of the distance from the Point to the Smithfield Street Bridge. There it was that the original Craig and O'Hara glass factory was set up and there, in time, sprang up other factories working with iron and steel. Monongahela Borough, which was erected in 1858 and which extended from West Pittsburgh to the Smithfield Street Bridge, was the home of the Clinton Iron Works, the Sligo Iron Works, the Sligo Glass Works, and the Pittsburgh and Lake Erie Railroad yards. It was orginally known as Sligo. Both Monongahela and West Pittsburgh, though at one time densely populated, are now almost devoid of permanent residents. Even as early as 1850 a few dwellings were beginning to appear above on the top of Coal Hill, now known as Mount Washington, and then called Gray's Gardens or Cowanville, while the hollow that now shelters the Castle Shannon Incline was peopled by a colony of miners. It was probably to this settlement that the name Millersville was applied. The Washington Road ran up the steep side of the hill about on a line with what is now William Street.

From Monongahela to Sixth Street was the borough of South Pittsburgh, set up in 1848, and dependent upon glass- and ironworks. Most of the land from the Smithfield Street Bridge to

Beck's Run had been warranted to John Ormsby before the Revolution and by him had been named "Homestead Farms." This man was an Irishman who had been educated at the University of Dublin, had come to Pittsburgh with General Forbes in 1758, and had kept a store and a ferry for many years. Ormsby left a son, Oliver, who succeeded to his father's business and who was active in the development of the South Side.

Dr. Nathaniel Bedford married John Ormsby's daughter, Jane, and inherited through her a tract of land that included the south bank of the Monongahela from Sixth to Seventeenth Streets. There in 1811 he laid out a town that he called Birmingham for his home in England, and there he lived like an English gentleman during his declining years. In Birmingham, made a borough in 1826, was continued the line of glass factories and ironworks that extended along the river. It was the first of the boroughs in Allegheny County created after Pittsburgh.

East Birmingham, sometimes known as Sidneyville, which extended to Twenty-seventh Street and was made a borough in 1849, possessed more glass- and ironworks. The borough of Ormsby, which extended from Twenty-seventh Street almost to Beck's Run, was not incorporated until 1868.

Before the Civil War several of the daughters of Oliver Ormsby lived in East Birmingham on the family tract of land between Twenty-first and Twenty-fourth Streets, each with her own house and beautiful well-kept gardens extending down to the river. In order, from west to east, they were Josephine Yard, who lived in the family homestead; Sidney Page, whose home was known as "The Dingle"; Sarah Phillips of "The Orchard"; and Mary Phillips of the "White House." Another daughter, Oliveretta Wharton, in later years occupied the Yard mansion. On the hillside above his sisters lived Dr. Oliver Ormsby, the only brother, in "Ormsby Manor," a typical country gentleman's estate with forests, meadows, and private race track. It was from this Oliver Ormsby that the borough of Mount Oliver took its name. Many of the names given to the streets of the South Side boroughs are those of members of the Ormsby families or of their relatives by marriage.

The growth of the South Side boroughs, as has doubtless been gleaned from the foregoing, was largely dependent upon the glass and iron industries. Coal-mining and coke-making were important supplementary industries. By 1853 the Economites had laid the Sawmill Run Railroad to Banksville, a distance of three miles, and their little coal cars were spinning downhill to the tipple on the Monongahela. It was the success of this road that is supposed to have encouraged the Economites to build the Pittsburgh and Lake Erie Railroad. The manufactories of the South Side originally obtained their coal from the hill at their doors, but when those veins were worked out coal was brought from points farther away. As early as 1837 the South Side possessed nine glass factories, seven ironworks, a foundry, and a white lead factory; they employed over nine hundred men, consumed 1,500,000 bushels of coal annually, and produced goods worth $2,500,000. The figures for 1860 are not available but the increase must have been large. At least the South Side had become so important a population center that the Birmingham Passenger Railway was built to afford easy access to the city, and the line was later extended to Mount Oliver.

XIX

Moral and Cultural Advancement

THERE is a story told of an old Scotsman named John Cameron who kept the best vegetable garden in Pittsburgh but who refused to sell produce on Sunday. It seems that General Jackson had stopped in Pittsburgh over the week-end and the landlord of his inn sent to Mr. Cameron on Sunday morning for some fresh vegetables. Cameron refused, and though the landlord came himself and threatened to withdraw his patronage the old man proved obdurate. "Well, let me go into the garden myself, and I will pay you Monday," begged the landlord.

"No!" returned the Scotsman. "It is far better to let General Jackson do without vegetables than to break the Sabbath."

When Cameron was asked, later on, how he managed his hotbeds on Sunday, he answered, "I judge on Saturday night, and raise the sash a little with a corncob for air."

"But were you never mistaken?"

"Oh, yes. One Sabbath morning I knew that frost was coming but I had no right to move the cobs on the Lord's day. The next morning about five hundred dollars worth of plants were frozen." He hesitated for a moment, then went on: "I never spoke of it before; perhaps some would not believe me, but that year I made more money off my garden than any other year of my life."

This spirit of absolute refusal to compromise on moral questions has always been a part of the religious marrow of western Pennsylvania. For more than a hundred years associations to promote the observance of the Sabbath have been strong and at various times have endeavored to "correct certain prevalent abuses"—such as the running of steamboats, canal boats, and trains on Sunday. Missionary work has also had a prominent place in Pittsburgh's church activities. From the very first, money was raised and volunteers were sent to the Indians and to foreign lands. From time to time an endeavor was made among the ministers of the city to provide for church services for the boatmen at the Point, and in the forties the more radical denominations sponsored a wave of street preaching.

The temperance movement was probably as characteristic of Pittsburgh morality as any reform and possessed more interest and dramatic vigor than most. A number of local temperance societies had been organized before 1830, but in that year the various societies formed a union and undertook a real campaign. The ministers of the city were active in the movement, of course, but many well known in other walks of life participated, among them the lawyers Charles Shaler and Walter Forward, and the publishers Neville B. Craig, Alfred Nevin, and Isaac Harris.

For more than a score of years the papers were filled with the activities of the Washingtonians, the Marthas, the Sons of Temperance, and the Society of Reformed Drunkards of Baltimore. A Mrs. Lusher ran a temperance hotel, the George Washington; even the proprietor of the Dravo House saw the light, dumped out his liquors, and laid in a stock of ice cream and lemonade. There were two temperance auditoriums, the Washington Ark, in Allegheny, and Temperance Hall, at the southeast corner of Smithfield Street and Diamond Alley. The latter heard many a rousing reformist lecture, abolitionist and feminist as well as temperance; and Frederick Douglass, Lucy Stone, Abby Kelly, William Lloyd Garrison, and Wendell Phillips are said to have spoken from its platform. Sometimes the irreverent boys and men of the town would climb upon the low roof and proceed to beat a tattoo or do clog dances while a lecture was in progress.

A favorite temperance speaker was Captain E. F. Pratt, a veteran of the War of 1812 and a reformed drunkard, who interspersed his talks with songs. One of his songs ran like this:

> And then I had nothing but rags to my back,
> My boots would not hide my toes
> The crown of my hat went flip, flip, flap,
> And you could tweak my rum-blossom nose.

During a drive in the spring of 1841 the pledge was signed by an "army of cold water men amounting to nearly 6000 persons," and at another time the entire Neptune Fire Engine Company signed *en masse* amidst a chorus of hosannas. Temperance parades were held frequently in an attempt to whip up enthusiasm. The Sons of Temperance, a secret organization with passwords and flamboyant regalia, was especially impressive on such occasions. Even the children, organized as Cadets of Temperance, paraded. One time, when the Cadets were marching, a tipsy spectator who was clinging to a lamp post was so impressed that he burst out to one of his companions: "Sam—hic—I say, Sam, let's take all these little fellows into Weaver's and—hic—treat 'em to all they can drink."

The temperance movement in Pennsylvania was only a part of a nation-wide struggle that reached its height in the fifties and that at one time or another succeeded in laying upon nearly a score of states more or less loose prohibition laws; they were fleeting in their effects, however, save in Maine. In Pennsylvania the temperance workers united in support of a stricter license law and finally put one through the legislature, but on the whole the movement in Pennsylvania did not meet with even the qualified success that it did elsewhere.

II

THE growth of Pittsburgh churches was slow until about 1830, when their strength suddenly began to increase with such vigor that within twelve years the number of church buildings had jumped from ten to fifty-five and the number of congregations from fifteen to seventy-six. It is of interest to note that of the latter, forty-six belonged to the various Presbyterian denominations. By 1855 the number of church buildings had further increased to eighty-four.

The very multiplicity of congregations forbids notice of more than a few. From 1811 to 1850 the Reverend Francis Herron was the pastor of the First Presbyterian Church, and his ministry was marked not only by the growth of the congregation but by its increased influence in the community. In 1853 a new church building was erected, and it continued to serve the congregation until 1903, when part of the lot on which it stood was leased for the McCreery store and a new church was built facing Sixth Avenue.

The Second Church, organized in 1804, occupied a number of sites before the present one on Eighth Street, to which it moved in 1905. Old Pittsburghers remember a dramatic incident that occurred on the night of June 6, 1850, in the church at 247 Fifth Avenue, when one "Demented Kelley" rode into the midst of the assembled congregation on horseback and shouted, "I come this time on a black horse, but I will come next on a red." That night the church building burned to the ground.

The Third Presbyterian Church, built in 1833 at the northeastern corner of Third and Ferry Streets, was a magnificent structure with massive columns and a steeple that towered 163 feet above the street, a landmark in the city until its destruction by fire in 1863. A new site at Sixth Avenue and Cherry Alley was then purchased and a Romanesque church built. In 1837 the congregation led a secessionist group from the mother church that formed the New School Assembly. The divisions were reunited, however, on November 12, 1869. On that historic morning the General Assembly of the New School marched from the Third Church down Sixth Avenue and turned on to Wood Street opposite the First Church. The General Assembly of the Old School then left the latter building and lined up on Wood Street opposite the other group. Then, in the sight of thousands of shouting spectators, the moderators of the two assemblies approached and shook hands, and the other churchmen quickly followed their example down the length of the double line. The men of the two united bodies then marched back arm in arm to the Third Church, and as they entered the building the choir and organ took up the hymn "Blow ye the trumpet, blow, the gladly solemn sound." Even though it was all carefully staged, the event was one of the most inspiring in Pittsburgh's ecclesiastical history.

The Episcopalians continued to worship in the "Old Round Church" from about 1808 to 1825. The Monongahela Bank Building now occupies the site of the church, which was in the triangular block bounded by Liberty, Sixth, and Wood. The congregation's most vigorous and successful rector was John Henry Hopkins, who had graduated from the iron furnace to the law to the ministry and who was later to become Bishop of Vermont. He built a new Trinity Church on the old Penn land grant that had hitherto been used only as a cemetery, and encouraged the establishment of new parishes, which proved to be the salvation of the Episcopal Church in the region. Pittsburgh became a diocese in 1865 under the energetic Bishop John B. Kerfoot, and it was during his episcopate that the present Trinity Church was built in 1871.

The Methodists continued to worship in one body at their Brimstone Corner edifice (at the southeast corner of Smithfield and Seventh) until 1829, when the quarrel over church polity that led to the formation of the Methodist Protestant Church became acute and the congregation split. The "Radicals" demanded a more democratic form of church government, and the "Old Side" upheld the traditional form. The latter had the church building, and to insure possession they changed the lock and posted a guard. Their rivals, however, jimmied a window and seized control, and the "Old Side" withdrew to the first meetinghouse on Front Street. The case was carried through the civil courts but was finally settled privately. The "Radicals" joined the Methodist Protestant Church and moved into a new building on Fifth Avenue.

St. Patrick's Roman Catholic Church had been erected at Liberty Avenue and Washington (Eleventh) Street in 1811. During the next twenty years German and Irish Catholics came in such numbers that the parish priest, the versatile and liberal Father Charles B. Maguire—who was a member of the faculty of the university and one of Pittsburgh's most popular after-dinner speakers—was able to begin a new and larger church on the west side of Grant Street between Fifth Avenue and Virgin Alley (Oliver Avenue). It was completed in 1834 and dedicated as St. Paul's Church. The old church was given to the Germans of St. Patrick's parish and was finally replaced by St. Philomena's Church. In 1843 Pittsburgh was made a diocese; the Reverend Michael O'Connor was made bishop, and his labors led to the erection of other churches in the following years. During the forties the cutting away of Grant's Hill had left the cathedral perched dangerously upon a hummock; when it was burned in 1851 work was immediately begun on a new brick structure, which served until 1901, when a new Gothic cathedral was erected at Fifth Avenue and Craig Street. The structure of 1851 was said to be second in size only to St. Patrick's Cathedral in New York City.

The oldest Jewish congregation in Pittsburgh is that of the Rodef Shalom Temple, which grew out of a society formed in 1846. Its members worshiped over the engine room of the Vigilant Fire Engine Company. There were about that time nearly a hundred Jewish families who lived chiefly between Market and Ferry Streets on Second and Third Avenues. In the group were two factions: the Germans, who belonged to the reformed wing of Judaism; and the Poles, who were strictly orthodox. In 1854 this difference led to a split and to the erection by the Germans of the first Rodef Shalom Temple on Eighth Street, now the Second Presbyterian Church. There the congregation worshiped from 1862 until 1907, when the second temple was begun on Fifth near Morewood. The Ladies' Aid Society and the Hebrew Benevolent Society, both founded during the Civil War, were active in relief work during that struggle.

III

JUDGED by the number of paintings exhibited in Pittsburgh, some from the brushes of men acknowledged to be masters, the people of the city must have been interested in art. Sometimes pictures were exhibited by the proprietors of the local museums, sometimes a collection was brought in by individuals who made a business of exhibiting pictures in different towns. The entrepreneur who was exhibiting hired a hall or a room in a hotel or private dwelling, hung his pictures, advertised in the newspapers, and waited for the populace to flock in at from twenty-five to fifty cents a head. Doubtless pictures such as Titian's "Venus" and Le Blanc's "Adam and Eve" drew large crowds, especially when ladies and gentlemen were admitted only separately.

Portrait and miniature painters visited Pittsburgh at frequent intervals. James Bowman, who had studied in Europe and attained some eminence, lived in Pittsburgh for awhile. James R. Lambdin, a Pittsburgh museum proprietor of many interests, was a portrait painter who had studied under Sully. Isaac E. Craig, the son of the editor of the *Gazette*, excelled in crayon sketches and landscape painting. He opened a studio in 1849 but soon departed for Europe, where he lived the rest of his life. Emil Foerster came to the United States as a boy, then later returned to Germany to study art. He established a studio in Pittsburgh just before the Civil War and was soon recognized as a portrait painter of considerable merit. L. Braun, a political refugee from Baden, and George Hetzel, a native of Alsace, were other artists of merit who settled in Pittsburgh. It is probable that the development of artistic interest in Pittsburgh owed much to the establishment of an art gallery and store in 1832 by J. J. Gillespie. There the artists named above and others gathered to inspect new pictures, and presently citizens of the town began going there for informal education in things artistic. By the winter of 1859-60 the Pittsburgh Art Association was holding annual exhibits of paintings, but it seems to have gone out of existence during the Civil War. In 1855 the Pittsburgh Academy for Instruction in Drawing and Painting was started, and ten years later the Pittsburgh School of Design drew a large clientele from well-to-do families.

The city's best-loved artist, and the only one of that time who has won national attention, was David G. Blythe. He was born near East Liverpool, Ohio, in 1815, and at the age of sixteen he came to Pittsburgh to learn the woodcarving business. After some years he served in the navy as a carpenter, and then he returned to East Liverpool, where he took up portrait painting. In 1845 he moved to Uniontown and soon became one of the town's most popular citizens. The death of his wife radically changed his outlook upon life; he became careless of his dress and manners and indifferent to the opinions of others. He was not an unsociable being, however, and was prominent and popular among the artists of Pittsburgh, where for several years he maintained a studio at 66 Market Street. His tall, spare figure, and unkempt red hair and beard were familiar sights in the Pittsburgh of the fifties; apparently his genius was appreciated, for his paintings and sketches were carefully preserved by those into whose hands they fell, and they are still sometimes exhibited.

During the Civil War he became a camp follower, content to beg his food and lodging from casually met soldiers, and although the Pittsburgh art dealer, J. J. Gillespie, had given him unlimited credit, legend has it that he drew only one dollar. He is said to have spent much of his time in guardhouses as a suspicious character, but at any rate he managed to bring back with him many sketches and fruitful memories. Between his excursions with the army he returned to Pittsburgh and filled in his sketches or painted the scenes he had witnessed. Shortly after the war, on May 15, 1865, he died of pneumonia brought on by malnutrition.

Blythe was an artist whose greatness was rooted in the independence that made it possible for him to criticize and even to poke fun at the conventions of a solemnly conventional age, and his best works are American genre paintings. Especially noteworthy are his pictures with such subjects as married life, in which a woman bends over the washtub while a strapping husband holds the baby; the post-office window, before which several discourteous citizens crowd, squeezing the crinoline of a struggling woman into a ludicrous shape, while in the foreground a snoopy individual looks over the shoulder of a man who is reading a letter; and the "Deacon at Prayer" at the table, while his small son, almost hidden by the tall back of a chair, holds the tail of a scrabbling cat. Someone has said that his humor was "lustily Elizabethan rather than sentimentally Victorian"; Blythe exemplified the boisterous and unrestrained laughter of the pioneer, who by then had passed far beyond the Mississippi, rather than the industrial middle class, whose staid morals influenced the conventions of life in his time.

IV

THE Pittsburgh Harmonic Society seems to have been organized about the time of the War of 1812 and was devoted to instrumental music. It seems to have been disbanded in 1818, but it was soon followed by the Pittsburgh Musical Society, which was organized to give special attention to sacred music. The growth of musical interest was very rapid and in the decade of the thirties there were probably half a dozen musical societies in the town. The Mozart Society, founded about 1838, was destined to have a long life during which it presented many orchestral concerts of classical music. The Pittsburgh Academy of Music was established in the forties for the instruction of the musically inclined. Pittsburgh boasted several composers. One of them, Henry Kleber, a composer of waltzes and schottisches, created one of the few ripples of scandal in the local musical world when he publicly horsewhipped the ministerial editor of a German paper for unjustly criticizing him. He is better remembered, however, as the musical mentor of Stephen C. Foster.

The reception accorded the famous "Swedish Nightingale," Jenny Lind, in November, 1851, caused more than a mere ripple of scandal. When she landed in the United States in 1850 the people of Pittsburgh were much troubled lest Phineas T. Barnum would not take her to Pittsburgh; in April of the next year a number of Pittsburghers decided to take no chances and went to Cincinnati to hear her. A Wheeling newspaper editor, humorously referring to the steamboat men's outcry against a new bridge in his city, announced jocosely that the "reason Jenny Lind does not go to Pittsburgh is that her reputation is so high she cannot get it under the bridge."

Finally, however, it was announced that she would sing in Pittsburgh on the evening of April 25. Masonic Hall, on Fifth Avenue (across from the site of the present Warner Theater), which seated eleven hundred people, was engaged. The tickets of admission were put up at auction; the first brought a premium of fifty dollars, and the total receipts from admissions was supposed to have been over eight thousand dollars. Jenny Lind arrived from Cincinnati by the steamboat "Messenger" on the morning of the twenty-fifth, and she was escorted by Barnum through an immense throng to a waiting carriage, which with difficulty made its way to the Monongahela House, where she was to stay.

That night not only was the hall jammed but the streets outside, and the near-by fences and vacant lots; even the roofs and windows of the surrounding houses were filled with the curious, who could easily see in because the windows of the hall had neither shutters nor shades. The managers had taken the precaution of boarding up the windows of the singer's dressing room, and there, on "magnificent furniture" loaned for the occasion by "our liberal townsman," J. W. Woodwell, she reclined during the orchestral renditions that made up the greater part of the program. The power of suggestion is shown by the write-up printed the next day in the *Post*: "She sang only as the angels sing in the courts of Paradise. Her voice is sweet as the warbling of birds. . . . When she smiles it seems as if a flash of light from Heaven shone upon her face!"

The *hoi polloi* without, however, were not as entranced as the editor of the *Post* and a few of them expressed their opinions (or at least their low standards of courtesy) by stones and vocal insults. When the recital was over the crowd lingered outside, probably more curious than anything else, but the stones that had landed on the boards at the windows had so frightened the songstress that she would not leave. It is said that a drayman named Keating finally pried some boards off the fence back of the hall and helped her through with several of her entourage, and took them on his dray by a roundabout course through Virgin Alley, Cherry Alley, and Water Street to the hotel. The company left early the next morning without waiting to give a promised second concert, but on November 13 Jenny Lind summoned the courage to return. The second appearance was not marked by any of the rude demonstrations of the first. It is said that the proprietor of the Monongahela House auctioned the sheets and pillow cases upon which Jenny Lind had slept and gave the money to charity.

V

STEPHEN COLLINS FOSTER was born July 4, 1826, in old Lawrenceville, the village that had been laid out in 1814 by his father, William B. Foster. The father was a struggling businessman and politician who spent his life, like most people, hoping for better days but forced to be content, like most people, with minor manifestations of the community's regard. Stephen was the ninth child and like other children in large families early became acquainted with the nip of financial worry, if not with actual want. From the very first he showed a passion for music, and he probably pursued its study under Henry Kleber, the young German who kept a music store in the town. Foster's first known musical composition, *Open Thy Lattice, Love*, was published in 1844.

The lad tried his hand at the negro minstrel songs that were so popular on the stage, and several of his compositions soon found their way into print. *Susanna* and *Lou'siana Belle* gave him the coveted start in the musical world. Against the opposition of his family the chances of a commercial career were thrown aside, musical writing was adopted as a vocation, and until 1860 he seems to have made a fairly good living from it. Meanwhile he married Jane, the daughter of Pittsburgh's Dr. Andrew N. McDowell, but they do not seem to have been well adapted to each other. Jane's formal, unsentimental, competent nature (she was later to earn a living as a telegrapher) must have been a sore trial to the dreamy, temperamental poet-musician, and doubtless he was as great a trial to her. As time went on he became moody and more than ever addicted to the social glass; these years, however, were productive of his best work. Contrary to common belief, he spent little time in the South except for a few brief visits to relatives in Kentucky and a trip to New Orleans.

The close of Foster's career should be painted in tragic rather than shameful colors. He removed to New York with his little family in 1860, a change that was to prove fatal. Tuberculosis had already fastened upon him and his health became rapidly worse; the quality of his work deteriorated and sales dropped; last of all, in his despondency he allowed the liquor habit to obtain complete control of him. Financial stringency forced Jane to return home to earn her own living, but there is no indication that she and Stephen were estranged. During the last months of his life the composer sank rapidly; an accident finally sent him to the charity ward of Bellevue Hospital, and there he died on January 13, 1864.

It is a fitting commentary upon the vanity of human ambition that many of the names of Pittsburgh's statesmen, warriors, and industrialists have passed from the nation's memory but the fame of one of the humblest and least assuming of her sons has been preserved in the hearts of all those who love the simple things of life—the humming of the bees in the garden, the song of the lover, the longing for the scenes of home and childhood, and the tinkle of the darky's banjo as he keeps time to the juba patters or plaintively yearns for the promised deliverance of the life beyond death. Stephen Collins Foster died in poverty and obscurity, without the knowledge that in his short life he had found the magic key that unlocks the chamber of the heart in which dwell the tender emotions, the simple joys, the poignant sorrows, and the workaday tribulations that make the human race one family. His was in a large measure a life of frustration and disappointment; his trusting heart was broken, perhaps by some that he loved, and at the end he seemed to himself and to those around him to be a failure. Perhaps that is why the world understands him—why his songs seem to be written in a universal language.

VI

IT WOULD be impossible here to follow in detail the histories of the many literary and scientific societies that flourished in Pittsburgh between 1820 and 1860. Names like Tilghman, Marshall, Wirt, Baldwin, and Franklin were commonly used as titles by the more literary "institutes." The scientific societies were the Pittsburgh Chemical and Physiological Society, the Pittsburgh Institute of Arts and Sciences, and the Philosophical and Philological Society. The Young Men's Society and the Young Men's Christian Association were religious in their interests and fought nobly the vanities of the world, particularly the theaters. In the thirties at least two gymnasiums were established "for Gladiatorial and Athletic Exercises, after the manner of the ancient Greeks and Romans."

The flower of literary institutes was the system of lyceums organized in 1836 by N. R. Smith as a part of a state-wide scheme that included several branch groups, among them one for young ladies, one for "young merchants," and one for children. The lyceums lasted at least until 1846 and were real factors in the educational growth of Pittsburgh. Apparently nothing was too erudite to draw the interest of the members of such institutions. There were lectures on all the arts and sciences, on history and letters, on commerce and industry. At one time or another Ralph W. Emerson, Henry W. Beecher, William L. Garrison, Horace Greeley, Horace Mann, Lucy Stone, George W. Curtis, Bayard Taylor, and Thomas H. Benton, not to mention a host of those less well known, lectured before Pittsburgh audiences. Fanny Kemble gave a series of Shakespearean readings during which, save for the sound of her voice, "one could have heard a pin drop." A Professor Bronson lectured on his "complete system of Mental and Vocal Philosophy," as a result of which one Le Roy Sunderland extracted a tooth from the jaw of a young lady while she was "under the magnetic influence." Phrenologists were frequent pests, and one time several of them visited the Western Penitentiary, examined the heads of the inmates, and guessed what transgressions had landed them there—sometimes with surprising accuracy. When Orson Squire Fowler, the greatest phrenologist of them all, appeared in town the *Gazette* irreverently remarked that all those who had faith in the "mapping off of the head" could have "their natural characters dissected by one in authority and the result set down in black and white."

On January 11, 1834, a meeting was held in "Mr. George Beale's long room" at Market and Second Streets to "determine upon the expediency of an historical society." Walter Forward was chairman, and a committee was appointed to draft a constitution and by-laws for the proposed society. Benjamin Bakewell was the first president. The society seems to have lapsed after a few years. Though it was revived in 1843 by the Reverend George Upfold, it died again in a short time. In 1858 another attempt was made, and a third society crippled along until the preoccupations of the Civil War put an end to it. In 1879 a fourth organization was started under the name of the "Old Residents' Association of Pittsburgh and Western Pennsylvania," with some of the men who had been prominent in the earlier societies as members. In 1882 the name was changed to the "Historical Society of Western Pennsylvania," and the roll was thrown open to others than old residents. Miss Marie Eaton and the Reverend A. A. Lambing were the chief inspirations of the fourth revival and it was through their incessant labors in laying a firm foundation, and through the later ministrations of such members as William H. Stevenson, Charles W. Dahlinger, and Emma Dare Poole, that the society was able to lay the jinx that haunted its predecessors and to survive to the present day.

Library facilities were not of the best, but from time to time special organizations or the owners of bookstores attempted to establish reading rooms. In 1825 an association of business men opened a library for the use of apprentices. In 1850 Colonel James Anderson established in Allegheny another apprentices' library, which, at the insistence of a lad named Andrew Carnegie, an employee of the Pennsylvania Railroad, was opened to all working boys. The most important of Pittsburgh's libraries was probably that maintained by the Mercantile Library Association, which seems to have been formed in 1847 by the union of several others and which twenty years later occupied a building of its own, called Library Hall, at the northwest corner of Penn Avenue and Barker Alley. In the seventies financial difficulties forced its discontinuance.

Pittsburgh's literary periodicals were few and struggling. Two physicians named J. Lewis and D. M. Kirkpatrick began in 1819 to publish the *Western Eclectic Repertory, and Analytical Review, Medical and Philosophical*, but though they received the good wishes of the enlightened there is no proof that they received much of anything else. In 1828 publication of the *Hesperus* was begun, and in 1834 one Alexander Jones announced that he would publish "a literary and miscellaneous semimonthly journal" under the title of the *Pittsburgh Mirror*. In 1839 the *Literary Examiner* and in 1841 the *Literary Messenger* appeared, and in 1845 the *Nautilus* was founded by E. Z. C. Judson ("Ned Buntline"). The *Albatross*, started as an antislavery paper, soon became the *Western World*. None of the above publications seems to have enjoyed long life or success. There were in addition a number of fraternal or religious magazines; the most famous of the latter was the *Pittsburgh Recorder*, which after a series of changes of titles and owners became the *Presbyterian Banner*.

Few of Pittsburgh's writers attained a great amount of national prominence. Henry Marie Brackenridge, the son of the redoubtable lawyer of Whiskey Insurrection days, was best known for his autobiography and his works on travel, history, and diplomacy. Jane Gray Swisshelm, the editor of the *Pittsburgh Saturday Visiter* and an incorrigible reformer, seems to have gathered about her a group of women writers who in 1875 gave in her honor a "blue tea"—blue decorations, blue flowers, blue invitations, blue ribbons on blue teacups, and a pair of blue stockings as a gift to the guest of honor. It was at this meeting that the Women's Club of Pittsburgh was formed—the first woman's club in Pennsylvania and the second in the United States, so it is said. Morgan Neville, son of Colonel Presley Neville, was editor of the *Gazette* and did some literary work, both prose and poetry, that showed promise that was never fulfilled. Wilkins Tannehill, who was educated in Pittsburgh Academy but moved to Nashville, was the author of a *History of Literature* that won wide praise. There were in addition a group of poets, novelists, textbook compilers, and ecclesiastical writers whose work was best known locally.

VII

DRAMATIC art in Pittsburgh labored for many years under the handicap of being considered not quite decent in many "respectable" quarters. As late as 1841 the editor of the *Gazette*, Neville B. Craig, wrote: "The fact is, there is not enough of a drama loving population in this city to support a respectable theatre, and we are glad of it. We think it speaks well for the good taste and morality of our inhabitants." Until well after the Civil War the theater was indeed a struggling institution in Pittsburgh, playing short seasons to audiences that were none too large.

The theater that had been erected before 1820 on the "old hay scale lot" on the north side of Third Street near Smithfield Street seems to have been Pittsburgh's only dramatic center until 1833, save perhaps for a few amateur performances in Lambdin's Museum. Samuel Young leaves a story of the old days: the theater was having such hard going that the owners rented out the basement to a soap-maker to help pay expenses, and they put on amateur performances without paying the license fee demanded by the city fathers. Upon one occasion during a performance there was a cry that the constables were coming, and the cast scattered in a hurry. One of the troupers dropped through a trapdoor in the stage and landed in a kettle of hardening soap. He was so frightened that he let out a yell that should have brought the constables running if they had been anywhere near, which happily was not the case. The unfortunate fellow had the soap cleaned from his clothes and went on with the show. It was in the same theater that Edwin Forrest played his first Pittsburgh engagement under a roof so open to the heavens that rain forced the members of the audience to hoist umbrellas.

The playhouse that was to engage the affections of Pittsburgh drama lovers for many years was the Pittsburgh Theatre, oftener known affectionately as Old Drury. It was built in 1833 on the lots now designated as 306-10 Fifth Avenue and at present occupied by the F and W Grand Stores. The building, designed to hold an audience of twelve hundred, was 57 by 130 feet, two stories high (though an old illustration shows a false third story facade), and stuccoed. There were five entrances in front; the middle three were overhung by an iron balcony bearing six or eight lamp standards. There were two tiers of boxes, rose colored and ornamented with gold, and each bearing the arms of the United States. The seats were covered with crimson and edged with velvet and brass nails, and the auditorium was lighted by eighteen chandeliers. The proscenium was surmounted by the arms of Pennsylvania. The admission to the box seats was ordinarily fifty cents, to the pit twenty-five cents, to the second tier boxes thirty-seven and a half cents, while the frequenters of the gallery paid twelve and a half. The two left-hand sections of the gallery were reserved for colored people. There were three bars in the house, all well patronized, or those who chose could go next door to the bar of the Falstaff House, presided over by portly Mr. Boston, who wore a bottle-green, pigeon-tailed coat, a plug hat, and an enormous cluster of stage diamonds. Dignified old Mr. Cheesman was the billposter, or rather he supervised his constant assistant, John, in the work. In later years, when the paint had become tarnished and the owners had grown careless, a negress and her numerous progeny cleaned the theater by sweeping out the programs and peanut shells, and settling the dust on the floor with a little water, which soon seeped into the dank, unventilated cellar.

The behavior of the audiences was, to say the least, most informal. Men removed their coats and kept on their tall beaver hats. A newspaper commentator in 1838 wrote: "The babel confusion and uproar, the yelling and cursing—swearing and tearing —the friendly interchange of commodities—apples, pignuts, etc., between the tenants of the upper boxes and pit, have become intolerable." The "gallery gods" seem to have been allowed to do about as they pleased since they provided a goodly share of the receipts; upon one occasion the manager put a strong police guard up on the balcony, but he was roundly hissed when he appeared upon the stage.

Old Drury started auspiciously under the management of Francis C. Wemyss of Philadelphia. No expense had been spared in providing scenery and costumes. Edwin Forrest was scheduled to appear in the third performance. The curtain went up at 7:30 P. M. on September 2, 1833, upon a performance of *Hamlet,* with Mr. A. Adams in the title role. Tyrone Power and Junius Brutus Booth played later in the season; the latter, as was too often the case, was beastly drunk during the performance. *Mazeppa, or, the Wild Horse of the Ukraine* was one of the attractions offered by the management, and it received the loud kudos of all who saw it. The favorite actor of the season, however, seems to have been a Mr. Parsloe, who was as surely traveling in a cast-iron groove as any modern Hollywood character actor. He was perennially cast as a monkey and appeared successively in that character in *Mushapug the Monkey, Jack Robinson and his Monkey,* in *The Cabin Boy,* and in *The Monkey Who Had Seen the World.* Finally, as a simian climax, in the character of *Jocko, the Ape of Brazil,* he made "his Grand Ascent from the Stage to the Gallery—around the House, and descended to the Stage."

As the season progressed Mr. Wemyss complained that the audiences almost invariably selected the worst actors as their favorites, while they would hiss from the stage anyone whose real-life traits they disapproved—for example, they would not allow a certain actor to go on with his performance because he wore white gloves on the street. The season ended on January 8, after 112 nights; it had not been a financial success, and thereafter Wemyss devoted his chief attention to managing a Philadelphia theater and provided only short seasons in Pittsburgh.

Old Drury proved to be a complete financial failure by 1840 and remained vacant for some time. In 1842 it was reopened by an English actress, a Miss Clarendon, who lifted Pittsburgh eyebrows by horsewhipping an insulter in the lobby of the theater. Later the theater was closed again. "Cause—want of support."

During the years from 1845 to 1851, when Charles S. Porter was manager, poor Old Drury descended pathetically from its first splendid promise. The wardrobe was so scanty that the cast appeared in costumes made up of parts ranging in period from William the Conqueror to George the Third. The gallery had to be closed during the cold weather, and a new policy of cheaper prices was instituted. Local playwrights were drawn upon for scripts and the tarnished galleries resounded to *Blanche of Allegheny; The Pittsburgh Fireman, or the Penn Street Heiress; Dr. Brodie's Pills, or the Way to Cure Him* (named for a local pill-roller); *A Squint at Pittsburgh;* and *1949, or Pittsburgh 100 Years Hence.* Pittsburghers could wish that the last script had been saved, even while returning thanks that the others have been lost. Once in 1849 when an opera troupe appeared in Pittsburgh the stock company of Old Drury nobly shared the boards with it in a double bill composed of a farce and Bellini's *La Somnambula*. For that occasion the free list was suspended, save for the gentlemen of the press.

From 1851 to 1858 "Governor" Joseph C. Foster was manager and somehow kept the house open most of the year. It was during his managership that on the night of November 17, 1853, *Uncle Tom's Cabin* was played for the first time in Pittsburgh. The war boom enabled William Henderson, who took charge in 1858, to clean up a fortune and retire. The building was sold in 1867 or 1868 for around ninety thousand dollars and for a time was the headquarters of the Democratic Club. It was then reopened under the managership of "Old Harry" Williams, a young man who always played the part of an old man. Presently a gaping hole appeared in the roof, and since the owner would not repair it, Mr. Williams decided to close. Christmas week was devoted to pantomines, as had been the custom for some years, and then on January 1, 1870, Old Drury closed its doors for the last time.

Old Drury was not the only theater in Pittsburgh during those years. The site of the Warner Theater on Diamond Street was occupied by a large playhouse known successively as the New National and the Apollo. The Pittsburgh Grand Opera House was erected on the spot in 1871, and there the divine Sarah Bernhardt played, as well as many others well known in their day. Christy's Minstrels, whose repertoire included many of the songs of Pittsburgh's most beloved musician, Stephen C. Foster, performed in 1845 in Duquesne Hall, over the post office. The changes in names and management of the theaters are too numerous to follow, but there were at one time or another an Ethiopian Opera House and an Athenaeum. One of the best known of the town's show houses was Trimble's Varieties, which put on in one bill as many as seventeen vaudeville acts.

The most popular of the ministrels who visited Pittsburgh was the famous "Jim Crow" Rice, who about 1832 began the vogue for negro characterization on the stage and created the "Ethiopian Opera." It was in Pittsburgh that Rice's theme song, "Jim Crow," was prepared for publication by William Cumming Peters. Eventually there were hundreds of stanzas to the song, but the chorus was always the same and was always accompanied by a peculiar hop called the "Jim Crow":

> First on de heel tap, den on de toe,
> Ebery time I wheel about I jump Jim Crow.
> Wheel about and turn about and do jis so,
> And ebery time I wheel about I jump Jim Crow.

Negro minstrelsy soon became so popular that the legitimate stage had difficulty in surviving. In Pittsburgh the trend toward negro songs had an important effect in directing the talents of Stephen C. Foster to that end, and gave the world a number of songs that were to survive long after the vogue that called them into being had passed.

XX

High and Low Life

THE life of Pittsburgh's streets was a never ending drama replete with color and human interest. At two or three o'clock in the morning the farmers' wagons began to lumber in from the country, and their iron-shod horses and heavy tired wheels hit the city's cobbled pavements with a crash. Milkmen soon appeared and began making the rounds of the retail establishments, leaving at each place an ungainly can of lacteal fluid that was often "as pure as water could make it." From the fertile market gardens on Neville Island or "Shirties" Creek appeared flat-bottomed "John boats," piled high with melons and green groceries and poled by husky lads with gnarled knuckles and shoulders bowed from stooping over the rows of vegetables. The hucksters appeared presently and drove sharp bargains with the countrymen for the produce that they intended to hawk from door to door later in the day. A hard life, perhaps, was this early rising, but once in a century there was a recompense—witness that morning in 1833 when the market people were regaled for an hour by a remarkable shower of meteors that lit up the entire sky from hill to hill and that a day later received elaborate electrical explanations from late rising editors.

About five o'clock sleepy-eyed clerks appeared from hidden

recesses within the stores and yawningly began to remove the heavy paneled shutters that closed the store fronts to marauders during the night. Later in the day these same clerks sped afoot through the roaring traffic to deliver packages at the swank homes of lower Penn Avenue. For his services, which might be required as long as seventeen hours on market days, the ambitious junior clerk received a measly three dollars a week, and it scarcely occurred to him that he might be underpaid. It was his firm determination to become a partner in the store and quite often his ambition was realized, especially if the owner had a daughter who was not too lovely to consider a rising young clerk. The merchants themselves had lost some of the youthful energy that had distinguished them in the days when they had been junior clerks with an eye on their employer's daughter, and the watchmen complained that they had to wind their spring rattles for ten minutes before the lazybones would get up. The inference that everyone must be out of bed before the watchmen went off duty casts an interesting sidelight upon the modern complaint against regimentation.

In those days the early bird didn't catch the worm. No one thought of opening the day with breakfast; instead of that everyone went to the shop or store first and put in a couple of hours at work. Draymen in their carts lumbered down to the wharves or the canal basins in the hope of receiving fat hauling contracts, and the Irish and negro roustabouts who had slept on the cotton bales on the decks of the steamboats took up their beds and walked them ashore. Carpenters were busily sawing and bricklayers' helpers were sweating at the mortar boxes before dawn. By six o'clock everyone was bustling about as though he was set to work throughout the day.

About seven o'clock there was a pause for breakfast. A contributor to the *Gazette* was roaming aimlessly about the town one morning musing on "our noble destiny and onward march to wealth, and usefulness, and honor" when he was met by "an immense mass of industrious, happy youth, just emerging from a large cotton factory to their homes and breakfasts. This pleasing sight . . . at once disclosed the grand secret, the *magical art* by which . . . all individuals, towns, cities or countries rise, and become flourishing and happy, viz: honest industry, prudence and economy—agriculture, manufactures, commerce, and enterprise, judiciously managed."

The early morning hours and those immediately after breakfast were utilized by housewives or their cooks for marketing. The well-equipped marketer was armed with a huge basket and a tiny silver butter taster, and perhaps was flanked by a small daughter bent on getting a glimpse of real life under color of learning the tricks of marketing. One had to be careful about grocers and country people or they would palm off bad eggs or slightly rancid butter. One had to learn to judge meat by its texture and appearance and not rely upon the butcher's assertion that it came from a blooded steer with a pedigree "as long as the moral law." When buying sugar one rubbed it between thumb and forefinger to detect sand; mackerel, "in half barrels for family use," had to be opened and then not purchased if it failed to pass an olfactory test; pheasants must be shunned at a certain season, when they fed on laurel and their flesh was therefore poisonous. Tomatoes, or "love apples" as they were called, rarely appeared in the market, because they were reputed to be rank poison, and of course the grapefruit, bananas, and pineapples of today were unknown, while oranges were rare and expensive and not at all satisfactory. Even the melons were often pithy and tasteless.

II

THE sights of workaday life must have been entrancing to the visiting country boy—perhaps lured to the city by the paragraph in the *Commercial Journal* that there was going to be an eclipse of the sun on the twenty-fifth, and "we hope our friends in the country will not fail to come to town that day and see it." When he passed a clothing store a man pacing along outside was sure to give the hayseed an ingratiating pat on the back and invite him in. There he discovered that, though twenty dollars might be asked for a suit, half an hour of patient sales resistance would often get it for seven. In the mayor's court a prominent medico and a covey of students might be on trial for body-snatching. A visit to the horse market at Eighth and Grant Streets would, in half a day, produce more jokes and ludicrous situations than all the rest of Pittsburgh put together, for the horsemen were proverbially a "cute race"; they lived by their wits and enjoyed a merry, even if turbulent, existence.

A walk through the teeming life of the canal basins to Penn Avenue and down that thoroughfare was always of interest. Perhaps there was a circus encamped on a vacant lot, and the countryman might well while away a pleasant afternoon there. A little farther down Penn Avenue, if it were late in the afternoon, disgusted boys could be seen carrying home their mothers' spinning wheels from a tea party. After the steamboats came into use their mates would fire a small cannon from the bow so that the hotel hacks and unoccupied carters could race to the Monongahela wharf at break-neck speed. Our country visitor, if he followed, might on occasion get a glimpse of draymen loading kegs of Mexican silver and gold for transportation to the canal.

If the day chanced to be the first of April the confusion of the city streets would be doubled by the rattle and bang of moving householders. In those days distances were not so great nor the furnishings of the average home so large in quantity but that many families could move without the aid of a wagon. Doubtless moving day was a joyous occasion, rivaled for excitement only by floods, holidays, and those rare times when flocks of wild pigeons lighted on the neighboring hills and the populace turned out to slaughter them by the tens of thousands. Moving day invariably had its quota of lost children and the bellman was kept busy going through the streets ringing his bell and calling the names and descriptions of the strays.

Floods, of course, always disrupted the orderly confusion of Pittsburgh's business and brought destruction and loss of life in their wake. The great flood of 1832, which reached a peak of 35 feet, was followed by lesser ones in 1852, 1861, and 1865. The factories often had to stop work and the idle workers lined the river banks excitedly watching lumber, coal boats, and houses being swept by. As the water rose higher anxious householders moved their goods to the second stories of their homes or took them to higher ground. The better residential district on lower Penn Avenue was not exempt, and on several occasions well-kept lawns were hidden by swirling waters, and sheltered little girls of the neighborhood could look down in envy from their bedroom windows upon their brothers paddling their canoes happily between mansion and carriage house.

A visitor from the country would also have taken note that the town bell was an important factor in Pittsburgh life until well into the century. It summoned the children to school morning and afternoon; it rang for council meetings; three times on Sunday it pealed out the call to church services, and on Wednesday evening it announced the hour for prayer meeting; it was used as the fire alarm, and its full tones in the night were the signal that woke the town into a frenzy of half-fearful but wholly exhilarating activity.

Loafing on street corners was a custom bitterly denounced by solid citizens, and merchants sometimes complained that the "loose and lewd remarks" of the loafers hurt business by making it unpleasant for ladies to pass. On the other hand, there were complaints about the women who stopped to gossip and obstructed the sidewalks with their spreading crinolines. It is a striking fact, however, that objections to loafing and drinking and other like sins arose from a presumption that they hampered business rather than from moral grounds. Traffic was freely permitted to raise its din in the city streets on Sundays, and when the First Presbyterian congregation petitioned for the right to have chains stretched across Wood Street during services the request was promptly refused. Streets and sidewalks were occupied by merchants for their wares, by builders for their materials, and by draymen as overnight parking places; stablemen kept their horses on the streets, used them when breaking in their colts, and held their auctions there. Anyone who complained through the columns of the newspapers was pretty sure to have a swift comeback from the offenders or even from the editors. In the German section just over the line in Bayardstown many of the residents put their chairs out on the sidewalks and spent the Sabbath in beer-drinking and social conversation, much to the disgust of those Anglo-American churchgoers who, with their wives on their arms, had to pick their way through.

III

VISITORS to Pittsburgh could choose from a goodly list of hotels. In the thirties the Exchange probably ranked first. It was located at Penn Avenue and Sixth Street, and boasted all the modern conveniences: a ladies' dining room, a double reading room, and an ice house. The cutlery was stamped with the name of the hotel, and the tables were furnished with French china. The servants, so runs an old account, did not wear wooden or iron-bound shoes, and the guests were not disturbed during the night, therefore, by the clatter incident to bringing in the luggage of late arrivals. The most modern touch was the advertisement of room and bath —the room on one side of the street in the hotel and the bath on the other in Concert Hall. It was at this hostelry that young Charles Dickens stayed during his visit in 1842, when the *literati* of the little city almost went wild in their welcome to him.

For almost three-quarters of a century after its erection in 1840 the Monongahela House was the leading hotel of Pittsburgh. The first building was destroyed in the great fire of 1845, but in 1847 a newer and better hotel was put up on the site, at the northwest corner of Water and Smithfield Streets. Among the guests during its long existence were at least six presidents: John Q. Adams, Andrew Jackson, Zachary Taylor, Abraham Lincoln, Ulysses S. Grant, and Theodore Roosevelt. King Edward VII, as Prince of Wales; Jenny Lind; and various assorted soldiers and statesmen, among them Henry Clay, Jefferson Davis, William H. Seward, William T. Sherman, Philip H. Sheridan, and James G. Blaine, all put up at the Monongahela House.

Country visitors of small means were not as likely to patronize the Exchange Hotel or Monongahela House as one of the scores of combination hotels and boarding houses that dotted the city. In these wayfarers' havens everyone was awakened at six o'clock by the vigorous beating of a gong. At mealtimes the guests gathered in the hall and when the dining-room door was thrown open

273

rushed in, seated themselves, and began eating. The bar served only strong drinks; beer was left to the Germans in their beer gardens. After 1837 the common rooms were lighted by gas, but when it was time to retire the guests took small lamps filled with "burning fluid" up the long dark steps to their rooms. In some parts of the city the lamps were hardly needed, for the glare of the iron mills and the coke ovens cast almost enough light to read by.

Every spring there descended upon Pittsburgh a horde of red-jacketed raftsmen who had come down the rivers with lumber or saw logs. Their journeys ended at Pittsburgh, or they put in there for some fun before they went on to Cincinnati or Louisville. The hotels near the bank of the Allegheny catered to such customers and must have witnessed many a large night as the lumbermen did their bucolic best to paint the town red. The Lion Hotel at Penn and Eleventh kept by Daniel ("in the Lion's Den") Herwig was one of these resorts, as was also the Red Lion Hotel on St. Clair Street, on the site of the Fulton Building. Ben Trimble's Varieties, near Horne's "trimming store," specialized in the type of Thespian entertainment preferred by the raftsmen, and doubtless there were other theaters of the same sort.

For years there was a legend of the Red Lion Hotel told around Pittsburgh's wharves. A half-breed in charge of a crew of raftsmen had abducted a white girl from near Freeport and was keeping her with him in the hotel, seeing to it that she had no chance to escape or to ask for help. Big Ellery Morgan, from the hills behind Kittanning, sensed the situation, and offered to gamble his winter's wages for her. The half-breed accepted and, surrounded by his comrades, began playing, but it was not long before Morgan saw that he was being cheated by a system of signals among the half-breeds. He whispered to the landlord to remove the girl to a place of safety, then threw the accusation of cheating in his opponent's face. The man drew his knife, but Morgan was too quick for him; with a single movement he kicked the table over and smashed the hanging lamp, then in the darkness began laying about with a chair. When the bedlam had quieted down and the landlord had brought a light, it was seen that the half-breed was dead and his seven comrades all disabled.

IV

THE Pittsburgh of the middle period was a city of quaint and amusing contrasts. The elite class was composed of successful businessmen and lawyers; the women possessed the culture and occupied themselves with books and art, children, society, and charity; the men, dignified and "respectable" in deportment, devoted themselves unceasingly to business, and drove hard, sharp bargains. Social consciousness had not yet reached the place where business recognized a primary responsibility to the community, although such a consciousness was budding; a man's first loyalty was to his business and to his partners, and if in serving their interests others were injured he recalled the old adage to "hew to the line and let the chips fall where they may."

Pittsburgh's business days were earnest, not to say tense. The consciousness that here was a great country and a rich region to be built up was ever present, and men felt that fortunes awaited them if their luck and their health held out. Joking among men of business, especially in business hours, was well nigh as irreverent as would have been the singing of *Yankee Doodle* in the First Presbyterian Church on Sunday. There were, indeed, a few unmoral souls who refused to take life too seriously. For many years a *bon mot* of Billy Price, the foundry owner in Pipetown, was retailed amidst appreciative chuckles. It seems that Billy met on the street one day a funeral procession with a coffin borne upon the shoulders of the pallbearers and headed, as was then the custom, by the medico who had attended the deceased. "Well, doctor," said the irrepressible Billy, "I see that like myself you are delivering your work." Gentlemen of the bar were sometimes exceptions to the prevailing "life is real, life is earnest" school; but then they frequently drank themselves to death. Doubtless they had their reasons.

It would have been difficult to draw a line between the middle and lower classes; perhaps it would best have been indicated by standards of conduct rather than by size of income. The lower class very definitely included the poorer and more shiftless Irish immigrants, the drinking, fighting draymen, the canal and steamboat roustabouts, the railroad "Paddies," the quarrelsome washerwomen and charwomen, and the lads who worked in the glass-houses and iron mills instead of going to school or who ran in gangs instead of working in their fathers' countingrooms or stores. It included also the laborers and semi-skilled workers, often of foreign extraction, who worked hard and faithfully, but who expected to receive a living wage for their efforts, and who gave a sympathetic ear to labor and socialist agitators and upon occasion "turned out" for higher wages or better working conditions and paraded the streets with an amusing yet affecting show of manly dignity. These were the backbone of the city's dissidents, the strikers and rioters, the followers of the strange doctrines of the equality of men and the inevitability of the class struggle, whose consistent votes for Jackson destroyed whatever faith in democracy the conservatives may have developed.

The middle classes were composed traditionally of the clerks, overseers, and most skilled workmen—men of some education and ability and of steady habits. They copied, in a small way the attitudes and customs of the well-to-do, and expected to rise into the class above them, either in their own persons or in the persons of their children. They believed, therefore, that all was right with the world; long hours and low wages they accepted uncomplainingly, their eyes fixed steadily on the future. Trade-unions generally found them unresponsive, the new philosophers of the Marxist school found them cold, and even the democratic gentlemen from the West found their temperature only a little above lukewarm.

v

ONE of the most fascinating aspects of the history of any city is the way in which the fine residential sections retreat toward the outskirts before the encroachments of commerce and industry and the once fashionable old mansions are taken over by the slums or torn down to make way for factories and warehouses. During the days when Pittsburgh first developed a well-to-do group Water Street was the preferred residential center, but by the time of the War of 1812 the members had begun to remove elsewhere. For a time there seems to have been no coagulate residential center for them, and they were to be found scattered on the back streets, on Grant's Hill, or in the surrounding country. With the rise of the great industries, however, lower Penn Street (now Penn Avenue), particularly between Third and Fifth Streets (now Marbury and Stanwix) was devoted to the mansions, stables, and servants' quarters of the wealthy. Those who dwelt on the north side of the street were able to extend their gardens through to the bank of the Allegheny.

Meanwhile a short-lived residential section of the socially elect had been built up in the neighborhood of the present Pennsylvania Union Station, but the coming of the railroad forced a flight from that location. Some moved to Bluff Street on Boyd's Hill, others to the "second bank" region of Allegheny on Stockton, Ridge, and Western Avenues, and still others to the Point Breeze neighborhood, then a lovely rolling country of fields and orchards. Many of those who belonged to the Third Presbyterian Church settled the "Third Church Colony" in Oakland, and a few moved to the woods of Squirrel Hill. The exodus to Sewickley Heights by some of the most wealthy citizens did not begin until late in the century.

Life on lower Penn Street was slow-paced, gracious, and dignified; the colony of businessmen that lived there constituted a quiet island of wealth and culture in the midst of a swirling sea of commerce and industry. The hoarse whistles of steamboats and factories and the clatter of the trains on Liberty Street were audible at all hours of the day and night, clouds of soot rained perpetually upon the well-kept flower gardens and the white party dresses of the women, and rows of "honeymoon cottages" encroached, in a demure but determined manner, upon the privacy of the neighborhood; still for fifty years the dwellers on lower Penn Street clung to the massive brick mansions that spelled stability and prestige for them, and even after the third generation had departed to Ridge Avenue, Sewickley, or Point Breeze many of the older people remained there to die.

Penn Street was "Third Presbyterian" in its early days, but in time the easier life within the "Creed" exercised its fascinations and the younger set began to take the "Shorter Catechism" and the sterner Presbyterian responsibilities less seriously or even to slip away to Trinity Church. The Steinway pianos in the high-ceilinged parlors were covered with sheet music bearing such titles as *Love in a Cottage* and *Leave Me Not Yet*, and the decorous maidens of Penn Street found excuses for frequent trips to the post office around St. Valentine's Day. Vanities such as perfumes and Paris styles ("Gents' and Boys' Clothing," as well as women's) found favor, and the "Balm of a Thousand Flowers" (which "prevents bad breath, cleans the teeth white as alabaster, gives a beautiful complexion—removing tan, pimples, and freckles —and makes shaving easy") found a ready sale to those who had lost their pristine Scotch canniness. New-fangled ways of doing things crept in. Camphene and lard-oil lamps took the place of whale oil and candles. The ladies took to tight lacing in spite of the warning that it caused red noses, and it became quite the thing for substantial citizens and their wives to pose stiffly before the daguerreotype—the "Pencil of Nature." Divorces even came hesitantly into style (though still frowned upon by most of the socially elect) and there are said to have been a dozen applications waiting before the court of quarter sessions in 1848.

VI

THE balls held on lower Penn Street and on the second bank in Allegheny were occasions to be remembered and described to future generations. Sometimes the program was varied by tableaux and charades, but always there was a remarkable display of refreshments. One old lady tells of being allowed, as a small girl, to glimpse the supper table at a party. There were "pyramids of maccaroons, buttressed with barley sugar, reaching almost to the chandelier, more pyramids of quartered oranges, with fountains of spun sugar veiling them, ice cream in ravishing shapes, a basket of flowers in natural colors just like the plaster casts the men sold on the streets, a rampant horse, a lion couchant, a pyramid of calves-foot jelly glasses, alternating pink and yellow, high openwork china dishes heaped with almonds."

The military balls that the Duquesne Grays or the Pittsburgh

Blues held in their armories were gala occasions, and there were "select hops" at the Exchange Hotel and the Monongahela House. The young people and even the matrons could doubtless enjoy them until two in the morning, but the sedate business-man, with his mind on the strenuous transactions of the morrow and with no place in the crowded ballroom to sit down and rest his weary feet, was much more inclined to consider "big parties big nuisances!"

If there was a social arbiter in Pittsburgh during the first half of the century it was probably the aristocratic and open-handed William Croghan, Jr., who on a visit to Pittsburgh had met and married Mary Carson O'Hara, the daughter of General James O'Hara. He finally settled in Pittsburgh and built "Picnic," a brick and stone mansion still standing on Stanton Heights. He had, in addition to his own extensive patrimony, a considerable inheritance through his wife, so that he was one of the wealth-iest men in Pittsburgh. He was readily acknowledged to be one of the handsomest men in the city as well as the courtliest; his wife and son had died in 1827 and 1828, and he had only a daughter, Mary, born in 1827, to inherit his fortune.

When Mary Croghan was a girl of fifteen she was sent to a select boarding school kept by a Mrs. McLeod on Staten Island. There, a year or so later, the middle-aged Captain Edward E. H. Schenley, a British veteran of the Peninsular Campaign, New Orleans, and Waterloo, and twice a widower, appeared on a visit and captivated the susceptible heart of the Pittsburgh heiress. The two were secretly married and departed for England—the third elopement for the captain. It is said that William Croghan fainted when he heard of his daughter's marriage, and Queen Victoria refused to allow young Mrs. Schenley's presentation at court for some years because she had been "a disobedient daughter."

The father finally forgave the Schenleys and they visited him at "Picnic." In the hope of persuading them to stay he built an extensive addition to the house, but he died in 1850 before it was quite completed. The Schenleys visited Pittsburgh occasionally and once spent five years there. As the result of Mary Croghan's runaway marriage one of Pittsburgh's largest fortunes is today held by a foreign family.

The social high spot of Pittsburgh's early history was the occasion of the visit of Lafayette in 1825 during his triumphal tour of the country. He approached Pittsburgh on May 30 by way of Lawrenceville, where he received a salute of twenty-four guns and breakfasted with Colonel Wooley in the arsenal. The road to the city was lined with the curious and crowded with military organizations. At the tollhouse at what is now Twentieth Street, Lafayette and Mayor John Snowden got into an open barouche drawn by four white horses and entered the city. They were followed by other carriages containing veterans of the Revolution and by a long procession of troops and citizens. On a vacant lot at the southwest corner of Penn and Tenth were gathered a great number of school children, each wearing portraits of Washington and Lafayette. From there on the children preceded the "nation's guest" and strewed flowers on the streets. Finally the procession halted at the Mansion House, on the northwest corner of Wood and Fifth (now the site of the First National Bank), which was to be Layafette's headquarters during his stay.

The day was well occupied by functions. There was a banquet at which Henry Baldwin, Harmar Denny, Charles Shaler, and James Ross spoke. In the evening there was a magnificent ball at the Pittsburgh Hotel at the southeast corner of Wood and Third Streets; invitations to it had been eagerly sought, and the possession of one was the final cachet of social distinction then and for many years to come.

Among other activities during the next two days, Lafayette visited the former home of his deceased aide, Presley Neville; lunched in the Barlow home on the second bank; went through the Bakewell glasshouse; and stood sponsor at the baptism of a child in St. Patrick's Roman Catholic Church. Finally, on June 1, Lafayette and his entourage left Pittsburgh for Erie. They were escorted out of town by the light dragoons, and the departure was an occasion of such melancholy to the citizens that Mrs. Thomas Barlow felt quite justified in writing to her sister that it "put her in mind of a funeral."

VII

THE number and variety of amusements in Pittsburgh increased amazingly after the War of 1812. Among the most popular were the museums, which were a diverting combination of the educational with the farcical and the morbid. At one time or another there appeared in these places the whole gamut of entertainment hokum: the "industrious flees," the armless wonder, the Siamese twins, the tattooed man, a fire eater "who also juggles, sings, and recites," General Tom Thumb, waxworks, Egyptian mummies, magicians, and a real Chinese woman with "astonishing little feet." There were phantasmagorias, dissolving views, panoramas, dioramas, and fantoccini in abundance, not to mention "Sinclair's celebrated peristrephic," which was not "a theatrical exhibition, so that no religious scruples need prevent any from visiting it." Napoleon fought the Battle of Waterloo a thousand times, was buried over and over again on St. Helena, and Moscow must have been a crisp, what with its many conflagrations.

Ventriloquists, mesmerists, clairvoyants, astrologists, spiritualists, and phrenologists held the public attention in turn. Evidently the art of ballyhoo was well understood; a Pittsburgh editor found himself being sued for questioning the genuineness of a handkerchief performance; and at another time the child clairvoyant, Tennessee Claflin, who professed to be able to cure diseases and tell where stolen property could be found, was arrested for conspiracy to defraud and was defended in court by no less a personage than "Glorious Tom" Marshall. Of rather more valid interest were the performances of Swiss bell ringers and the exhibition of a planetarium.

The "Glorious Fourth" in 1835 was marked by the "Grand Ascension of a Splendid Variegated Silk Balloon" under the guidance of the intrepid aeronaut, Mr. Richard Clayton, from a specially constructed amphitheatre at Penn and Tenth Streets, when a "living quadruped" was let down in a parachute. The celebration was marred by the collapse of a grandstand that injured a number of spectators, and one woman was said to have died as the result of the accident. Clayton made other ascensions in his trusty "aerostat" in 1837, 1839, and 1840. Before the last one he advertised his intention to cross the Alleghenies and carry letters and newspapers with him. Alas for all his elaborate preparations, which among other things included a car in the form of a boat to be used in case he was driven out to sea and forced down. He landed ignominiously at Tarentum the evening of the day of his departure.

Circuses, which visited in the city frequently, usually camped in the vicinity of Penn Street and the canal. Their menageries, performing ponies, trained lions and elephants, rope dancers, strong men, and equestriennes were highly attractive, but in 1840 the Pittsburgh Moral Society rather spoiled the sport by having the appearance of female stunt riders banned in order to avoid "the slightest possible shadow of obloquy." In 1824 there was a serious riot when some rowdies stoned a building at Third and Ferry in which a circus was performing. The besieged circus men put up a good defense and finally drove off their attackers, shooting and killing a citizen named Hartzell in the process.

Prize fighting was not unknown, but was looked upon as a brutal sport, and a bout was likely to be raided by sheriff or constables. Cock fighters were also in danger of police interference, but for some reason bear baiting, hog worrying, and dog fighting seem to have been permitted; perhaps the followers of these sports were cautious enough to leave the confines of the towns and to "fix" the country law officers.

A sport engaged in by young men who could afford the equipment was boat racing. For years the rivalry among the boat clubs was intense, and on more than a few occasions the town took the races so seriously that thousands of people lined the shores to watch them. Each club had its distinctive color or colors, and it must have been a striking sight to see the gay-shirted oarsmen bending to the task. Every club had pleasure barges as well as racing craft and frequently went on picnics, sometimes accompanied by the young ladies. Cricket was another sport popular in the fifties, and several cricket clubs were formed and a number of match games played with teams from other cities, but by 1860 cricket advocates had to admit that its popularity was giving way to baseball.

There were in the vicinity of Pittsburgh a number of dinner-dance resorts, and they were well patronized, though Victorian standards demanded that young couples be accompanied by chaperons, except perhaps in the daytime. Rosedale Gardens, in Manchester, possessed "beautifully embellished" grounds from which a view could be had of the Ohio; the patrons ate strawberries and cream and listened to the orchestra the while they looked out across the river. Sweeny's Mount Emmett Hotel overlooked the village of Allegheny and was a place much patronized for its chicken and waffle dinners. Hartman's Tavern near Woods Run was reached by a stage that ran from the Exchange Hotel and that afforded a delightful moonlight ride along the shimmering ponds of lower Water Lane, now Western Avenue. Mrs. Hartman, the genial hostess, set an excellent table, served the best of home-made wines, and her guests were free to roam in the five acres of grounds planted with trees and shrubbery, or to rest in the grape arbors between dances. Hartman's was one of the favorite termini for sleighing parties.

There were other resorts in abundance. The Yellow Tavern near Lawrenceville was popular with the young and its dance floor was seldom unoccupied. Shakespeare Gardens, near Penn and Shady, was famous in the forties and was distinguished by what would now be called a floor show. It is said that the famous circus clown, Dan Rice, first became stage-struck while working there as a lad, and he began his career by acquiring a half interest in a performing pig.

Anniversaries were celebrated with much noise and feasting. New Year's Day was punctuated with the reports of firearms, and oldsters noted sadly that the custom of making New Year's calls was falling off. January 8, the anniversary of Jackson's victory at New Orleans, was for a time a patriotic occasion second only to the Fourth of July and was celebrated by banquets and parades; one winter when the Monongahela was frozen over the Jackson Blues held their parade on the ice. An annual winter event, for some time at least, was the parade of the "Snag Marines," an organization of steamboat officers. Horse-drawn yawls, placed on runners and decorated with flags and bunting and headed by one containing a band, paraded the streets to the vast delight of the youngsters.

In the thirties the "Pyrotechnical Association" set off fireworks from boats on the Monongahela, apparently for the sake of the entertainment rather than to celebrate Independence Day, for they seem to have missed that occasion. The Fourth was marked, however, by parades, banquets, and speeches and various political functions. By 1853 young America had discovered and put the firecracker to such efficient use that the mayor felt obliged to issue a proclamation forbidding their use on the Fourth.

Summer also brought muster day, the annual occasion upon which by law every able-bodied man had to practice drilling in order to be ready to fight and to die for his country. The growth of a professional army had long since reduced the muster to an absurdity and the men usually chose to treat it as such. They assembled on Herron Hill with wooden swords and guns, broomsticks, or wooden cannon. Some even wore bonnets and skirts and blacked their faces with burnt cork. A commander was elected and a desultory drill performed, perhaps a straggling march was made through the streets, and then the hilarious troops might take it into their heads to chase their commandant out of town. Usually the muster ended at the Oregon House, near Grant and Fourth, which was renowned for its liquors and the prodigality with which it dealt them out to thirsty warriors.

XXI

National Politics on a Local Scale

THE so-called "Era of Good Feeling" brought little of that tender quality to the politicians of Pittsburgh, and the newspapers, as usual, were in the thickest of the fray. In 1820 a journalistic observer wrote: "We have been somewhat amused of late with the *triangular warfare* carried on between the Pittsburgh newspapers—the editors of these papers are all *grand dignitaries* of the empire—one is *alderman*, another *prothonotary*, and the third *sheriff* of Allegheny county. But *we* say nothing! When the big folks fall out—we little folks have nothing to do but *look on*." The three editors referred to were respectively John M. Snowden of the *Mercury*, Ephraim Pentland of the *Statesman*, and Morgan Neville of the *Gazette*. The last-named paper had been edited by John Scull, its founder, until 1818, when he retired and left the management to his son, John I. Scull, and Morgan Neville, the son of Colonel Presley Neville. Young Scull soon resigned and Neville was sole editor, probably until 1824, when he removed to Cincinnati. In 1829 Neville B. Craig acquired the *Gazette*; it had always been the conservative organ of the community, but under him it became a veritable fugleman of political and moral propriety.

Neville B. Craig, who was the son of Major Isaac Craig and

Amelia Neville Craig, was born in 1787 in Bouquet's redoubt, and he was educated at the Pittsburgh Academy and at Princeton. He was admitted to the bar in 1810 and was at various times during his life city solicitor of Pittsburgh, a member of the state legislature, and a local historian. He was a man of "fixed principles," scrupulously honest, enthusiastic in his support of Pittsburgh's industrial and commercial progress, and intensely conservative in his moral and social outlook. Toward his political antagonists he was intemperately bitter and sarcastic, and they came to refer to him as the "green-eyed monster," from the green eyeshade that he always wore in the office. He wasted no time on frivolity, spent slavishly long hours at his work, and supervised his employees with a rough paternalism that was meant to be kindly. Craig considered the theater a bad moral influence and forbade his employees to attend.

In 1833 the *Gazette* became Pittsburgh's first daily, an example that other papers were not slow in following. Under Craig the *Gazette* was in turn conservative Democratic, Antimasonic, and Whig, and after his retirement in 1841 to the rural fastness of what is now the Bellefield section of Oakland and the accession of David N. White as editor, the Whig allegiance continued until the formation of the Republican party, when it joined with the new alignment.

The chief rival of the *Gazette* was the paper which, as the result of a series of consolidations and changes of ownership, was known successively as the *Commonwealth*, the *Mercury*, the *Mercury and Allegheny Democrat*, the *Mercury and Manufacturer*, and the *Post*. During these metamorphoses the paper ranged from a nonpartisan stand at the beginning to violent Jacksonianism in the thirties, and with the advent of the *Post* banner title it became pro-labor. Perhaps that policy was good business in a day when every other paper in Pittsburgh was anti-labor or avoided the problem of labor relations. John M. Snowden, the editor of the old *Mercury*, was not only a newspaper man but a banker, an alderman, mayor of Pittsburgh from 1825 to 1828, and finally associate judge of Allegheny County. The *Post* was one of the most progressive papers in the city and was the first to use the new "electric telegraph" for the reception of news dispatches.

A third important newspaper in Pittsburgh's middle period was the *Dispatch*, founded in 1846 by Colonel J. Heron Foster. It was the first successful penny paper in the West and, of course, was rather small in size at first. Unlike most other papers of the time, it owed allegiance to no particular party but was independent in its attitude toward both local and national problems. At any rate it seems to have prospered and at one time probably had as large a circulation as all the other Pittsburgh papers combined.

These three were by no means all the newspapers published in Pittsburgh. In 1850 there were said to be nine dailies and eighteen weeklies. The rise and fall of journalistic enterprises was rapid and only a few attained any permanent place in the community. In 1841 the *Chronicle* began an existence that was to prove undistinguished for several decades. The *Pittsburgh Saturday Visiter* (spelling justified by Dr. Samuel Johnson's dictionary), published from 1847 to 1857 by Jane Grey Swisshelm, was one of the most flamboyant in the cause of reform, particularly in its advocacy of women's rights and its opposition to slavery.

Pittsburgh's first Sunday paper was published by George Youngson of the *Mercury*, February 1, 1848. It was scarcely off the press before it was met by the loud and unanimous opposition of the churches. The crusading Mrs. Swisshelm was first to break a lance when she launched an attack in her *Visiter:* "We have taken a good look at it—its romantic stories, poetry, and love songs, theatrical intelligence and commercial news, its two columns of jokes with the old joker at the head—its compliments to Mrs. Swisshelm, Thorns' bear, Talkrand's death and St. Paul's piety, and various other things, all fixed up for Sunday reading. Take a look at it, all of you who can, and see if it does not present almost as much variety as American Christianity itself. Fact is, it is about as good a portrait of our Sabbath-talking-about, Sabbath-breaking, Church-going, rum-selling, loud-praying, manstealing, heathen-converting, heathen-making, purity-preaching, concubine-keeping, psalm-singing, orphan-grinding, church-building, soul-selling, revival-manufacturing, God-defying piety, which we have ever met with in our life." In vain the dismayed Youngson tried to explain that the paper was printed on Saturday and only issued on Sunday. Eventually he had to change his banner title to *Saturday Mercury* or run the risk of having his regular edition ruined.

The *American Manufacturer*, begun in 1830 by William B. Conway, a follower of the notorious Frances Wright D'Arusemont, was frankly an anti-religious paper, and the churches and the other papers of the town regarded it as a Caliban. Probably Conway thought of himself as a Puck—at least he took a Puckish delight in tormenting his critics. In 1838 "the vile and speckled reptile" was made secretary of the newly organized Iowa Territory and the paper was taken over by Zantzinger McDonald and some associates, who made newspaper life interesting for some years by their embroilments with other publishers. The *Gazette* finally absorbed the sheet in 1842.

In spite of the violent disputes among the newspaper men of Pittsburgh they seem to have been friends outside business hours, much like the rival attorneys who drink together in a pothouse, and there was a continual friendly shift in the alignment of publishers and editorial writers. On one occasion in 1846 George Youngson and L. Y. Clarke were jailed together, the first for libeling the second, and the second for assaulting the first. They shared the same room and the same bed. "They appear to agree very well," noted an observant journalist.

This fellowship was well illustrated in 1847 at the height of the political troubles of the Mexican War period, when the printers of Pittsburgh held a banquet. Neville B. Craig was the toastmaster on the occasion, and the climax of the evening was the giving of a toast that included the names of all the leading newspapers of the city: "The printers of the *Olden Time* who help to unfurl the proud *Banner* of the *Stars and Stripes:* May their successors *Advocate* their principles and *Chronicle* in their *Gazette* to the *American* people that the *Spirit of the Age* requires them to *Post* their *Daybooks* and *Journals* and receive a *Dispatch* by *Telegraph* to prove a welcome *Visitor* to the *Manufacturers* of the *Iron City*."

II

THE political battles of the twenties in Pittsburgh were largely waged between the adherents and the opponents of Andrew Jackson. In 1824 Edward Patchell, a forcible backwoods preacher, organized western Pennsylvania for Jackson ("on the straight course," as he termed it), while Henry Baldwin was "praying good God, good Devil not knowing whose hands he might fall into." In spite of the lukewarmness of the old line leaders Patchell was able to write his hero that "I have reduced the Lousie party here from ten thousand to something less than fifty, and they are chiefly the antient and notorious wire workers, they are the office holders and office hunters, and all they can do now is grin and show their teeth."

Pittsburghers agreed in the main in the support of the protective tariff, and the supposed defection of Henry Clay from the system that he had fathered was received with widespread indignation. In 1825 Patchell and a Jacksonian editor were indicted "for inciting a riot—that is to say for holding out inducements to other persons, to roast an effigy of a Kentucky Gambler [Henry Clay] over a burning tar barrel." The affair came to nothing, even for the sixty witnesses who had been summoned, for the county commissioners refused to pay their fees.

Two years later the protectionists of Pittsburgh, headed by men like Walter Forward, Charles Shaler, Christopher Magee, Neville B. Craig, and Ephraim Pentland, gave a dinner to Clay in the Anchor Paper Mill. There were over six hundred diners present to hear Clay when he rose to respond to a toast. "As the silver tones of his voice first began to fall upon the ear, breathless silence succeeded to the acclamations which his rising had created. But when sentiments of exalted patriotism, wrought to the highest coloring by the strength of his genius, rolled with all the modulations of intense feeling upon the auditory, the excitement could not be restrained; reiterated applause broke from all parts of the assembly, and the orator was obliged again and again to stop until the desire to hear produced silence and calmness." At the conclusion of his address Clay offered the following toast: "The city of Pittsburg; the abundance, variety and excellence

of its fabrics attest the wisdom of the policy which fosters them."
Among the toasts were these: "Alexander Hamilton—The first
advocate of protective duties"; "The Woolen Bill—Let us feed,
clothe and protect ourselves"; "The Anchor Paper Mill—The
only American factory ever stopped through Henry Clay. It
stopped one day to honor him who prevented it from stopping
altogether."

By 1827 Jackson sentiment had grown to such an extent that
most of the regular party leaders of Pittsburgh hopped on the
bandwagon. On July 4, 1827, a Jackson dinner was held at which
John M. Snowden, William Wilkins, and Henry Baldwin were
present and after which the last, standing on a pile of British
cannon captured at the Battle of Lake Erie, read the Declaration
of Independence in the justly famous Baldwin manner. Pentland
enlivened the presidential campaign by issuing the so-called
"Coffin Handbills," which by cartoons and statements brought
into relief Jackson's supposed complicity with Burr's treason,
his activities as a duelist and slave trader, and his execution of
militiamen. In the end, however, Pennsylvania's vote was gained
for the victor of New Orleans by the cautious assurances of his
managers that they favored the protective tariff, although the
South was assured that they opposed it. Jackson's ascension to
the presidential chair was the signal for the beginning of a new
and more bitter struggle.

III

THE overwhelming victory of the Jacksonians in 1828 left their
opponents prostrate and almost hopelessly divided and opened
the way for the rise of one of the peculiar political and social
phenomena of American history—the Antimasonic party. The
alleged abduction and murder of William Morgan in New York
in 1826 by Masons in retaliation for his threatened revelation
of their vows was the beginning of the Antimasonic agitation.
In western Pennsylvania there was already considerable distrust
of secret organizations on the part of the radical sects among
the Germans and Scotch-Irish, and the Pluymart and Emmons
bank robbery and the mysterious jail breaks and final pardon of

the former, a Mason, were well remembered. The result was that the opponents of Jackson both in Pennsylvania and in the northern states in general saw an excellent chance to turn his democratic adherents against him by posting him as a member of an aristocratic secret organization. The leader of this attempt in Pennsylvania was the brilliant and unscrupulous Thaddeus Stevens, who had already gained fame as the father of the public-school system of the state and was currently building new political fences with the graft from the Pennsylvania Public Works.

The Antimasonic movement in Pittsburgh was in full swing in 1829, and the strength of the party was indicated by the success of Harmar Denny in a special congressional election that year. The *Statesman*, then edited by a Mason, John B. Butler, took up the cudgel for Masonry, even though his paper was an anti-Jackson publication, and "Green-eyed Monster" Craig swung his *Gazette* into the Antimasonic ranks. The supposed Masonic ritual was published, and the Masons were the unfortunate butts of ridicule from the stage, and of vituperation from the pulpit. The lodges began to decrease both in numbers and in membership, then members began to drop out and lodges to surrender their charters, until finally Lodge No. 45 was the only one left in Pittsburgh.

Anne Royall, the redoubtable and eccentric enemy of evangelical Christianity and the self-appointed champion of the Masons, made a visit to Pittsburgh during the height of the excitement and left a scorching indictment of the city as "that barbarous, ignorant, smoky, pitiful, rascally, dirty, dingy, silly, murderous, anti-masonic, vagabond village." It was no wonder that someone proceeded to horsewhip her, and then, when brought into court, escaped with a twenty-dollar fine.

In 1832 the Antimasonic party's political bias was proclaimed by the humorous and revealing fact that it nominated a Mason, William Wirt, for president. Allegheny County was carried but Pennsylvania and the nation were lost, and "Old Hickory" entered upon another term in the White House.

Meanwhile the Whig party was taking shape as the champion of anti-Jacksonism. A "Meeting of the Foes of Usurpation," three thousand strong, held in a factory yard resulted in resolutions against Jackson. The Young Men's Whig Association, formed in 1834, adopted a remarkable resolution that should throw light upon the moot question as to whether history repeats itself. "Resolved," it read, "that *we have so marked* the insidious encroachments of the executive of the United States—we have seen the present incumbent of the Presidential chair enter office with promises of 'retrenchment & reform' and we are now witnesses of an enormous annual increase of expenditure, and have learned to construe *his* 'reform' into an unblushing distribution of offices and posts of honour as 'Spoils of Victory.' . . . We have seen him lay his hand upon the Currency of the Country, and the sources of its prosperity dried up—desolation and ruin spread over the land by the operation of an 'Experiment' in political quackery . . . . he claims the power to construe the Constitution as he 'understands it,' and to execute the laws in conformity with such construction."

By 1835 the Jacksonians of Pennsylvania were so divided that the Whigs and the Antimasons were able to elect as governor broad-beamed and good-natured Joseph Ritner, "the Wagoner of the Alleghenies," and thus set Thaddeus Stevens in the position of dictator at Harrisburg. An investigation of secret societies was begun as soon as the legislature convened, but it struck a snag when subpoenaed Masons refused to testify; try as he might, Stevens could not get the legislature to punish them for their stubbornness. The Antimasonic party in Pennsylvania was ruined and never again exercised any very potent influence. It had, however, served its political mission by opening a breach in the Democratic ranks and pointing the way toward the organization of an effective party of opposition. The corruption of the Stevens regime and the revulsion that came as a result of the panic of 1837 led to the victory of the Democrats under David R. Porter in the gubernatorial contest of 1838. In Pittsburgh the victors celebrated by parading through the town and then over a bridge of boats to a sandbar in the Monongahela, where roast ox and freely flowing whiskey combined to make them forget the years of defeat.

IV

THE presidential campaign of 1840 has long been recognized as a prime example of the power of ballyhoo in American politics. The principles of the Whigs may have been conservative, but their nomination of William Henry Harrison, the "hero" of Tippecanoe, their adoption of the homely log cabin as their campaign emblem, and their loud and long lip service to the principles of frontier democracy won enough votes to carry the day.

The hard times then existing gave people plenty of leisure time to devote to politics and they proceeded to enjoy the campaign with a will. Log cabin tabernacles were "raised" at various points and enthusiastic meetings were held in them. Liberty poles came back into vogue. Whig horses and riders were garlanded with strings of buckeyes, and streamers bearing the words "Two Dollars a Day and Roast Beef" were displayed in advocacy of the protective tariff, which was promoted as the cure for hard times. A Pittsburgh newspaper house began printing a weekly that was called *The Old Granny That Delivered the Frontier from the British Proctor, and His Host of Mercenaries and Savages*—a title coined from Harrison's nickname and from his activities in the War of 1812. A rally in October, said to have been attended by thirty thousand people, was addressed by the vice-presidential candidate, John Tyler, and by Walter Forward, Pittsburgh's own orator and former congressman. Forward was later rewarded for his campaign services by the post of secretary of the treasury.

The Jacksonian Democrats were led by the able William Wilkins, who as a congressman and senator had been dubbed "the iron knight" because of his advocacy of tariff protection for Pittsburgh manufacturers. Wilkins had also been a federal judge and a minister to Russia, and he was allied by marriage to the politically potent Dallas brothers, George M. and Trevanion B., and the three were often spoken of as "the family" by their enemies. Wilkins had yielded to expediency to the extent that he had voted for the compromise tariff of 1833 (which was designed to keep South Carolina in the union) and had thereby alienated his high tariff friends. The fact that in 1839 he ran for three elective offices was used against him, and he was dubbed the "Bashaw with three tails"—an epithet that stuck to him during the campaign of 1840.

The Harrison victory was celebrated in January by a reception to the successful candidate when he passed through Pittsburgh on his way to Washington—a brilliant contrast to the day when, as a callow young lieutenant, he had signed in Major Craig's book a receipt for the issuance of a flatboat for the transportation of men and supplies down river to the Indian wars.

v

THE politics of the forties were so badly mixed that voters could scarcely be blamed for not knowing where to cast their influence. The Whig party had profited by its victory of 1840 for only one month, for the death of Harrison placed in the presidency the arch-Democratic (though anti-Jacksonian) John Tyler. The Whigs, who had never been united on much of anything beside their hatred of Andrew Jackson, found that they had to cope not only with the Democrats but with the remnants of the Antimasons and the new Liberty and Native American parties. The Clay-Polk campaign of 1844 was waged bitterly by both sides. Though he lost the nation, Clay carried Allegheny County by a narrow margin, and that only, said the Democrats, because Whig coal merchants hired all the Democrats they could find as crews for their coal boats and floated them down river on a water-rise that came providentially just before the election.

Nevertheless, from 1840 to 1853 Pittsburgh was a Whig stronghold. The party's advocacy of industrial and commerical progress through the tariff and the expansion of railroads accorded with the local spirit and made it more popular than the political factions that were more interested in women's rights, secret societies, or slavery.

The Mexican War was entered upon with enthusiasm by the Democrats and not quite so whole-heartedly by their opponents, save for those who were fascinated by the glamor of expansion. Several of Pittsburgh's swank marching companies, including the Duquesne Grays, the Jackson Blues, the Irish Greens, and the German nondescripts, led by such local celebrities as General Alexander Hays and Colonel Samuel Black, had been mustered into service and had departed for Mexico amid the cheers of the citizenry, with ranks so well filled that two companies could scarcely cram on a steamboat. The reformers of Pittsburgh were openly contemptuous. "Our gallant volunteers are surely going to Mexico to kill women and children," wrote Mrs. Swisshelm. "This is too plain to admit of proof, and that woman they shot at Monterey while she was carrying bread and water to dying men, and binding their wounds with her own clothes, is one witness at the bar of heaven to prove it there. The weakness of the enemy has allowed them to get into their country, desolate their homes and bombard their churches, all for glory, as an Irishman knocks down his friend for love. Well, those who do not die there will doubtless return completely besmeared with glory. Those who leave their families to the charity of the world will know that this winter, or while the war fever lasts, they will be kept from starving; after that their wives can sew for twelve and a half cents a day to support themselves and children."

A year and a half later the soldiers returned "besmeared with glory," but with ranks so depleted that a single steamboat easily carried a regiment. Wooden legs, empty sleeves, and angry red scars—beyond these their gains were few. The war did much to jolt Pittsburghers out of their absorption in industrial progress by turning the spotlight on the slavery issue; antislavery sentiment began to grow as it became evident that slaveholders meant to profit by the annexation of alien soil. The old parties, afraid to face new issues, fell into a state of innocuous desuetude and the lunatic fringe that is always in evidence when an era of social and economic change is in the offing became louder and funnier—as witness Mayor Joe Barker.

VI

DURING the forties Pittsburgh was afflicted by a rash of street-preachers, most of them uncouth and ignorant and each fanatical upon one or two reforms or social panaceas. Joseph Barker was by far the most prominent of the group. Nothing is known of his origin or background; not even his birth date is known, though he was old enough to have had a son in the Mexican War. When he first became known as a soap-box orator around 1840 his chief subjects of interest were Antimasonry, opposition to politics and politicians, and Native Americanism and its concomitant, anti-Catholicism. His final admonition to his audience on one occasion was not to trust politicians, "not even Joe Barker himself, if he comes sneaking about." The *Post*, in recounting the incident, dryly nodded approval and added that "this was the most wholesome advice he gave during the whole speech."

Barker's home was in rough and tough Bayardstown and, so far as surviving information indicates, he had no visible means of support, although he held petty public offices under the Whigs for short periods. He was, however, always clean shaven and made a good appearance in his neat white neckcloth, stovepipe hat, and cape. He possessed a remarkable influence over the rowdies of the neighborhood, and they gathered every Sunday to hear him preach from the canal bridge and on other days at the Diamond or one of the markets. He was usually followed by Hugh Kirkland, who had once been a Presbyterian preacher, but who was now Joe Barker's yes-man and document-bearer. Whenever Barker wanted to emphasize a telling point he would shout, "That's true, isn't it Kirkland?"

"Every word of it," Kirkland would reply, "and I have the papers here to prove it." Then he would take a paper from his bundle and pass it around, not the least embarrassed that it had nothing to do with the point at issue.

Joe became such a nuisance that he was arrested for speaking on the steps of the Catholic cathedral and spent thirty days in Mount Airy, but he was far from feeling chastened. Finally in November, 1849, a drunken man at another street service started a riot that soon spread to Barker's stand at the canal bridge. Barker had been delivering an anti-Catholic harangue that was even more intemperate than usual, and as the result of the riot and his speech he soon found himself indicted for obstructing the streets, using obscene language, and causing a riot. Barker was promptly tried before Judge Patton, convicted, fined $250 and costs, and sentenced to a year's imprisonment.

The furor caused by Barker's trial and imprisonment made him a public hero, and he was immediately put forth, perhaps at first as a joke, as a candidate for mayor in the election that was to be held on January 7. Few worried about the situation and the *Chronicle* doubtless spoke the mind of the respectable element when it said that the "people generally know him, and we are willing to leave him in their hands." The vote was large for a municipal election, and when it became apparent that Barker was gaining (there were no secret ballots then) the Whigs turned in and helped him. The result was the election by a plurality vote of an inmate of the county jail to the mayoralty.

It was late in the evening when the last vote was counted, but a torchlight parade was started at once. The crowd gathered about the jail and threatened to break down the door unless the successful candidate was produced, and the sheriff promptly liberated his prisoner. Barker was then hoisted on the shoulders of the mob and carried to the mayor's office, where Mayor Herron was ejected from his chair and Joe Barker deposited therein. The next morning the judges hastened to release him legally until a pardon arrived from the governor, when the new mayor was inducted into office. Someone with a sense of humor saw to it that Judge Patton administered the oath of office.

Barker made a good impression at first by abandoning his street-preaching and sticking to business. Obstructions were cleared from the streets, much to the consternation of businessmen. The mayor with two assistants carefully tested the weights and measures in the city markets. On one occasion an irate butter woman, whose stock Barker found light in weight, threw a pound of the squashy stuff in his face. "Pick it up men," said Joe, wiping his face as he turned away, "it's good enough for the poor."

On another occasion, soon after Barker assumed office, a colored woman named Belle Lowes was brought before him for drunkenness. She was an old offender and doubtless an acquaintance of His Honor. "Well, Belle," said the mayor, "what have you to say for yourself?"

"Well, Mayor," replied Belle, "I believe I was drunk."

"Then I shall have to send you to Mount Airy for twenty days, Belle," said the mayor.

Belle objected to this and there followed an amusing colloquy as to the relative expense of sending her up once for twenty days or four times during that period.

"Well," said the mayor finally, "what would you have me do then?"

"Do?" replied the indignant Belle, "Why, you know well 'nuf what to do without ax'n me. What does the Bible tell you: 'Do justice and love mercy.' Do what your own conscience says."

"Well," replied the imperturbable mayor, "my conscience says twenty days. Next case."

In those days steamboats carried German bands to attract and to amuse passengers. In 1850 one steamboat installed a calliope, which had been recently invented by a Pittsburgher named Jenigen, and it drowned out all the German bands on the water front. An indignant rival captain went before Mayor Barker and asked that he issue a restraining order against the owner of the calliope. Barker listened to his argument and then answered like a true Native American: "The calliope is an American institution, and the brass band is a damned imported Dutch institution. I am for America all the time. Get out!"

Barker had scarcely taken office before he opened a feud with the police committee, of which he was a member but which was not under his control. On one occasion he fired all the watchmen in the morning and then reinstated them before night. Each morning, after hearing the cases that had accumulated during the night, he would deliver a lecture on the intransigence and general incompetence of the council, the police committee, the courts, or upon some other aversion. Finally in October matters came to a head. Barker accused several policemen of misconduct and removed them from their positions. The police commissioners attempted to reinstate the men, but were themselves clapped into jail by the mayor. Barker was then arrested by the sheriff and released on bail. Presently there were two rival police forces patrolling the town and they were soon more interested in clubbing each other than in preserving the peace. After a riot between the two factions the mayor was again arrested and he gave bail for two thousand dollars, at the same time disclaiming "all responsibility for these disorderly persons who have been running the streets for some nights past with maces in their hands." An amusing tempest in a teapot followed: several more suits were brought against the mayor; the two sets of watchmen continued on duty. Perforce a truce was entered into. The mayor's men cared for the lamps and cried the hours, while the committee's men marched around in a body and attended to disturbers of the peace. Barker resumed his soap-boxing habits and explained his case on the street corners. In the end, however, the mayor submitted quietly when the county court decided against him and discharged his private force.

Barker ran for mayor the next January on the "Reform" ticket but polled only about a quarter of the vote; his successful rival was John B. Guthrie. Mrs. Swisshelm, who also ran for mayor in the same election, polled only three votes. Barker soon sank into obscurity. He was thrown out of the Pennsylvania senate chamber when he tried to make a speech and was from time to time arraigned for trying to speak on the streets of Pittsburgh. Several times he was placed in the Mount Airy health resort. Once a wag won a silver cup in a contest for his conundrum:

"Why is ex-Mayor Barker like Joseph in Egypt?"

"Because he was taken out of prison to rule the people."

During the fifties Barker seems to have gone from bad to worse. His harangues became even more unprintable, drunkenness was added to his faults, and symptoms of epilepsy became marked. He still retained a great deal of influence with the people, and it is said that when popular opposition to the building of a street railway on Penn Street developed, Joe Barker, in the secret employ of the railway company effectively smothered the malcontents. On the night of August 2, 1862, while returning with a group of companions from a war meeting at Middletown, he was killed by a train a short distance below Manchester.

XXII

Prelude to Strife

PERIODS of social unrest and change are sometimes characterized by a multiplication of reformers, each with a panacea that he sincerely believes will cure the woes of the world, and of quacks with plausible—and profitable—economic nostrums. The forties and fifties bred a vast number of these peculiar doctrines, some of them good and some of them bad, but each of them was advocated with deadly, humorless earnestness by its devoted adherents. There were the Antimasons, the Mormons, the Native Americans, the phrenologists, the socialists, the Millerites, the Fourierists, the Spiritualists, the free-traders, the tariff advocates, the temperance people, the abolitionists, and the feminists. Some of them had their origin before 1840, but all except the first reached their flower after that date.

All of these theorists and reformers had a hearing in Pittsburgh at one time or another, but after the fall of the Antimasons the last four named above were by far the most prominent. A Millerite called Brother Fitch spent some time in Pittsburgh in 1843 but apparently left after converting only a few women to his belief that the world was to end in 1849; Minersville had a short scare brought on by reputed spirit rappings; Sidney Rigdon, who was prominent in the founding of Mormonism, was for a time a Baptist minister in Pittsburgh; the Fourierists did some soap-box preaching; and the German Workingmen's Association issued a socialist paper for a while under the editorship of a Mr. Backofen. Joe Barker and his long-haired prophets skipped about from this nostrum to that panacea, and professional viewers with alarm and peripatetic carpenters of a new era visited the city often in search of twenty-five cent admissions. More sincere (though perhaps not as cerebral) lecturers came, and teetotaler John B. Gough, ex-slave Frederick Douglass, serene philosopher Ralph Waldo Emerson, constitution-hater William Lloyd Garrison, and bloomer-clad feminist Lucy Stone, all graced Pittsburgh platforms. There was, however, one Pittsburgher who exercised so great an influence in both the feminist and abolitionist movements as to deserve special consideration. She was Jane Grey Swisshelm.

II

"THE *Pittsburgh Commercial Journal* has a new contributor who signs her name 'Jane G. Swisshelm,' dips her pen in liquid gold, and sands her paper with the down from butterflies' wings." This notice in an exchange in the late forties marked the emergence of the woman who was for twenty years to be the stormy petrel of American radical journalism. Surely no woman ever had a more vigorous training in personal conflict and misfortune for the role that she was to play.

Jane Grey Cannon was born in Pittsburgh, December 6, 1815, and spent her early years in an atmosphere of rigid Presbyterianism in Pittsburgh and Wilkinsburg. At the age of fifteen she became a schoolmistress, an occupation she followed during the greater part of the next eight years. In 1836 she married James Swisshelm, a young farmer whose family owned the land on the site of modern Swissvale, and the groom's parents immediately began a campaign of alternate blandishments and abuse to win her to Methodism. At first James Swisshelm, who was a large man physically but who was weak in character and initiative, stood aloof or even sided with his young wife; finally he was won over by his parents and joined with them in their attempts at coercion. In 1838 the young couple departed for Louisville to make their own way, but the attempt was a complete failure so far as the husband was concerned; they were forced to rely upon Jane's earnings as teacher and seamstress. The experience was not wholly fruitless, however, as it was there that she developed her crusading antagonism to slavery.

In 1839 Mrs. Swisshelm returned to Pittsburgh to nurse her mother during a last painful illness. The share of Mrs. Cannon's property that was left to her daughter became, under the Pennsylvania law of that day, the property of James Swisshelm, and he immediately began to use its income to improve the lands and mills of his widowed mother in Swissvale; he even put in a claim against Mrs. Cannon's estate for wages for his wife while she was nursing her mother. During the succeeding years Jane Swisshelm taught school and kept house for her husband's family; in spite of the nagging of his relatives, the period was for her a time of intellectual growth, and during her convalescence after a serious illness she composed some articles for the *Spirit*, an antislavery publication of Pittsburgh.

Articles and poems, principally on abolitionism and often intensely personal and sarcastic, continued to flow from Mrs. Swisshelm's pen. The Mexican War was a ripe subject for attack and she did the job effectually. In later years she related that when "Kossuth was on his starring tour in this country, he used to create wild enthusiasm by 'Your own late glorious struggle with Mexico'; but when he reached that climax in his Pittsburg speech a dead silence fell upon the vast, cheering audience."

Meanwhile Mr. Swisshelm's mother's property was waxing fat upon the improvements that Jane's money enabled her husband to make, but Jane had no claim upon it and there was every prospect that at the death of her mother-in-law the property would be divided among James and his brothers. Jane sued her husband to force him to allow her to control her own income, but when it occurred to her that her misfortunes might have been divinely sent to force her to do something toward righting the wrong that forbade a married woman to own property, she resolved that "instead of spending my strength quarreling with the hand, I would strike for the heart of that great tyranny." She borrowed law books from Judge William Wilkins, took legal advice from Colonel Samuel Black, and after a period of intense study began to publish in the *Daily Commercial Journal* a series of articles on the subject of a married woman's right to hold property that exercised a profound influence in bringing about an early change in the Pennsylvania property laws. All this time she was living under the roof of her husband's mother.

III

ONE day toward the close of the Mexican War Mrs. Swisshelm received word that the *Albatross*, Pittsburgh's latest venture in abolitionary journalism, had expired. Like a "lightning flash" the thought struck her that she would found a successor to it. To her surprise her husband favored the project. However much he might have abused his rights over her, he had remained a consistent admirer of her intellect and trenchant powers of expression; and the family campaign to convert her to Methodism had been made not merely to save her soul and get peaceable control of her property, but to turn her into a flaming evangelist.

Mrs. Swisshelm's *Pittsburgh Saturday Visiter* was published in the office of the *Commercial Journal* and was destined to remain under her guidance for ten years, from 1847 to 1857; it doubtless owed its long life to the fact that it was subsidized, probably by the eminent Pittsburgh philanthropist, Charles Avery. The *Visiter* was a four-page weekly, headed by the scriptural motto "Speak unto the children of Israel that they go forward." The commotion wrought by the sheet, not only in Pittsburgh but throughout the nation, was amusing. Fair woman had at last abandoned the sacred precincts of the home and invaded the realm of politics, which by divine fiat was sacred to men! "No sooner did the American eagle catch sight of it," wrote Mrs. Swisshelm of her paper, "than he swooned and fell off his perch. Democratic roosters straightened out their necks and ran screaming with terror. Whig coons scampered up trees and barked furiously. The world was falling and every one had 'heard it, saw it, and felt it.' "

The paper was immediately adopted as the local organ of the Liberty party and plunged into the political melee with rolled sleeves and tucked up skirts. The first blow was struck at a judge who had gone out of his way to punish a local newspaper man for criticizing a proslavery decision. Mrs. Swisshelm wrote that a "great legal luminary," until recently visible in the Pennsylvania heavens, had suddenly disappeared and could not be located until she had built a crooked telescope through which one could look around corners—then, behold, the "luminary" had been found "almost sixty degrees below our moral horizon."

The antislavery battle was waged in this vein for ten years, and there were also excursions into the field of women's rights. In the latter Mrs. Swisshelm was interested chiefly in the attainment of property rights and not so much in equal rights in every walk of life. Bloomers were an abomination to her and she despised women's rights conventions. It was, indeed, a task for her to confine her publication to her two main interests, for every crack-brained theorist considered that a woman journalist should naturally propagandize for his pet plan. "Turkish trowsers, Fourierism, Spiritualism, Vegetarianism, Phonetics, Pneumonics, the Eight Hour Law, Criminal Caudling, Magdalenism, and other devices for teaching pyramids to stand on their apex were pressed upon the *Visiter*, and it was held by the disciples of each as 'false to all its professions,' when declining to devote itself to its advocacy."

In the end the *Visiter* yielded, not to its foes, but to the bad business management of Mrs. Swisshelm's partner, her brother-in-law. The behavior of her husband had meanwhile remained so odious that she resolved to leave him and thus give him grounds for divorce. Accordingly in 1857 she moved on to Minnesota and to new journalistic adventures, which were to be followed by service as a nurse in the Civil War and then by a period in the capitol city as the firebrand editor of a radical Republican journal. Finally in 1866 she returned to Pittsburgh and there lived quietly until her death in 1884. Strangely enough, her last years were spent in what is now Swissvale in the home that had once belonged to her husband's family.

IV

THE antislavery cause that Mrs. Swisshelm so ably championed seems to have run in Pittsburgh about the same course that it did in other northern cities. The American Colonization Society had advocated the gradual transfer of the negro to the African home of his ancestors, but it was not active enough to ship out annually more than a fraction of the natural increase of the race. The Pittsburgh branch of the society was organized in the First Presbyterian Church in 1826 and survived through a humdrum existence of twelve or fifteen years.

Meanwhile Allegheny County was receiving each year additional numbers of free negroes and runaways, who formed a colony in a squalid section of the Hill, which was promptly dubbed Hayti. As early as 1835 there were sporadic race riots, and on one occasion a white mob went so far as to pull down several tenements. The leading negro of Pittsburgh was a barber, J. B. Vashon, who it was said might have passed for a Spanish grandee. The colored people, under the guidance of leaders like Vashon, or white philanthropists like Charles Avery, formed educational societies "for the purpose of dispersing the moral gloom" that enshrouded the race. Probably such organizations accomplished some good, though it is difficult to judge at this late date.

In the thirties abolitionist societies began to be formed in Pittsburgh and were immediately offset by societies called "Friends of the Integrity of the Union." The flagrant expansion of slave territory as the result of the Texas annexation and the Mexican cessions did much to promote the antislavery cause in Pittsburgh, but it was hardly respectable until after the passage of the Fugitive Slave Law of 1850 and the Kansas-Nebraska Act of 1854. The Fugitive Slave Law resulted in a sizeable exodus of Pittsburgh negroes; it was said that in the month of September alone over two hundred left for Canada.

Pittsburgh's rugged terrain made its vicinity an ideal hiding place for runaways and it early became a station on the underground railway. The red brick hospital of a Dr. John Ball on Boyd's Hill (now St. Mary's Hall of Duquesne University) is said to have been a refuge for fugitive slaves. Here, it is told, there once came a poor runaway still wearing the chains that had been riveted upon him. He soon died as the result of his hardships. The more supersititious residents of the Bluff claim that his ghost still haunts the old building and that the rattling of his chains can often be heard at night.

A businessman of the time, William Stewart, has left a description of an incident connected with a fugitive. "The bridge at Niagara Falls," said he, "is the haven to which we send all hunted slaves. On a Sunday morning I was just starting for church when a well known knock touched my door. I knew at once that church for me was in another direction. I opened my door, leisurely went out and turned to the right towards the east. About a block away there was a little covered carriage that was very much in use in Pittsburg at that time. They were called dearborns. When I left my own house there was a gentleman walking between the carriage and me. We did not speak to each other, but he turned down the first street. The curtains of the dearborn were all rolled up and no person but the driver could be seen. I was in charge of the dearborn. It was made with a double bottom and the slave was lying flat between the upper and lower bottoms. The driver kept going on very leisurely. There was a ferry about where the Fortieth street bridge is. We both got on the same ferry, but the driver never changed words with us. He was one of our wealthiest citizens and was wearing a fine pair of false whiskers. After we crossed the river the driver drove on the tow path of the canal. Finally the dearborn and the man in sight turned on a road running across Pine creek below Sharpsburg. There another man came out of a house. The new man took his place, while the first took another direction, no one having spoken a word since we started. The dearborn was then driven into a lonely place in the woods, where there was a 'station' provided with all manner of disguises. Provided with these the slave was started on his way to Niagara. After leaving Pittsburg they were scarcely ever captured."

In a city so close to the border of a slave state there were bound to be cases where local negroes, perhaps really runaways, were claimed by former masters. Sometimes no resort was made to the courts, but instead the slaves were kidnaped and secretly taken out of town. The animosities engendered by the Fugitive Slave Law led to several serious clashes between abolitionists and slave-catchers that were aired in the courts; the latter nearly always won, as was indeed inevitable under the law. On one occasion a southerner and his wife who were passing through Pittsburgh with a colored nurse were mobbed on their way to the steamboat landing by several free negroes in an attempt to rescue the slave girl. They managed to reach their boat only under police protection. About the same time the colored servants in a hotel spirited away a negro girl, the servant of guests there, but released her when it turned out that she was free.

v

THE winter of 1852 and 1853 was severe in western Pennsylvania. Queues of shivering, thinly-clad unemployed gathered at doors of soup houses maintained by Pittsburgh's charity workers; enthusiasts with economic mare's-nests in their hair found a ready hearing from idlers hard pressed to fill up their hours; disgruntled Whigs, still smarting from their defeat by the Democrats under their handsome figurehead, Franklin Pierce, admitted that the inexorable logic of events was leading to direct conflict over the issue of the extension of slavery to the newly-won territory. Some of them even admitted that sooner or later they would have to stop hedging and take a stand on the hated issue that had thus far been left to radicals like Mrs. Swisshelm.

In some strange manner there had grown up that winter a coterie of men of ill-assorted political opinions who met in the grocery store of David C. Herbst at the northwest corner of Third Street and Cherry Alley. Probably they met there because it was convenient for most of them, because Mr. Herbst always kept a good coal fire in his stove, and because when they sat around on counters and nail kegs the cracker barrel and a wedge of York State cheese were always handy. Significantly enough, they were all substantial business men. David N. White, still a Whig, was proprietor and editor of the *Gazette*, Rees Fleeson was connected with the *Dispatch*, and Robert Riddle of the *Com-*

mercial Journal had been a sponsor to Mrs. Swisshelm and had experienced her sarcastic thrusts when he deviated from the straight and narrow path of abolitionism. There were, in addition to these journalists, "Mine Host," John M. Crossan, of the Monongahela House; ex-mayor William J. Howard, then federal pension agent; the attorney and Mexican War veteran, Captain Charles Naylor, once of Philadelphia; and a handful of men who were prominent in the metal manufacturing businesses.

There were in the group men of all political complexions and the long winter evenings were filled with acrimonious debate. As men of affairs most of them felt that business was being injured by the wrangle over slavery as well as by the threat of the competition of slave labor with free labor in the new territories, and it was finally on the principle of opposition to the extension of slavery that the group united and projected a new political party, probably intended to be active at first only in the local field. When the matter of a name for the new organization was brought up a number of suggestions were made, but at length Captain Naylor rose and said, "Our country is a great Republic; why not name the new party 'Republican,' without prefix or suffix?" Naylor's proposal met with instant approval, and the new party was named, at least as far as Pittsburgh was concerned.

The Pittsburgh Republicans took issue with the extension of slavery more because they were seeking the welfare of industry than because they were concerned about farmers and free laborers. The labor elements of Pittsburgh, at that time more vocal than they had ever been, seemed to recognize the economic bias of the Republican group. Robert Riddle, who was at the moment running for mayor, backed by a coalition of Whigs and Antimasons, was jeered by an amusing ditty in the columns of the *Post:*

> Sing hey diddle, diddle!
> Hurrah for Bob Riddle!
> The man for the working men he!
> He smiles in their faces
> With all his best graces
> As friendly as friendly can be,

But when fortunes frown
And the *wages come down*
And labor is trodden in dust,
The proud "upper ten"
Claim the *Journal* man then
And ever he's true to the trust.

Opposition to the extension of slavery almost sprang from the soil of the northern states, and clubs similar to the Pittsburgh organization mushroomed independently in many places. The name Republican, for obvious reasons, was a favorite with these groups, and as early as 1854 candidates were running for Congress under that label. State conventions were held in Wisconsin and Michigan during the same year, and on September 5, 1855, a Pennsylvania Republican convention was held in the city hall of Pittsburgh, which then stood on the eastern Diamond.

By the summer of 1855 there was on foot a definite movement for the consolidation of the disparate Republican state organizations, and in November Salmon P. Chase, the new Anti-Nebraska governor of Ohio, met David N. White in the Monongahela House to discuss the matter. As the result of this and other conferences a Republican national convention was called to meet in Pittsburgh on February 22, 1856.

The convention was held in Lafayette Hall near the southwest corner of Wood Street and Fourth Avenue. The hall, which was a plain rectangular structure with galleries along the sides, was decorated with flags and the portraits of prominent Republican men. A high dais flanked by massive columns was reserved for the leaders. Although the convention was a mass meeting attended by volunteers rather than delegates, it included many men whose names were to be prominent in the new party, though truth compels the admission that those most prominent at the time cannily watched from afar. Present were the witty Zachariah Chandler of Michigan, the crusading Henry J. Raymond of the *New York Times*, the future vice president Oliver P. Morton of Indiana, and Horace Greeley with the *Tribune* sticking out of his pocket, iron-rimmed spectacles pushed up over a massive forehead, and Galway slugger whiskers trembling with fervor. The abolitionist firebrand, Joshua R. Giddings, and the Reverend Owen Lovejoy were also there, as well as David Wilmot of "Proviso" fame, and Passmore Williamson, who had recently been clapped into a Philadelphia prison for refusing to deliver up a runaway slave. The presiding officer was F. P. Blair of Maryland.

The organization of the new party and the speeches attendant upon its birth occupied two days. The convention was opened with a prayer by Owen Lovejoy, who called upon the Almighty in no uncertain terms to remove the unholy national administration from power. The speeches that followed blew hot and cold; the majority of the members of the convention were plainly realistic politicians carefully feeling their way upon the important issue, questioning whether the North was ripe to stand forth openly against the dominant slave power. Horace Greeley, who had been sojourning among the timid politicians in Washington, advised caution, but Giddings countered with a story: Two pious brothers, Joe and John, took up a farm in the West. At family prayers the first day Joe outlined to the Lord the ways in which he wanted the project to prosper. When it came John's turn to pray his petition was short and simple. "Oh, Lord," he said, "we have begun a good work; carry it on as you think best, and don't mind what Joe says." During the laughter that followed Lovejoy took the rostrum and began an inflammatory address in which he declared war to the death. The issue of Know-Nothingism came in for its share of attention. German immigrants, who were almost to a man opposed to the extension of slavery, were well represented in the convention and made a plea for a party stand against the nativist movement.

Progress was made, however, despite the caution of many of the leaders. A national executive committee was appointed and a convention was called for June 17, 1856, in Philadelphia, to nominate candidates for president and vice president. A ringing "Address to the People of the United States," sounding a call to battle against the extension of slavery, was introduced into the convention just before it closed and was adopted with nine rousing cheers.

XXIII

The Sinews of War

THURSDAY, December twenty-seventh, 1860, two o'clock in the afternoon of a crisp day: the great portico and steps of the courthouse, the grounds about the building, and Grant, Diamond and Fifth Streets were jammed with thousands of Pittsburghers—not a good-natured throng, but sullen and even angry. Presently a large, bewhiskered man, who looked very much the born leader, shouldered his way through the courthouse door and down the steps to the balustrade of a platform overlooking Grant Street. At his appearance there was a murmur from the crowd that soon swelled into an articulate shout of "Moorhead! Moorhead! Speech! Speech!"

The big man raised his hands and the cries died away. "Fellow citizens," he began, "your moderation and liberality of feeling in the past has given me reason to be proud that I am a Pittsburgher; the alacrity with which you have turned out as one man when your country is in danger, does you the utmost credit. We have met here today to consult upon the best method of meeting the latest movement of the government—that of moving the cannon from Allegheny Arsenal to the South. May I as one who desires moderation, counsel that we meet this crisis peaceably. Whatever South Carolina may have done, let nothing be

311

committed here that resembles an overt act of treason. Let the
guns go. I am anxious that we preserve our reputation as union-
loving, law-abiding citizens. When the tug of war does come—if
come it must—I know that my constituents will show the same
alacrity which they now exhibit in maintaining the integrity of
the Union, not only by expressions of sentiment but by the exercise of physical force."

General Moorehead's address was interrupted from time to time
by applause and during the final burst of hand-clapping another
man stepped forward—a man whose keen eyes, long nose, and
jutting jaw were recognized as those of the anti-railroad lawyer
and ardent Republican, Thomas Williams. When quiet had been
restored he read a long series of resolutions deprecating the war
department's policy of arming the South but disavowing any intention of illegal interference. Few dissenting voices were heard
to the adoption of the resolutions. Meanwhile a lad who had
been wriggling through the press now managed to make his way
up the steps and thrust a bit of paper into the hands of Mr. Thomas J. Bigham, editor of the *Commercial Journal*. The editor
glanced over the message, then stepped forward with raised hand.

"Gentlemen," he said, "I have here a telegraphic dispatch
dated Philadelphia, December twenty-seventh. It reads thus:
'Fort Moultrie was last night evacuated by Major Anderson, who
first spiked the guns. He states that he had withdrew——"With-
drawn, you mean," shouted a voice in the crowd——from that
post in order to allay discussion and to strengthen his own position. It is said that a train has been laid to blow up the fort, but
the report is doubted. Several military companies have been
ordered out, and a collision is not improbable.'"

During the reading of the dispatch the excitement of the crowd
increased to such a pitch that at the end those in the back could
scarcely understand what was said. From that moment pacifica-
tory resolutions were of no avail. Pittsburgh had resolved that
no weapons should leave her wharves to arm the South for the
impending conflict.

As a matter of fact, Secretary John B. Floyd of the war department had ordered over a hundred big guns shipped to two

Gulf forts that were not yet nearly completed and were in no condition to receive them—guns that had really been cast years before, though it was officially claimed that they had been made expressly for the forts. President James Buchanan and the other officials of the national government were deluged by protesting telegrams from Pittsburgh committees, mass meetings, and prominent citizens. The commandant of the arsenal, Major John Symington, though he must have been conscious of the reasons for the department's haste, tried to obey orders. The guns and their military escorts, however, were halted on the streets by angry crowds and in one case were delayed for several hours, though no violence was offered. Thereafter the movement was slowed down by Major Symington until he should hear from Washington and only a few guns were actually loaded upon the waiting steamboat "Silver Wave," before the orders were countermanded.

II

THE crisis brought about in Pittsburgh by the attempted removal of the guns made that city a hotbed of opposition to secession long before the remainder of the North was stirred out of its apathy by the firing on Fort Sumter. In the previous November Abraham Lincoln's vote in Allegheny County had been more than double that of all his opponents combined; it was the result of the Republicans' support of the two principles most popular in Pittsburgh, free labor and the protective tariff. When he read the returns in Springfield Lincoln is said to have turned to a friend and asked, "Where is this State of Allegheny?"

It was, therefore, a great occasion for Pittsburgh when Lincoln stopped there over the night of February 14 on his way to the inauguration in Washington. Elaborate preparations were made to meet the official train in Allegheny and to escort Lincoln and his party through flag-decked streets to the Monongahela House. Shops and stores were closed, and countrymen and townsmen crowded the streets all day. Unfortunately the train was delayed for several hours at Freedom; an interim there was passed by the president-elect in shaking hands and conversing with the members of the assembled crowd. A huge teamster named Henry

Dillon stood back to back with Lincoln to be measured; the latter proved to be two or three inches taller and said laughingly to Dillon, "Oh! I could eat salt off the top of your head."

By the time the guns on Monument Hill and Boyd's Hill announced that the train had reached Pittsburgh a rain had set in, but the procession through the streets was made as planned. Several elite military companies (the crack Duquesne Grays refused to parade in honor of a Republican) under General James S. Negley led the way, and the Lincoln party and the officials and councils of the two cities followed in carriages. The crowd gathered about the Monongahela House was denser than it had been on that day in the previous October when the Prince of Wales, later to be Edward VII, had favored Pittsburgh by making an overnight stop. General Negley's troops fixed bayonets and cleared a path into the hotel, but even there the crowd was so thick that the president-elect and his family almost had to be carried up the stairs to their rooms.

Presently the repeated calls for him induced Lincoln to come out of his room and try to excuse himself from speaking by promising to make a speech the next day. "Say something about Allegheny County," someone shouted. At the mention of the county that had given him such a thumping majority Lincoln's eyes brightened, and he replied, "I have a great regard for Allegheny County. It is the banner county of the state, if not of the entire Union." At this someone called, "No *rail*ery, Abe." The pun was met by a burst of applause and shouts of "Good for the rail-splitter!" and "Split another rail, Abe!" Meanwhile the rain-soaked crowd in the street was crying "Lincoln! Lincoln! Come out and show yourself, Abe!" Finally he went out on the balcony and excused himself until morning, saying "I have made my appearance now only to afford you an opportunity of seeing as clearly as may be my beautiful countenance." Under cover of the laughs he called "Good night!" and retreated to his room.

The rain continued throughout the night, but nevertheless thousands of people assembled in the drizzle well before eight-thirty and waited impatiently under a sea of raised umbrellas. Lincoln finally appeared on the balcony and was formally welcomed to the city by Mayor George Wilson. The president-elect spoke for half an hour to an attentive audience. He declined to commit himself upon the policies with which the national crisis would be met because he felt that the situation had not yet fully developed. He did, however, express the opinion that the crisis was an artificial one, existing only in the minds of the dissatisfied, and that it would be solved if both North and South would meet the issue calmly. The latter half of his address was devoted to a discussion of the tariff during which he spoke of labor as "the true standard of value" and approved protection of American industry and labor.

The speech has lasted so long that the departure for Cleveland had to be hurried. Soldiers made a way for the city's guest through the halls of the hotel to the waiting carriage. The streets along the course back to Allegheny were so thronged with people that the carriage could scarcely get through, and Lincoln was forced to stand most of the way to acknowledge their cheers. That ride was long remembered as having been the occasion for the wildest demonstration of enthusiasm that Pittsburgh had ever seen.

III

THE news of the attack on Fort Sumter was clicked off the telegraph wires in Pittsburgh on the evening of Friday, April 12, 1861. Feverish excitement prevailed, and hundreds of people remained on the streets most of the night discussing the situation and waiting for further news. Special dispatches were read in the theaters and the accounts of Major Robert Anderson's defense were received with wild applause. In one theater a man leaped to his feet and cried "I'm a Democrat, but three cheers for Major Anderson." They were given with a will.

The day after the fall of Fort Sumter a mass meeting at City Hall presided over by William Wilkins provided for a Committee of Public Safety of one hundred members that should supervise the measures taken to aid in meeting the crisis. Subcommittees immediately began to recruit troops in response to Lincoln's call for volunteers, to feed and equip men, to care for their families, to expedite the forwarding of war munitions to the front, to intercept contraband shipments, and provide for home defense. The actual opening of war brought even the Duquesne Grays to the support of the government. The Republican marching clubs known as Wide Awakes reorganized as military companies and drilled under whatever former army officers and sergeants they could find, while the already existing military organizations polished their swords and rifles in preparation for combat. Camp Wilkins was hastily established on the county's fairground near Penn and Twenty-sixth Streets, but the soldiers were soon moved to the new Camp Wright at Hulton on the Allegheny River. Camp Howe was established in Oakland and reports and newspaper accounts refer at various times to other camps—Linden Grove, Brooks, Copeland, and Reynolds. During the war Allegheny County furnished a total of twenty-four thousand men to the army and navy—not a bad showing for a population of one hundred eighty thousand which was largely engaged in essential industries. The most prominent officers given by Pittsburgh to the army were Major-General James S. Negley, Colonel Samuel Black, who fell at Gaines's Mill, and General Alexander Hays, who was killed during the Battle of the Wilderness.

The first troops left Pittsburgh on April 24. A review had been planned on the Allegheny Commons but a heavy rain forestalled that and the troops plodded ingloriously through the mud to the Pennsylvania Railroad depot, where the women filled their knapsacks with small comforts and eatables and bade them tearful farewells. Other companies were not slow in following, while even greater numbers than were accepted for service at the front remained in camp, fearful that the war would be over before they could get into battle. A gay Fourth of July was celebrated by a parade in Allegheny of the organizations left about the two cities, for it had not yet become evident that a long, grim war was in prospect. The Battle of Bull Run on July 21, however, brought that fact home to the nation and a new purposefulness now took the place of the recent holiday spirit. The former half good-natured contempt for "rebels" was replaced by bitter hatred, and there were even those who were ready to compare the struggle to the one recounted by Milton in *Paradise Lost*, between the

good and the bad angels. There was no longer danger that any
ardent volunteer would fail to get the desired whiff of powder
smoke; industrialists, laborers, and relief workers tightened their
belts for "a long pull, a strong pull, and a pull all together."

IV

THE part that Pittsburgh's industries took in the prosecution
and winning of the Civil War has seldom been realized. The manufactories of the city prospered. Locomotives and freight cars,
heavy artillery, small arms, ammunition, clothing (too often
shoddy), steamboats, coal, and thousands of head of cattle and
hogs left the vicinity in a steady stream. The Mississippi ram
fleet was largely Pittsburgh built, it was armed with Pittsburgh
guns, and the engines were fired by Pittsburgh coal. River and
ocean monitors slid down its ways and splashed in the yellow
current of its rivers. The manufacture of armor plate became a
leading industry, which has kept its importance to the present.

Pittsburgh's cannon were the giants of that day. The Fort Pitt
Foundry alone furnished 1,193 cannon (or fifteen per cent of the
government's artillery) which were valued at about $1,600,000.
Some of them were gigantic twenty-inch Rodman guns, the largest that had yet been made with the exception of a stone-throw-
ing bronze cannon at the Dardenelles. The large Rodmans each
weighed fifty-six tons, were twenty feet long, and fired one-thou-
sand-pound projectiles. The Rodmans and columbiads cast at
the Fort Pitt Foundry were sometimes rolled out of the yard on
timbers by the use of windlass and crowbars and were hauled to
the railroad or to steamboats by a twenty-four-horse team. It
seems that only a certain John Sample could drive the team and
so important were his services that when he was drafted for the
army a substitute was hired to take his place in the ranks. The
cannon were regularly tested at Tarentum, and that town gained
the sobriquet of "Bangtown-on-Allegheny."

The lists of smaller weapons and miscellaneous supplies furnished by Pittsburgh are even more imposing. About ten per cent
of the projectiles bought by the government were manufactured
in Pittsburgh. Gun carriages, wagons, harness, blankets, and

tents were among the other contributions. During the four years of the war nearly 5,500,000 tons of coal were mined in the vicinity of the city.

One of the most important manufactories of war munitions in Pittsburgh was the government-owned Allegheny Arsenal. As early as July, 1861, the arsenal was employing four hundred hands and was engaged in making bullets, cartridges, and horse equipment. The danger of explosion was always present there and at one time the commandant discharged two hundred boys on the plea that they were persistently careless with matches, and he hired girls in their places. That the dread of explosion was not unwarranted was demonstrated on September 17, 1862, when the building known as the laboratory blew up. The cause of the disaster was never determined, but the structure was demolished and about seventy-five boys and girls were blown to bits or charred beyond recognition. Public indignation at what was considered the neglect of the arsenal officials was great and they were severely censured by a coroner's jury.

The Civil War was an important stimulus to the development of Pittsburgh's industries. The manufacture of ordnance and firearms ceased at the close of the war, but the heavy steel and foundry work went on. The military demand for railroad iron was succeeded by an era of phenomenal railroad building and by increased demands for bridge iron, and the impetus given to the manufacture of armor plate was continued as modern navies came into existence. The war also gave Pittsburgh's industrialists a rigorous training in precision methods, and that was the heritage that was to give them a running start in the period of cutthroat competition that followed the war.

v

THE Civil War was for Pittsburgh a succession of joyful celebrations at the reception of good news from the front and of periods of gloomy despondency when there was a defeat or when a movement of the Confederate army seemed to threaten the city. The first scare came during the first spring of the war when Lee and McClellan were swinging back and forth in West Virginia. Another scare came the next year at the time of Lee's first invasion of the North. The greatest, however, was during the Gettysburg campaign in 1863, when no one could have persuaded Pittsburgh that the Confederates would not soon be pouring through the mountain passes to lay waste the great source of northern supplies.

It was expected at first that a raid by the Confederate cavalry leader, J. E. B. Stuart, was inevitable, but fear soon expanded the raid into an attack in full force. On Sunday, June 14, the manufacturers and businessmen met at the Monongahela House and agreed to suspend business in order to send their men to work on emergency defenses for the city, so that the invaders might be welcomed "with bloody hands to hospitable graves." Fortunately plans had already been drawn up and all that remained to be done was to execute them. The next morning several thousand men paid at the rate of $1.25 a day by their employers and armed with their employers' picks and shovels, gathered near the Monongahela House to be assigned to their sectors. The redoubts and batteries as constructed occupied a line extending along Coal Hill from Temperanceville (now West End) to Beck's Run; from Gazzam's Hill, above Soho, in an irregular line over Herron Hill, Bloomfield, and Stanton Heights to the Allegheny River opposite Sharpsburg; and in Allegheny from Uniondale Cemetery to Troy Hill.

There were about ten thousand men engaged on the fortifications at one time or another, and the work went on incessantly until the Fourth of July saw its completion. Boys received seventy-five cents a day to carry free beer and hard cider to the men; like boys on a lark the men were not always observant of property rights and in a few cases raided the grocery stores and swept them clean of food. The cannon foundries were robbed of ordnance, which was sent posthaste to the gun emplacements, where the black mouths of the cannon soon grinned out toward the country across which it was expected that the Confederate columns would advance. Meanwhile the militia and the home guard had been mustering and the streets presented a lively and martial appearance. On June 25 a telegraph operator with the

Confederate cavalry that had occupied McConnellsburg wired to Pittsburgh that they were on their way to seize the city. The threat heightened the excitement among the more impressionable citizens, though of course nothing ever came of it. The completion of the fortifications was hailed with relief, and it was boasted that Pittsburgh had become a second Gibraltar and that not even the combined forces of the South could take the city.

The danger, however, evaporated almost as quickly as it had arisen. The retreat of Lee's broken legions from Gettysburg was not only the turning point of the war but it removed from Pittsburgh the last serious threat of invasion. General John H. Morgan's cavalry raid into Indiana and Ohio in the same month as Gettysburg caused a flurry of excitement, and the first families hastened to bury their silver to keep it from "Mr. Morgan's men." But the capture of the last of the raiders near New Lisbon, Ohio, however, put an end to that scare, and Pittsburghers safely went on about their business for the rest of the war.

VI

WHILE Pittsburgh furnished the nation with the sinews of war in a measure out of all proportion to the population, contributions to special services to soldiers were even more remarkable. The guns of Fort Sumter had scarcely been silenced before agencies were being organized to care for soldiers. The Subsistence Committee of the Committee of Public Safety, with Thomas M. Howe, the copper and iron magnate, as chairman, and with B. F. Jones and William Thaw as prominent members, began to collect food and money and to furnish meals to soldiers in transit. Most of the work of the committee was carried on by volunteers from among the women of the city. A dining hall was fitted up in a warehouse at Penn and Ninth Streets, near the Pennsylvania Railroad depot; here and at the old city hall in the Diamond, during a period of more than four years, over four hundred thousand meals were served at a cost that averaged about five cents per meal—not a very large allowance, but the food was substantial. Sick and wounded soldiers were cared for in the Soldiers' Home at 34 Liberty Street and it is estimated that to this haven at one time or another there came approximately one hundred thousand men.

As early as October, 1861, a committee of citizens had established with government aid the United States Sanitary Commission to receive donations of clothing and medical supplies, and the committee had appointed Jacob Glosser as the Pittsburgh agent. At the reception of the news of the battle of Shiloh two steamboats were chartered by the Pittsburgh Sanitary Commission, loaded with surgeons, nurses, and supplies, and sent down river under the direction of Felix R. Brunot. Similar aid was sent from time to time to other battlefields, and the Sanitary Commission came to perform somewhat the same functions as the modern Red Cross. In April, 1863, the Christian Commission under the chairmanship of the Reverend Herrick Johnson took over part of the work of the Sanitary Commission and the hospital activities of the Subsistence Committee, and it carried them on until the end of the war. Its functions might be compared to those of the Y. M. C. A. in a more recent war. Meanwhile facilities had been established, partly at public expense, for the care of soldiers' orphans and dependents, though there was considerable complaint that the maintenance was not only inadequate but badly administered.

In the long roster of names of Pittsburgh men and women who are remembered for their humanitarian work during the war none stands higher than that of Felix R. Brunot. He was born in 1820, a grandson of Dr. Felix Brunot, one of Pittsburgh's early physicians, and was educated as a civil engineer. His fortune, however, was amassed chiefly in railroad investments and in the steel business and was acquired early enough in life to enable him to devote much of his time to philanthropy. Time and again Mr. Brunot led parties of surgeons and nurses to the battle lines, and upon one occasion in 1862 he was captured with a field hospital and incarcerated for a time in Libby Prison. Between such expeditions he devoted himself to the raising of medicines and supplies, and he served upon many important committees. After the war he became interested in Indian welfare, in Christian education, and, for that matter, in a hundred other charitable activities.

It is, however, for his war work that he is chiefly remembered; during the terrible years of conflict he was the mainspring of Pittsburgh's humanitarian activities.

During the last year of the war Mr. Brunot devoted himself to the Pittsburgh Sanitary Fair, which was held, like those in a score of other centers, to raise money for war work. The lumber used in the buildings of the Cleveland fair was purchased and buildings were erected on that part of the Allegheny Commons known as the Diamond. The fair was opened on June 1, 1864, as the climax of a grand parade from the Monongahela House to Allegheny. Mr. Brunot presided and the assembly was addressed by Pennsylvania's war governor, Andrew G. Curtin. The buildings then thrown open to the public were revelations of delight, and Pittsburgh oldsters have never tired of recounting their magnificence.

There were several main buildings: the Mechanics' Hall, the Audience Hall, the Floral Hall, the Bazaar, and the Dining Hall. There were also a Swiss Cottage and a building for the exhibition of live stock, and the second floor of Allegheny's new city hall was devoted to an art gallery and to the Old Curiosity Shop. The Monitor Building bore a vague resemblance to the famous warship *Monitor* and contained a miniature lake with an island in the center. A model fleet moved about under its own steam and staged a mimic battle with several water batteries located on the island. Another feature of the fair was a program of tableaux, which included scenes of Lalla Rookh listening to Fermoz, "a saucy Basque girl confronting the gay Henry of Navarre, all in clouds of tarletan," and the "Artist's Vision" posed charmingly by "a dainty blonde, slightly above medium height, slender, graceful, lovely."

Much of the money raised by the fair was received from the sale of books, shawls, jewelry, and other articles of interest or value that were donated by individuals for that purpose. As her contribution to war relief it is said that one young lady, who had been given a diamond ring by a brother who had later been killed in battle, gave the ring to be sold. By chance William Thaw, the railroad executive and philanthropist, heard of the sacrifice, bought the ring, and gave it back to her. With this romantic incident began Thaw's courtship of Mary Copley.

The Sanitary Fair proved to be a phenomenal success and was said to have raised a higher per capita sum in relation to the population than any other fair in the country. Though the fair lasted for only eighteen days it cleared three hundred twenty thousand dollars. The war ended before the sum could be expended and two hundred thousand dollars of it was eventually handed over to the Western Pennsylvania Hospital as the nucleus of an endowment fund.

VII

THE war years in Pittsburgh were a time of frenzied money-making and unselfish devotion; of high prices and high rents offset by high wages; of mass meetings in the town hall being addressed by fat stay-at-homes and passing grandiloquent resolutions rejoicing in victory or piously dejectant in defeat; of repeated calls for thirty-, sixty-, ninety-, and hundred-day volunteers, for nine-month and three-year men, of fabulous thousand-dollar bounties, and of many stilted presentations of swords and colors; of muffled drums at military funerals and black veiled women praying in the churches; of receptions to generals, some of whom had but yesterday been tanners, or politicians, or German revolutionists, or who had been engaged in doling out blankets and notions to red-skinned horse thieves; most important of all, it was the time when national ideals crystallized and Pittsburgh took its place, not as the metropolis of a section, but as a city in a nation.

The streets and public utilities fell into decay while the citizens prospered; petroleum waste dumped into the rivers by the refineries was pumped into the city reservoirs and no one seemed to care save those who had to drink it; complaints were rife that the negroes, elevated at the thought of being the cause of a civil war, were becoming lazy and arrogant. Jeff Davis was hung in effigy, and anyone who publicly expressed sentiments different from those popularly held was ridden out of town on a rail if he were fortunate enough not to be locked up in the penitentiary

323

with Morgan's raiders. In short, Pittsburgh was like any city in war time—cruel, arrogant, intolerant, selfish, and bombastic, but also uncomplaining, self-sacrificing, fervently patriotic, and gripped by a mystical idealism that would stop at nothing.

Soldiers were everywhere, crowding the theaters and hotels, some gallantly escorting demure, crinolined young belles, others quarreling drunkenly in pothouses. Every steamboat that landed at the wharf had its quota of sick, wounded, furloughed, or discharged boys in blue; even the freight trains sometimes had soldiers swarming on the tops of the cars. Children made it a patriotic duty and pleasure to wave at the passing defenders of their homes; little Margaret Wade, who had forgotten her hankie, slipped out of her pantalettes and waved them in wild abandon until she was captured by a horrified relative, who was unaware that the small disregarder of the proprieties was, as Margaret Deland, to become one of America's great novelists.

The theaters had never been so generously patronized. Variety shows were the favorites, but plays and operas were well attended. War topics were treated in the drama; *McClellan's Dream* and *Southern Rebellion by Land and Sea*—the latter with panoramic scenery and gunboats for local color—drew large crowds. Great panoramas of the battle fronts were unrolled before admiring audiences at twenty-five cents a head and the queerer their names the more custom they drew, whence the appearances of the "panametra" and the "polopticomorama."

Baseball, quoits, aquatic sports, and gymnastic exercises swept the country, and even the young women began in greater numbers to ride horseback, though one editor sagely remarked that they were traveling too fast through the streets. Sports actually became respectable and people smiled at the story of the banker who had considered a certain young man a bad risk because he played cricket of evenings. Lecturers seemed to throng the platforms of arriving trains. Henry Ward Beecher fired the first oratorical gun of the war, Edward Everett pulled out all the stops of his eloquence, Emerson drifted into town for a peaceable lecture on "Clubs," and John B. Gough stopped off to take a whack at the devil and John Barleycorn. Those who went to hear Artemus Ward lecture on "Sixty Minutes in Africa" were thoughtfully warned that he was a humorist, and that his subject would have "nothing to do with what he will talk about." Santa Anna's leg (wooden) was exhibited in a store window, and General Grant, cornered at the city hall, submitted in a bored manner to having his hand pumped several thousand times by admiring citizens.

The end of the war was marked by a series of delirious celebrations. The thunder of saluting cannon seemed to hang always over the city; men drunk with joy and whiskey sang hymns and drinking songs indiscriminately from the customhouse steps; courts were adjourned *sine die;* Fifth Street in the evenings was crowded with parading fire engines and jubilant crowds, and citizens went in continual peril of falling rocket sticks.

Then like a pall descended the news of Lincoln's assassination. Theaters and business houses were closed, the newspapers came out with deep black borders, and men and women went sorrowfully about the streets in mourning. People were in no mood to have the memory of their martyred hero insulted; a milkman who said that Lincoln should have been killed four years before was barely rescued by the police from hanging, and another man who expressed like sentiments had a bucket of yeast thrown in his face by a "lady" standing nearby. The Amazon then proceeded to knock him down with an ax handle and might have killed him if he had not fled. Numerous meetings were held and countless resolutions of sorrow were passed and published.

But the war was over. The veterans were rapidly discarding blue shoddy for black broadcloth, and a city with eyes intent upon expanding commerce and industry paused for only a decent interval. The raftsmen came down the Allegheny once more on their winter's haul of lumber and logs and drank and danced the nights away in the water-front hotels. Keen-eyed young men were edging their way into the board rooms of the iron factories, and the whistles of ever larger numbers of locomotives echoed over the spreading web of railroads that made Pittsburgh their center. "Free soil, free speech, free labor, and free men" were realities. The shackles that had bound the industries of Pittsburgh were broken and the great age of expansion was about to begin.

INDEX

INDEX

Index

329

at Fort Pitt, 63, 70
Indian expeditions, 68, 69, 71
Bower Hill, burned, 119
Bowman, James, 254
Boyd, John, 114
Boyd's Hill, 114
Brackenridge, Alexander, 237
Brackenridge, Henry M., 164, 166, 169
 writings, 232, 262
Brackenridge, Hugh H., 111, 112, 159, 168
 political activties, 105, 112, 172
 in Whiskey Insurrection, 117-128
 Modern Chivalry, 160, 161
Brackenridge family, 244
Braddock, Edward, expedition and defeat, 27-37, 40-42
Braddock Road, 28, 234
Braddock's Field meeting, 120-123
Bradford, David, 120, 121, 124, 125, 127
Bradford, William, 124, 127
Braun, L., 254
Bridges, 199, 205, 206
Brimstone Corner, 158, 252
Brison, James, 109, 176
British, in Ohio Valley, 11, 12, 46
 during Revolutionary War, 93
Brodhead, Daniel, 91, 95, 97, 99
Bruce, Robert, 215
Brunot, Dr. Felix, 163, 321
Brunot, Felix R., 321
Bullett, Capt._____, 50, 51
Burd, James, 58
Burr, Aaron, 181
Bushy Run Battle, 69
Business depressions, 147, 153, 184, 199, 219, 292
Butler, Richard, 73, 91, 92
Butler, Thomas, 123
Butler, William, 73, 82
Butler, Pike, 242

Cadets of Temperance, 250
Campbell, John, 73, 80, 82, 84, 86, 103
Canals, Erie, 185
 Cross Cut and Ohio, 193
 Chesapeake and Ohio Canal, 194
 See also Pennsylvania Canal
Cannon manufactories, 238, 317
Carnegie-Illinois Steel Corp., 30
Carnegie Steel Company, 243
Castle Shannon Incline, 245
Catholic church, 31, 44, 45, 158, 252
 cathedral, 253
Caveat, James, 84

Celoron de Blainville, 11, 18
Central High School, 216
Chapese, Henry, 106
Charitable projects, 158, 213, 214
Charter of Pittsburgh, 201, 202
Chartier, Peter, 8
Chartier's Creek Hospital, 94
Chartier's Old Town, 8
Chislett, John, 204
Cholera epidemics, 212
Christy's Minstrels, 266
Churches, 110,250-253
 missions, 249
Citizens Passenger Railway Company, 240
Civil War, effect on Pittsburgh, 311-325
 relief groups, 315, 320, 321
 camps, 316
 fortifications, 319
Claflin, Tennessee, 281
Clapboard Democracy, 175
Clapham, William, 66
Clark, George R., 96, 99
Clarke, L. Y., 288
Clay, Henry, 289
Clay industry, 148
Clayton, Richard, 281
Clinton Iron Works, 221, 245
Clow, James, 109
Clymer, George, 94, 101
Coal Hill, 105, 245
Coal industry, 148, 247
"Coffin Handbills," 290
Coke industry, 221, 247
Collins Township, 202
Collot, Victor, 108
Columbia Railroad, 192, 197
Commonwealth, 180, 286
Conestoga wagon, 137
Connolly, Dr. John, 74, 76, 83, 84, 86, 96
Contrecoeur, Pierre de, 18, 23-25, 30
Conway, William B., 288
Copeland, Thomas, 150
Cotton industry, 221, 223, 226, 227
Councils, common and select, 201, 202
Courthouses, 109, 204, 231
Covenanters, 158
Cowan, Christopher, 150
Cowansville, 245
Craig, Amelia Neville, 286
Craig, Isaac, 112, 115
 at Fort Pitt, 100, 106-108
 business activities, 130, 140, 147, 285
Craig, Isaac E., 254

Trollope, Anthony, on Pittsburgh, 202
Tulleken, John, 58
Turnbull, William, 106, 115
Turnpikes and turnpike companies, 137, 186-188
Turtle's Heart, Indian, 66, 68
Tustin, James, 168, 233
Tyler, John, 294

United States Bank of Pennsylvania, 195
United States Marine Hospital, 212
University of Pittsburgh. *See* Pittsburgh, University of
Upfold, Rev. George, 261

"Valley Forge," vessel, 190
Van Braam, Jacob, 14, 21, 22, 26
Vashon, J. B., 305
Vaudreuil, Marquis de, 46
Vaughn, Maj. _____, 58
Viele, Arnold, 8
Vigilant Fire Engine Company, 156, 253
Villiers, Coulon de, 26
Vinal, Rev. William, on Braddock's defeat, 36, 37
Virgin Alley, 204
Virginia, claims to Ohio Valley, 16
land policy, 71, 77-79
Revolutionary War regiments, 90, 93
See also Pennsylvania-Virginia controversy
Virginia Path, 4
Virginia Provincial Convention, 91
Visitors and Lecturers to Pittsburgh, 249, 260, 273, 301, 309, 324

Wabash Railroad, 197
Wages, early nineteenth century, 150
mid nineteenth century, 224
Waggoner, Capt. _____, at Braddock's defeat, 34
Wallace, George, 169
War of *1812*, effect on Pittsburgh, 141, 152, 153, 166, 182
Ward, Edward, 10, 23-25, 38, 71, 86, 101
Warden, Isaac, 245
Wards, in city, 202
Warner Theater, site, 266
Washington, George, expedition to Venango, 14-16, 20-22
at Fort Necessity, 25, 26
with Braddock, 29, 34-36
with Forbes, 48
interest in western lands, 76-79
Washington Ark, 249

Washington Country, erected, 100
in Whiskey Insurrection, 119, 120
Washington Hotel, 249
Washington Road, 245
Washington Street, 103
Water Lane, 283
Water Street, 276
Water systems, 156, 206, 207, 323
Quarry Hill reservoirs, 207
Ross pumping station, 244
Watson, Andrew, tavern-keeper, 109, 110, 120, 126
Watson's Road, 194, 234
Waxwork exhibits, 168
Wayne, Anthony, 108
Wayne Street, 103
Weber, Rev. Johann W., 110
Weiser, Conrad, 3
Welch, George, 111
Wemyss, Francis C., 264, 265
West Augusta District, 100
court, 84
West End, 245
West Pittsburgh, 245
Western Avenue, 283
Western Electric Repertory and Analytical Review, 261
"Western Experiment," vessel, 130
Western Gleaner, 162
Western Iron Association, 222
Western Missionary Society, 159
Western Penitentiary, 242
Western Pennsylvania, described, 1-12
population in *1775*, 72
Western Pennsylvania Hospital, 212, 323
Western Theological Seminary, 242
"Western Trader," vessel, 131
Western University of Pennsylvania. *See* Pittsburgh, University of
Western World, 262
Westmoreland County, erected, 79
in Pennsylvania-Virginia controvery, 80, 81, 100
Wharton, Oliveretta, 246
Wheeling, commercial rivalry, 140, 184
Whig party, 289-294, 308
Whiskey Insurrection, 113, 117-128
effects, 145, 172, 173
White, David N., 286, 307, 309
White Eyes, Delaware chief, 92, 94
Wilkins, John, Jr., 121, 151, 176
Wilkins, John, Sr., 104
Wilkins, William, 151, 152, 169, 180, 235, 290, 293, 303, 315

MAPS

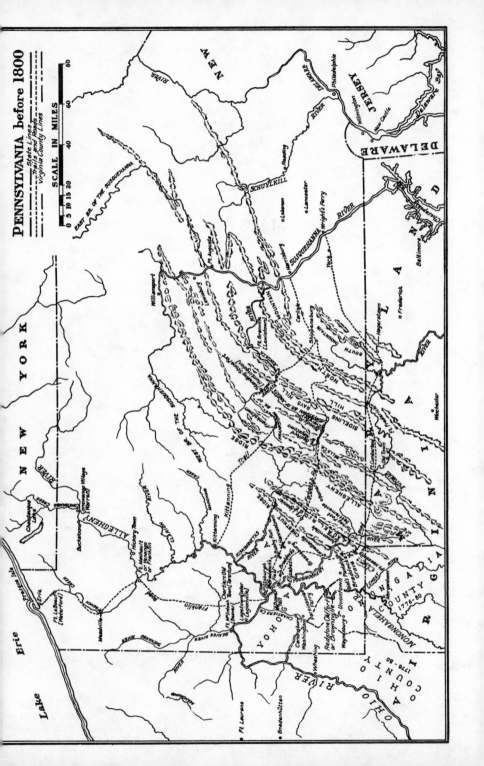

PENNSYLVANIA before 1800

State Lines
Trails
Virginia County Lines

SCALE IN MILES
0 5 10 15 20   40   60   80

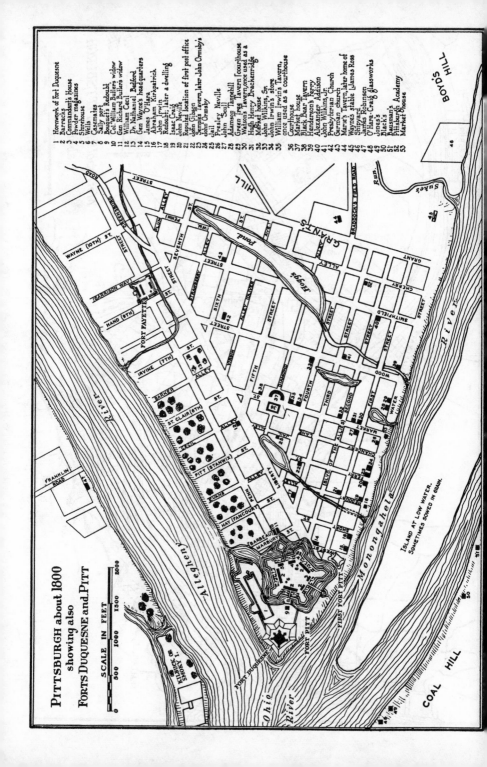

PITTSBURGH about 1800
showing also
Forts DUQUESNE and PITT

SCALE IN FEET
0   500   1000   1500   2000

1 Hornwork of Fort Duquesne
2 Barracks
3 Commandant's House
4 Powder magazines
5 Storehouse
6 Wells
7 Casemates
8 Sally port
9 Bouquet's Redoubt
10 Col. William Butler's widow
11 Gen. Richard Butler's widow
12 William Cecil
13 Dr. Nathaniel Bedford
14 Gen. Wayne's headquarters
15 James O'Hara
16 Alexander Kirkpatrick
17 John Irwin
18 Redoubt, later a dwelling
19 Isaac Craig
20 John Neville
21 Reputed location of first post office
22 John Gibson
23 Semple's Tavern, later John Ormsby's
24 John Ormsby
25 Jail
26 Presley Neville
27 John Scull
28 Adamson Tannehill
29 Green Tree Tavern [courthouse
30 Watson's Tavern once used as a
31 Hugh Henry Brackenridge
32 Market house
33 John Wilkins, Sr.
34 John Irwin's store
35 William Irwin's Tavern,
   once used as a courthouse
36 Courthouse
37 Market house
38 Black Bear Tavern
39 Henderson's Ferry
40 Alexander Addison
41 John Wilkins, Jr.
42 Presbyterian Church
43 German church
44 Marie's Tavern, later home of
45 Wayne's stable [James Ross
46 William Irwin
47 Abraham Kirkpatrick
48 O'Hara Craig Glassworks
49 Shipyard
50 Jones's
51 Black's
52 Bausman's
53 Pittsburgh Academy
   Market house

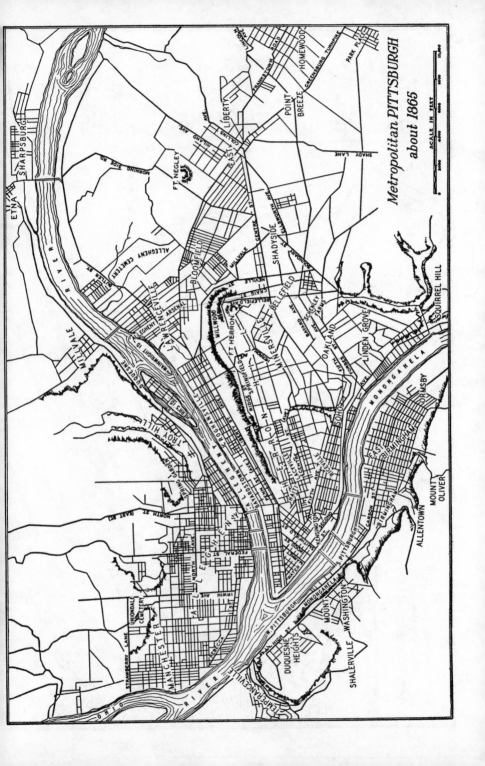

Metropolitan PITTSBURGH about 1865

SCALE IN FEET